Falling...in Love
with San Miguel

Falling...in Love with San Miguel

Retiring to Mexico on Social Security

Carol Schmidt and Norma Hair

SalsaVerde Press
Laredo, Texas

Back cover photo by Jon Sievert

This book is a companion to the website *www.fallinginlovewithsanmiguel.com*, which contains Carol Schmidt's ongoing blog on daily life in San Miguel, Norma Hair's blog on cooking at high altitudes, Frequently Asked Questions (FAQs) about San Miguel, SMA news, photos, links and forums.

Preassigned LCCN: 2006906833
ISBN-13: 978-0-9787286-2-5
ISBN-10: 0-9787286-2-9

SalsaVerde Press
Laredo, TX
www.SalsaVerdePress.com

Printed in the United States of America

CONTENTS

Introduction

Is it still possible to retire to Mexico on average Social Security and have a better quality of life than in the United States? Yes. Well-meaning friends told us we'd be kidnapped or killed, that banditos would pick us off the moment we crossed the border, that prices had skyrocketed in Mexico just as high as in the States. We'd be bored, we were too old to learn Spanish, we couldn't have internet or American TV, we'd die from turista and poor medical care.

On the other hand, some believed the fantasy that we could live like millionaires on a few bucks.

We were sure none of that was true from our travels through parts of Mexico, but we were not so sure we would be happier living there. We are. This journal started out as one year's letters to friends and relatives in the States describing our retirement in San Miguel de Allende. It now includes more than four years' experiences, and tells all about our new life as we moved to Mexico.

It is not a how-to guide but a love story. In the process of falling in love with San Miguel, Carol fell literally on the cobblestones and irregular sidewalks her first day in town and once or twice a year ever since—San Miguel's nickname is "the city of fallen women." Norma, who has never shuffled her feet, was lucky her first four years until a slanted wet tile got her. Just scrapes and bruises so far.

We include the prices of just about everything we bought (using an average 10:1 peso to dollar exchange for convenience, though the conversion rate has ranged from 9.2 pesos to the dollar to 11.7 pesos to the dollar during our four years). We describe the mishaps we made struggling with Spanish, our cultural adjustments, even our poor decisions, such as relying on the internet for an over-priced, sight-unseen rental.

Along the way we lost about 40 pounds each in those four years, walking more and eating better, although we had started to diet several years before the move and had each lost close to 100 pounds already. We can still go up 25 pounds practically overnight during a holiday season or vacation before we catch ourselves again—this is a serious lifelong struggle.

We were not sure how we could keep the weight off in the States, even though our goal had always been a gradual and permanent change in lifestyle, not a short-range diet guaranteed to fail. We feel much more optimistic that we can stay in control here with the walking and abundance of inexpensive fresh produce.

We'll never be insurance chart thin, but we are healthier today than we ever were in the States, and have gone off several of the medications we'd been told we'd need to take the rest of our lives. We've survived one life-threatening medical crisis (based on pre-existing conditions) with the help of the Mexican health care system, though we had to return to the States for a major surgery. Phoenix doctors said the Mexican doctors had done everything right.

We've made new friends who include a much broader range of people than we had ever known before. We don't often meet those who are buying the million-dollar homes here, however—San Miguel is many cities, many tales, many parallel universes, and sometimes expats are the five blind men describing the elephant. This is solely our story.

We're freeing our creative sides and letting go of our rigidities. Encountering occasional cases of the *mañana* philosophy is no longer frustrating but freeing. Usually. What is important in life anyway? Mexico has given us new answers.

For those who are worried about retirement on average Social Security income alone, this is the journal of two women who are living much better and much happier in Mexico. It all started as a three-month vacation to escape the 100-degree-plus summer in Phoenix…

1

May

Norma has convinced me to spend this summer in a small artsy town called San Miguel de Allende in central Mexico, 160 miles northwest of Mexico City. After every frustrating board meeting of our homeowners association over the past year, she's come home to disappear into the internet, exploring Mexico. The HOA members are hostile to her because, as treasurer, she got the dues raised and says "no" to some members' costly pet projects. One man at another homeowner's association here in Phoenix actually did kill a board member, smuggling a gun into a meeting! Five years from now, when the HOA still has enough money, no one will remember to thank Norma.

I've been ignoring this new fascination of hers, not thrilled with Mexico myself from our occasional weekend vacations in Ensenada ever since we met in 1979. She'd taken her kids camping down the length of Baja after the new highway that opened in 1973 made it possible, and they all loved it.

The family has a dog and pony show of stories of one boy smuggling home lizards which suddenly crawled out of the air vents as Norma drove, and the time he didn't boil the coral he'd collected and wriggling worms greeted Norma when she opened the cooler at home, and of the time Mexican soldiers had to tow their old Pinto across a flooding river, and of rushing across the border after every trip to hit McDonald's before it closed. Norma and her three kids can chuckle all night recalling their Baja escapades.

One of her sons, retired early after 20 years in the Navy, now spends six months of the year living in his RV on Baja beaches, still surfing. Norma's grandson seems to be following in his steps.

My earlier experiences in Mexico were less pleasant. In 1970 my then-husband and I took a "hippie honeymoon" in a van we'd converted to a camper, moving from Detroit to LA via Quebec, Alaska, and Mexico City. It didn't help that to Mexican border guards he looked like mass murderer Charles Manson, who had just been captured, and in those days we had to bribe our way a lot.

Nor did it help that the starter on our van was going, and every morning we had to convince a pickup truck full of Mexican workers to push our automatic transmission van up to 35 mph so that we could get started. I was petrified the whole ten days we spent in Mexico, and not so sure the honeymoon or the marriage had been a good idea. Neither was.

No, my view of Mexico is nowhere near as positive as Norma's. But she's convinced me that this artist colony called San Miguel de Allende will be different. She's pushing the artsy aspects of the city as her hook.

We're taking our two cats and our white Shih Tzu, Lacey, along for the three months. Our neurotic dog is joined to us at our ankles; boarding would destroy her. The cats are no trouble, they'll just ride in the cat carrier adjoined to their covered litter box for the ride. We all survived full-time RVing for three and a half years, so they're used to traveling.

We have to get International Health Certificates for each of them within 72 hours of crossing the border, so we have appointments with a vet who says he has the required papers on hand, first thing tomorrow morning. We should cross the border at Piedras Negras within the time limit if all goes well. Otherwise we'll find a vet near the border for new ones.

I hate that drive across desolate West Texas. Norma always turns on Rush Limbaugh from 11 A.M. to 2 P.M. to keep her awake—he makes her so mad she's hitting the steering wheel as she drives, fully alert. The rest of the hours we play Broadway show tunes on CDs. Norma should have been a gay man. Singing "Bali Hai" as we drive through the desert helps.

We made it! The ride wasn't bad at all through the States. We'd done it often enough RVing. Norma planned everything to the nth degree from advice on the internet, but she worried anyway as we approached the border. She planned the itinerary so that we'd hit Piedras Negras at 7 A.M. Sunday for the least possible traffic, and it worked out. No questions, *nada*, right through. Lacey didn't have time to challenge the guards.

But we knew the real challenge could be at the *Aduana*, 30 miles down on Highway 57, the main road that goes all the way to Mexico City, and which is supposed to be a toll road all the way but isn't. Still, it was a very good road. The *Aduana* is where you get your tourist visas and a permit to bring your car into Mexico, and you pay any duties on what you're bringing into the country.

By 36 miles according to our odometer, Norma was worried that somehow we had missed the *Aduana*, or we were on the wrong road. She insisted I go into the next business we saw and ask directions. She says I'm better at Spanish than she is. That's not saying much. Next stop: a bar. Sunday morning. It's open. Gulp.

Me: "*¿Habla inglés, por favor?*"

Two men: "*No.*"

Me: (Deep breath.) "*¿Por favor, donde está la Aduana?*"

They, laughing: "*Una milla.*" (I think..)

Me: "*¿Derecho derecho?*" (Straight ahead?)

They: "*Si.*"

Me: "*¡Gracias!*"

And thus concluded my first exchange in Spanish in Mexico. (Not counting the time 20 years ago that I tried asking an Ensenada bartender to bring me *agua*, water, but by mistake I kept insisting, *aqui*, here.)

Norma was so proud. I was trembling. But did I hear them right? Was it *milla*, mile, or *mil*, a thousand, or *millón*, a million? Couldn't be a million anything, unless they were putting me on. A thousand miles? Impossible. A thousand meters? Could be. Probable, even.

Or they could have been saying a mile for my benefit rather than using meters. Either one, the *Aduana* should be close.

It was, right around the next bend. I was even able to answer questions: truck or car? (We took a chance an SUV was a car.) Will both of you be driving? Yes (though I'm so terrified driving in strange places I doubt that will happen.) All of Norma's advance planning paid off. We were through. I stopped shaking.

Norma laughed out loud a few minutes later when we drove over a tarantula crossing the road. We didn't mean to hit it, but if we had to hit anything, a big spider would come in second only to a snake. (She did deliberately run over a snake once in Portugal that had the misfortune of crossing the dirt road just as we approached—she hates snakes.)

I hadn't heard her laugh that freely since she'd been elected HOA treasurer and our lives went to hell. It still feels as if we've sprung from jail! I'm already dreading going back in three months. I feel freer in Mexico already.

Norma took what she thought would be a shortcut to Highway 57, and we ended up touring an industrial park and seeing thousands of newly made Ford Fiestas waiting to be transported.

We came across a stretch of real poverty, families living in 6'x 6' cardboard shacks out in the desert, selling rattlesnake skins that hung from clotheslines by the road, dozens of identical stands attempting to lure the cars whizzing by. Later, we saw dozens of identical stands selling *fresas y crema*, strawberries and cream. At gas stations dozens of kids offered the exact same packets of chewing gum for sale. At other stops we were rushed by women dressed almost identically selling the exact same kinds of rag dolls in Indian costumes. "*No, gracias*" to all.

I kept seeing signs that didn't seem to fit anything in my Spanish-English dictionary and which weren't covered in our two conversational Spanish classes back in Phoenix. I decided they were verb tenses. *No tire basura*—don't throw tires here? No, *basura* is trash, so *tire* must be some tense of throw.

Vulcanizar is to vulcanize, my dictionary said, but variations on the word were painted on shacks with stacks of tires out front. I was pretty sure the signs weren't talking about Star Trek's Vulcan Dr. Spock. A car tire is *llanta*, I remembered from our Spanish classes. None of the Spanish words for rubber are anything like "vulcan" but we decided the word had to have something to do with something rubber, which may mean repairing inner tubes. Do any tires today have inner tubes? And that's how we spent the 10 hours drive from the border. Guessing.

Pemex is the government-owned gasoline monopoly and the stations appear regularly, so we had plenty of places to stop and get a snack and walk the dog. Many of the restrooms charged two pesos, about 20 cents, to get in, or an attendant handed you six squares of toilet paper with one hand and expected something like two pesos in the other. (Reminder to self: always keep plenty of tissue in purse.) And we learned the joys of no toilet seats. Diet Pepsi? Forget it, I guess we'll be drinking Diet Coke from now on. (That's changing—Pepsi is making giant inroads into Mexico.)

Eventually we came to the Holiday Inn in San Luis Potosí, the only place we'd found on the internet on the whole route that said it took pets. To stop or not: it was late afternoon, and we didn't want to be driving strange roads coming into San Miguel in the dark.

It's not good to drive after dark in Mexico anyway. Free range livestock can be on the road. People often change tires right on the road because there are no shoulders. But the hotel looked like a luxury high rise, and we couldn't imagine smuggling the cat carrier and litter box through the lobby. We drove on.

It started to pour. We were really exhausted, especially from all the worries we'd had leading up to this morning's border crossing. We turned back.

"*No perros,*" the clerk insisted, and I asked to see the manager, who spoke some English. I cried. I sobbed. I told her the hotel's internet site said they took dogs. Tiny Lacey was *muy pequeña*. She relented. And the hotel had a back wing like a one-story motel with a guard at the entrance to the secure parking lot. He didn't notice us smuggling in the cats. We were home free.

Not exactly free—the hotel charged $108 US for the room, and we're the Motel 6 type. That chain definitely takes dogs. But the hotel dinner for two was $12 U.S. with tip! When we got the menus I saw the price of $35 for enchiladas and had to ask the English-speaking waiter whether the prices were in pesos or dollars. Only 35 pesos, $3.50 U.S., for an entrée in a hotel restaurant seemed too cheap, and 35 dollars seemed too expensive, even in a very nice U.S. hotel. They'd have to be really fantastic enchiladas. It was pesos. Of course. What was I thinking, I was in Mexico, did I really expect the prices to be in U.S. dollars? Apparently some part of me did.

And I'd been warned by the tour books to expect the cup of hot water and a jar of instant Nescafé if I ordered coffee. (That's changing, too—businesses with many U.S. customers are starting to brew café Americano. Brewed Mexican coffee often has caramel, cinnamon and/or chocolate added.)

The turn off to San Miguel from 57 is hard to find. We'd been told to look carefully before all overpasses for the small sign, San Miguel one way, Doctor Mora the other. We wondered who was this Doctor Mora that he should have traffic directed to his offices? (Later we learned his role in Mexican history.) The semis with tall double trailers made it difficult to spot the sign, but we did.

Lovely drive through the countryside and through a rough and tumble small town (Los Rodriguez) that fit every stereotype I had of what a Mexican village would look like. It seemed to be having an open market day, with stalls selling fruit and barbeque and fresh whole chickens and rustic ceramics. Or maybe it looked like that every day. We were still guessing.

We were stuck following a semi loaded with broccoli. Spears kept falling off the uncovered truck at every turn and every *tope* (speed bump). Kids appeared out of nowhere to scoop up the broccoli spears in the truck's wake. Then, miles of farmland.

Traffic started to build. The landlady had written to look for the huge red "GNC" and "G" signs, for the international vitamin store chain and Gigante, a supermarket. Yes, there they were. And suddenly we were on a roundabout, a *glorieta*, they're called in Mexico.

Round we go, not sure where to get off. Nobody stops at the *Alto* signs entering the glorieta unless they're going to hit something. They miss us. Horns blare. I'm frantically trying to correlate the handwritten directions from the landlord with the landmarks I'm supposed to see. Okay, turn here, I tell Norma. She swerves. More horn blowing.

Deep breath. We're going downhill. Literally. But we seem to be doing all right. Bump, a *tope*. Bump, another. Okay, hang on. We're coming up on a sharp left turn, and there's a big round mirror hanging at the intersection, apparently to tell drivers what's coming around the corner. A bus! Help! It will never make the narrow turn! Cars around us come to a stop. We do, too. The bus makes it without even slowing down. Deep breath. Keep going.

Everything is going fine. We relax a bit. First sight of San Miguel is of a much larger town than we expect. We know from the books the city population is about 80,000 and the regional population is 140,000, but sprawled down a hillside the city looks even bigger. Church spires and domes dot the landscape. A tinge of lavender spreads like mist down the hills. Must be jacaranda trees in bloom. We've missed those since leaving LA twenty years before.

Norma admits she's scared driving through such narrow streets with no traffic lights—San Miguel is a national historic monument and no traffic lights are allowed in Centro. Police direct traffic at many intersections, and the drivers seem polite at other corners, allowing one car from each direction to go in turn. Far cry from LA or Phoenix. I think Phoenix held the U.S. record for number of stoplights run, with resulting deaths and injuries.

As we come to the top of another hill, I feel as if I'm at the top of a roller coaster. But on a roller coaster you're pretty sure you'll make it. My heart is in my throat. I can see Norma's knuckles clenched on the steering wheel.

We come across plodding burros loaded with burlap sacks being led down the same streets as cars. They take precedence. The sidewalks look too narrow even for burros.

San Miguel's altitude is 6,400 feet. We've already started to get breathless during the two-day climb up onto Mexico's central plateau. Now we're panting. Or is that fear of driving? Rather, fear of crashing?

The colors are so bright! Reds, golds, maroons, roses, turquoises, teals. Norma is jumping up and down in her seat against her seat belt, squealing, "It's Disneyland! It's beautiful! I can't believe it!" Of course she knows it is insult to call a bustling region that is home to some 140,000 Mexicans a Disneyland, as if it were designed just for tourists, but I admit it, I feel that way, too.

Norma is getting into the rhythm now. Pick and crawl is the driving pattern. At least nobody's speeding. They couldn't.

The cobblestones are beautiful! The light is so bright! The internet said this was an artists' town because the light somehow is spectacular, maybe because of altitude and lack of pollution, and I see it. I feel as if I am looking into a kaleidoscope. The colors, the colors everywhere! I picture my palette with the fanciful names of paints that are more than dried dabs here: burnt sienna, yellow ochre, sepia, ultramarine blue, cerulean green, indigo, lemon yellow, alizarin crimson...

Back in Phoenix, our homeowners association rules declared that the exteriors of all park models had to be shades of white and beige, and in retaliation we'd painted our living room interior with one wall raspberry, the next terra cotta, the next peach, and the fourth lemon, with a teal leather sofa. An abstract rug, a wall quilt made by Norma, and one of my paintings tied the vibrant colors together. We made sure to leave our drapes wide open so that golf carts (bored retirees looking for rules violations to report) turning the corner past our park model would veer in shock at the rainbow. Here we'd fit right in. In fact, we'd read one person's explanation to confused relatives on why she'd moved to San Miguel: "Here the people think I'm normal."

Nothing clashes. Every house is a different color, or two or more colors. Every shade of bougainvillea crawls up and over walls and fences. The ceramics would seem gaudy in the States. Walls of rock that would cost a fortune to build in the States serve as spacers, hiding what look like ruins. Many homes have plain fronts, wood doors with small tile numbers the only sign it is a home. But where those doors are left open we can see splendid courtyards inside, with terraces and gardens and patios and fountains and twisting wrought iron stairwells and arches everywhere.

⧜⧜

Even seeing these plain facades throughout town, our first glimpse of our apartment for the next three months is devastating—faded wood, locked tight garage doors. What have we done? We have to drive around the block to keep circling on this one-way street until a parking place opens up. Not many of those in this town. I've read there are at least 7,000 cars in Centro fighting for 1,000 parking spaces and parking meters are to be installed some day soon. (Four years later the parking meters aren't here yet. "Soon" is a relative term.)

Finally someone pulls out as we round the bend again. We're stopped. More deep breaths. I hear rustling in the cat carrier. A tentative "Meow?" Lacey has to take a quick walk. She is excited and nervous about the new smells. Ummm, we inhale, too. Is that roast pork carnitas?

Our directions say to call the landlady when we arrive and she will come open the gate. Public phones are disappearing almost as fast in Mexico as in the States, victims of cell phones, and the few we see require phone cards. Finally I find one in a beauty shop that takes coins—but only three one-peso coins, and we have incorrect change. We'd gotten a thousand dollars changed into pesos back in Phoenix but we'd used what coins we had coming down. Mistake.

Thus we get our first introduction into the perpetual scarcity of coins in Mexico, since you need them for everything. Small stores rarely have *cambio*, change, and no one would change my ten-peso coin, the smallest I had (about a dollar U.S.).

Finally I see a storefront with shelves lined with junk food. In my rush I don't notice that the stairs go down, that the entrance is sunken below sidewalk level with no warning. I'm falling. I jam my knee. I pay no attention to the sudden pain and manage to keep from catapulting into the store. I remember San Miguel's nickname because of its cobblestones and rugged sidewalks: "The city of fallen women."

Seeming to cower behind the shelves is a huddled old woman. Maybe she thought I'd fall on her. She's about 4' 6", in a dark dress almost to the floor, her head and shoulders covered in a navy wool scarf (called a *rebozo* in Mexico) even though it's about 90°F. April and May are the hottest months in San Miguel. She sells me a lollipop for two pesos. She only has seven pesos change. Luckily they are seven one-peso coins, not fives or twos. I have to convince her I'm thrilled to get the seven pesos.

She seems distressed by the entire encounter, almost as if she thinks I'm going to rob her. What did I do wrong? I must be oozing anxiety. I'm ecstatic to get the small coins in my hand, to hell with being one peso short, and I head back to the beauty shop phone. My aching knee makes me remember my twisted descent into the store. The red lollipop is mango with chile. I was expecting strawberry.

Answering machine message. Damn! We sit in the hot car in our desirable parking place and reassure the cats and Lacey that we are at our new home. We have no idea when the landlady will arrive, but we'd better just stay put. Drivers slow as they pass by, eyeing our parking space, wondering if we're leaving soon.

Within ten minutes the landlady opens the gate—she says she'd been in the bathroom—and we get our first glimpse of the complex and our apartment. No water-saving xeriscape desert landscaping of gravel and cactus here, as we had left in Arizona. Blazing scarlet and orange bougainvillea blooms are everywhere, and lush, loose beds of cosmos laden with heavy pink blossoms circle two mossy stone fountains.

The complex has six one- and two-bedroom apartments and one three-bedroom casa. Ours is the smallest apartment for $400 a month, not much bigger than the 400-square-foot park models (small manufactured houses) that more and more RVers were putting up on our RV park lots, as we all tired of traveling and became year-round Arizona residents. We'd built an Arizona room onto our park model and had a total of 700 square feet living space. We're used to compact living—our last RV was 300 square feet and we lived in it for more than three years. But even so, this apartment is really small.

It has rough slate blue cement walls, terra cotta tile floors, dark beams on a whitewashed brick ceiling, wrought iron fixtures, carefully hung mirrors to make it look larger, a fireplace just the right size to put the hooded kitty litter box to keep the cats from running up the chimney, bright prints, and striped Mexican blankets on the "sofa" (just a thin mattress on a wood slab on four flimsy legs) and double bed. The 13-inch TV on a rickety stand gets a few Mexican channels via a rabbit ears antenna. Turning on the shower gets the entire bathroom soaked.

The landlord has stocked the bookshelves with paperbacks and copies of *The Nation* periodicals. In one of the posts when we were arranging the rental on the internet he'd said he was from Detroit, where I was raised, while Norma grew up a few miles away in Pontiac. Aha, a copy of *The Insider's Guide to San Miguel* by Archie Dean, that someone said was *must* reading.

The landlady made us sign a list of the contents of the apartment that she warned would be closely checked when we left, for damage and theft. I was expecting a more easy-going welcome, not a U.S.-style contract. But then we're renting from Americans. We are here to enjoy San Miguel and won't be spending much time in our apartment. Already we were making excuses to ourselves for what we wouldn't say to each other was a dismal apartment.

We're told a maid comes in twice a week, included in the $400 a month rent, and she will do our laundry for $5 a load. She hangs it to dry on the rooftop. A woman who has a long-term lease of the studio apartment in the rear garden owns three cats she lets run loose within the complex, with a sign on the front gate asking tenants and visitors to not let any of her cats out onto the street. The flyer has a photo of each cat. We'll put up photos of our cats, too, so if Calicat or LucyFurr gets loose there is hope they will get caught before they reach the street. We have big red ID tags on their collar with this address and *recompensa*—reward.

Lacey loves the garden. Green grass again, cool on her feet, after all that Phoenix gravel. A friend, Nancy, who used to live in the same RV park but moved back to Ohio, has rented an apartment in the same complex. When we first told her we were coming to San Miguel for three months, she announced she was going to come, too. At first we weren't thrilled—this was to be our private getaway—but it is good to see her. It's like homecoming. We haven't seen her in years, and she is astounded at how much weight we've lost, about 100 pounds each.

Yes, my father's death two years before had changed my emotional state so much that suddenly I was able to diet. Norma had started to cut back slowly two years before that. He'd lived with us for six years and then down the street in a retirement home for another. But we're not thinking in terms of a short-term diet, we're in this for the long haul life-style change, and we think three months in a hilly town where everybody walks a lot will jolt our systems to the tune of another 10-20 pound loss. After the initial drop in any weight loss program, every pound is a struggle, and it only takes a couple hundred calories a day either way to make for a slow loss or a slow gain. We'd love another jump-start. Nancy has been losing weight, too, and wants to lose more. The three of us chatter away as if we'd never been apart. Nancy is a link between our old lives and our new reality for three months.

Nancy caravanned with us when we all were full-time RVers, and our pets know each other well. Our dogs sniff and race around each other, old friends, both animals becoming more comfortable with their new environment even as we watch. Nancy got here first. The gardener gave her a big welcoming bunch of cut flowers and fresh herbs this morning when she admired his work.

꿔

I really should be saying how horrible this place is, to keep anyone else from coming. Jack Nicklaus has announced he is building a $25 million golf course resort near here, though we are reassured it may never happen. (Four years later, it hasn't, though we hear another company is interested in the property. There is one golf course here now, Malanquin.) The few people we have met already are worried San Miguel will lose its charm and be overrun with gringos.

"Gringo" is not usually a derogatory term here, used for all U.S., Canadian and European tourists and residents. When a Mexican does use the term derogatorily, you know it. Sometimes we're called "the foreign community," or foreigners, sometimes we're "expats." Sometimes we're "Americans," or U.S. citizens from *Los Estados Unidos de America*, though Mexico's full name is *Los Estados Unidos de Mexico*, so that technically makes them "Americans" from *Los Estados Unidos*, too.

More often we're called *Norteamericanos*, but Canadians here remind us they're Americans from the North American continent as well, and Mexico is in North America, too, not Central America. For that matter, Central and South Americans are Americans, too. Technically we shouldn't simply call ourselves "Americans." But the politically correct distinctions seem important only to me in every day conversation.

Houses here are as costly as in Phoenix and even more. Most houses I see advertised are $160,000 and up, way up, many in the millions of dollars. Our $400 U.S. rent for a small apartment is great for an internet listing, but we've been told we can find something cheaper to rent by walking the streets and looking at signs in windows and flyers on utility poles.

We're happy where we are, we're so centrally located, despite the dismal apartment. We just wanted to have someplace for sure when we arrived, even though people said that we should wait until we got here to find a cheaper place. We were delighted to find something for only $400. But right now we're thinking our cave is overpriced.

Costs of U.S. imported goods are higher than in the U.S., while local goods are much cheaper. Diet stuff is almost non-existent, and few lines have unscented products, as far as we've seen. We both took antihistamines after the maid used some heady floral-scented cleanser on our floors. The landlady said the water from one faucet in the laundry room has a reverse osmosis purification system so we fill pitchers there every morning for our day's drinking and cooking. I've already forgotten a few times and put my toothbrush under the tap faucet.

We're told to buy a big navy blue bottle of Microdyn and put a capful in a large bowl of tap water and let produce soak in it for 20 minutes—unless the produce is going to be boiled for 20 minutes or totally peeled like a banana.

I also keep forgetting to put used toilet paper into the wastebasket rather than flush it down the toilet—the landlady warned us Centro plumbing is usually pretty old and overworked. She says the San Miguel water is now chlorinated but sometimes the aged Centro pipes for clean water and for sewage can leak into each other, so drinking and cooking water should be bottled or purified.

The maid brings her toddler to work, and the little girl plays in the garden all day while mama cleans. Her older brother joins her after school. I finally figured out how to tell the maid to not let our pets out and to use only unscented soaps on our laundry and cleaning. Norma has found some acceptable cleaning products someplace that don't make her sinuses swell.

The gardener lugs probably 40 buckets of water from the fountain each day to water each plant in the garden—I don't know why he doesn't have a hose. Because I can say a few words he thinks I speak better Spanish than I do and rattles back at me. How often can I say, "*Repete, por favor, mas despacio*" (please repeat, more slowly)? A lot.

⌇⌇⌇

I'm happy to find an English language daily newspaper here with several pages of U.S. news and better international coverage than the *Arizona Republic*.

My knee really started to hurt once we got unpacked. The landlady says she can call a doctor who will charge maybe $20 for a house call. I'll try Advil. One of the places I am eager to see when my knee feels better is the Biblioteca. The library, run by an elected board of directors, half gringos, has 45,000 books, half in English. A $10 U.S. a year membership gives book loan and voting privileges.

In the courtyard are Spanish-English conversations Tuesday and Thursday afternoons, where we can improve our language. Up a ramp is a café, a salon with a heavily-orange-toned mural painted on all four walls, and a theater that seats 81. Upstairs are a computer lab and the newspaper offices for Atención, the local bilingual weekly newspaper geared mostly to telling English-speaking residents and tourists what is going on in town.

After my experiences editing the newsletter back in the RV park, I am going to stay as far away from writing anything but letters as I can. Our new philosophy is, Norma can't add and I can't write. We've learned: no good deed goes unpunished.

Norma is out exploring while I rest my knee. She says her favorite activity is simply sitting in the Jardin and people-watching. I caught glimpses of the wedding-cake Parroquia in the Jardin as we were coming in.

What an exquisite church! It glows rose-pink in the afternoon sun. The legend is that in 1880 a self-educated Indian architect, Zeferino Guitiérrez, was inspired to design a new front façade for the 17th century church from postcards of European cathedrals, and he showed the laborers what to do by drawing in the sand. I have no idea if the legend is true I'm trying to absorb everything I hear and read and will sort it all out later.

Her first trip out alone, Norma came home with a backpack of goodies for $20 U.S.: four beef tamales in corn husks, the biggest pineapple I've ever seen, a kilo (2.2 pounds) of still-hot corn tortillas, ten flour tortillas, cooking oil, two heads of garlic, and half a kilo each of limes, tomatoes, assorted green chiles, onions, avocados, queso fresco (white Mexican melting cheese), loose eggs in a plastic baggy (only one broke coming home), margarine and rice. Norma found one storefront that carried only corn tortillas, one sold only flour tortillas, another fruits and veggies, another chicken and eggs, another cheese and sausage. So much for a trip to one supermarket for everything you need. In Phoenix we'd go into Safeway for eggs and spend $75 on nothing.

Norma is going whole hog and making guacamole the Mexican way—roasting the chiles, tomatoes, onions and garlic on a *comal* (flat griddle) until blackened, then peeling and chopping them, and adding mashed avocadoes with lime juice, salt and pepper. She's been studying Rick Bayless's Mexican cookbooks. She fried her own tortilla chips and steamed the tamales for our first home-cooked meal in Mexico. Tomorrow she'll make omelets and the next day quesadillas, with food left over, all for $20 U.S.

As she walked Norma saw a milk delivery truck where people brought their own containers to be filled by kids in the back of a pickup, ladling the unpasteurized milk from aluminum vats. No thanks, too many Michigan farmers got sick on unpasteurized milk when I was a kid.

We'll stick to the processed variety in stores, including an ultra-pasteurized variety sold here in unrefrigerated paper cartons that keeps for weeks (for families with no refrigerator), as well as the usual refrigerated varieties sold in paper cartons like in the States. Yes, there is low-fat milk, and even an occasional brand for those who are lactose-intolerant.

Norma says there are two U.S. chain stores—Blockbusters and Domino's, well camouflaged in traditional Mexican architecture and located outside of the historic Centro. (But the visual of a dozen Domino's small home-delivery motorcycles in front of the store, with big red signs advertising two for one Tuesdays, was jarring, she reported. A Mexican sandwich shop had a similar rack of delivery scooters, though.) We read that many major U.S. chains, including Costco, Wal-Mart, Sears, and Office Depot, are in Querétaro, an industrial city of nearly a million about 45 miles away. I can't imagine we'll want for anything.

We didn't bring our desktop computers, which aren't allowed across the border on a tourist visa, though I hear that rule is expected to loosen soon. We have our old laptop with no modem, so we have to find an internet café, whatever that is. The guidebooks say San Miguel has lots of them.

Later, Norma stumbled across one internet café within a few blocks, but the computers all had Spanish language keyboards and the owner spoke only Spanish. Our two conversational Spanish classes back in Phoenix are not nearly enough. She managed to read the signs in the internet café that said the cost to use the computers was ten pesos, about a dollar an hour.

So she found another café a few blocks farther, which offered pastries and coffee to the dozen or so customers using the computers that encircled three walls of the shop. Price for internet service: $23 U.S. for 10 hours, or $2.30 an hour. It's much more upscale, and closer to Centro, than the Mexican-owned internet café, and therefore more expensive. I think that's the general rule: aimed at gringos in Centro, double the price. She'll take the floppy I'm loading on the laptop back there tomorrow. She estimates she walked five miles today. I limped to the bathroom and fridge.

First impressions: we absolutely love San Miguel de Allende (SMA from here on). We find it one of the liveliest walking towns we've experienced, with some feeling of Paris, Rome and Madrid, people bustling on foot everywhere. I prefer cities where people actually walk around, like San Francisco and Santa Monica and New York, but we can't afford them in the States. We've been preparing to live on only average Social Security after we sell our Arizona park model, so those traveling days are over. Norma still has some additional income but it will end when she turns 65 next year. And if we hadn't had so many medical bills through the years that ate up our savings plans, we might have more retirement and vacation options. It's been tough compared to our high-income days back in Los Angeles.

Many SMA stores are open 10 A.M.-2 P.M., and 4 P.M. to 7 P.M., shutting down 2-4 for siesta. Some restaurants seem to be open either for breakfast and lunch or lunch and dinner, no siesta. Several have live music after 9 P.M. We never went out to live music in Phoenix because it was a lengthy drive and cost plenty. Here we can walk to all kinds of music for a few bucks.

Tiny streets—this city was founded in 1542, and the historic Centro neighborhood, or *colonia*, was laid out for burros and horses. Narrow sidewalks are hardly enough for me to feel comfortable walking in some places, but Mexicans walk two across. On some even narrower sidewalks I hold my breath when a bus passes.

"*Con permiso*" is what you say to get someone to move for you. When you say, "*Gracias*," people say, "*De nada*," for nothing, it was nothing, as our conversational Spanish teachers said they would. Seems kind of self-deprecating, compared to "You're welcome."

Latin Americans and those from many other countries have a different sense of space than we do, feeling fine being an elbow's distance away while we want an arm's length. I did that backup dance all through grad school in Chapel Hill where my roommate was from Puerto Rico.

I remember a joke about a research study done to find how much distance between people those of different nationalities find comfortable. Supposedly a Spaniard sitting alone in a room reading a paper would feel intruded upon if another person sat on the arm of his chair and read his paper. An Italian would complain that his space was invaded if the other person stood behind him and read his paper over his shoulder. An Englishman would be uncomfortable if another entered the same room, and a German felt invaded if someone else walked by outside the room. I'm half German (the other half French-Canadian). Norma is German and English.

And the sidewalks are irregular, with utility poles often growing right out of the middle of an already narrow walkway. Steps into a shop may take up half of the sidewalk, or, even more dangerous, as I encountered our first hour in town, steps may lead down into a store or home at a lower level than the sidewalk, with no guardrails or warning. If you're watching only your feet, you can run smack into a windowsill at forehead level jutting out into the sidewalk space.

Steps and curbs are not at regular heights, and I see very few curb cuts for wheelchairs. (How quickly we got used to seeing curb cuts in the States—I was thrilled the first time I saw a young woman in a wheelchair zipping along in West Los Angeles around 1975 when curb cuts first were required. Many people say Mexico is like the U.S. in the '50s on social issues.)

Shoe stores sell something called the San Miguel sandal, designed and made by a local woman, who nicknames them "combat cocktail sandals." They have wide elastic straps across the instep and ankle and come in every color and pattern. I think they're ugly. I'm going to stick to my Teva sandals originally designed for hikers and boaters to walk on rocky creek beds. That is, when I'm walking again. I'm already feeling nervous about falling.

We rented a secure parking space in a hotel parking lot across the street for $30 U.S. a month. Several bus lines stop right in front of our apartment complex. Our first day here, before we (or rather, Norma) unpacked and shopped, and before I gave in to my aching knee and went to bed, we took a chance on the buses to find a restaurant for dinner.

Our friend Nancy wanted to go out, too, so we ventured together onto the first bus that came along. It said *Ruta 3 Centro*, and we were in Centro, so how wrong could we go? Fare is four pesos, about forty cents each.

A boy about twelve collected fares every so often and got to ride shotgun next to the driver, half-hanging out the open door. No safety signs, "Passengers must stay behind the yellow line." It was definitely not a first-class bus, but at least no chickens or goats filled the aisles and no one hung off the roof, my expectation. Comfy enough.

The bus stopped at a school playground to allow mothers to collect their kids and board again. What public bus in the States would do that? Many of the kids were drinking some sort of colored liquids from clear plastic bags with straws.

Suddenly the bus was outside the city limits and we had no idea where we were or what we would do now. We had visions of trying to find a phone someplace to call a taxi, with our insufficient Spanish—and insufficient knowledge of where we were, to even tell a taxi driver where to come get us. We sweated it, worrying what to do, but the bus simply made a U-turn in a Mexican housing development entrance and returned the same way.

The driver wanted us to get off at the final stop but relented and simply charged us another four pesos each for the return to town. Through all this worry we never saw a restaurant we could agree upon. Norma has a touchy tummy, and she was taking no chances.

Back in Centro, we got off at a hotel that said it had a restaurant inside—and Norma laughed. It was the same hotel where she'd rented the car space a few hours earlier, a courtyard and parking lot away from where we had started. At Bella Italia, in the courtyard of the Hotel Sautto, Nancy and I shared a seafood platter of mussels, shrimp, calamari and oysters steamed in spicy wine sauce for dipping crusty French bread, $10 U.S. each, and Norma raved about her salmon in vodka sauce over penne for $9. Not as cheap as we'd hoped, but, after all, it was a restaurant within a hotel. (Bella Italia has since moved down the street to the Plaza Colonia, and Bacco, another Italian restaurant with a genuine wood-fired pizza oven, took its place in the Hotel Sautto courtyard.)

We're going to Harry's, a New Orleans Cajun/Creole restaurant nearby, to celebrate as soon as my knee heals. I'm mostly just reading about the town, Norma is doing the exploring, but she says she's seen Chinese, Italian, Spanish, French, sushi and Lebanese restaurants within cheap cab or bus range or walking distance. Cabs are only 20 pesos, about $2.00 U.S., by day within Centro, more at night or if you telephone them to come rather than flagging one down.

I'm learning about the dozens of volunteer programs to help the community and am glad to see expats giving back to the community. My fear was that all the foreigners would live in their own gated communities and not mix, but it seems as if most are doing volunteer work and trying to be a part of the community, even if not always succeeding.

The weather is heavenly, about 85° F highs, and at night we use a thin blanket. We're about to enter the rainy season, we've been warned, but that usually means an hour-long shower in the late af-

ternoon or early evening, from June to October. Or so the tourist
books promise. The landscape is pretty green already, especially compared to Phoenix. I've read SMA gets about 25 inches of rain a year,
compared to 7.5 for Phoenix. It's still considered high desert.

Have I mentioned I love it here already, even from bed, even in
this cramped apartment? The landlord sings Italian operas all morning long as he paints the courtyard walls yet another shade of red,
the children play so well (in our Arizona gated senior housing kids
did not exist), and it is a joy to look outside at the hummingbirds in
the bougainvillea and hear fountains tinkling in the background.
Norma is in ecstasy. It is so good to see her happy again.

Finally I am able to walk. We took a taxi to the Biblioteca and
I got a temporary card by putting $10 U.S. on deposit so I could
check out a bunch of light mysteries. Their "new books" section is
pathetic, some five-year-old books shelved as "new." I do miss the
Apache Junction library section of all the current New York Times
best sellers. But there is plenty to read for a lifetime. The latest *Atención* calendar section also has plenty to do for a lifetime.

Cautiously I said the words over dinner at Harry's: "What to
you think about the possibility of our moving here?"

Norma sat bolt upright in the booth: "Thank God! I've wanted
to move here ever since I started reading about it on the internet!"
She almost cried in joy. "It had to be your idea."

So her mind is calculating how we might do it. Maybe it's just
a dream. Norma is good at making dreams come true.

At Harry's I had the best fried oysters I've ever had (quarter-
sized crunchy ones with a Creole dipping sauce, not the tennis ball-
sized ones of the Pacific), and jambalaya on the side. Norma had a
spicy pasta dish with Cajun sausage and shrimp. With drinks and
tip, total bill was $25 U.S., half of what we would have paid at our

favorite Cajun restaurant in Scottsdale, and just as tasty. And Harry's is considered an upscale restaurant here.

We could have gotten lobster thermidor and paid $38 each, though, with wines of every price. We'll have to search out the cheaper restaurants; this one will be for splurges only, though I adore it already.

It's International Brotherhood Week featuring concerts each night in the Jardin (town square). Tonight was an Andes band playing sparkling flute notes and rhythms on instruments we'd never seen, made from sea shells, tortoise shells, wood percussion and gourds. At least 400 people, almost all Mexican, relaxed on the dark green wrought iron park benches or crowded near the temporary bandstand. Kids of all ages danced around, turned cartwheels, and squirted each other with purple foam stuff from spray cans.

Half a dozen mariachi bands in gold-embroidered and brass-buttoned costumes wrangled invitations to play from those sitting farther back in the Jardin from the Andes band that was playing up front on a temporary stage. I asked and found out that the going rate is $10 U.S. a tune.

Occasionally a mariachi band would find someone to hire them to play "Malagueña," "Besame Mucho" or some song I didn't recognize. I think I saw one band member roll his eyes when yet another gringo asked for "Cielito Lindo" and its chorus of "Ay ay ay ay."

I was jealous of the Mexicans who asked for and sang along to spirited songs I'd never heard before. For them, the mariachi bands seemed to be really enjoying themselves, not phoning it in.

The gringos were the funniest. I saw four Ché and three Spider-man T-shirts today, plus assorted costumes straight out of Montmartre or Ghiradelli Square where artists tempt passersby to have their portraits painted. A couple of guys our age looked like background singers for "Margaritaville," though they weren't drunk, just a bit dissolute, flirting with young Mexican women who ignored them.

A dancing couple took to the street in front of the band for a while. I can't identify a samba from a rumba or anything else so I don't know what dance they were doing (now I know it's salsa), but the crowd applauded. One blonde beauty walked by, model-perfect, all in black, looking like Candice Bergen in *The Group*. I'm showing my age. Bo Derek in *Ten*. I'm still showing my age.

Many women, foreign and Mexican, did walk alone, which surprised me. One young Mexican woman sped by on a motor scooter, hair flying, no helmet, not minding the cobblestone-induced bouncing. A guy with a toddler clinging to his waist rode by on a four-wheeler ATV.

Most of the young girls wore plaid Catholic school pleated skirts, white blouses and knee socks, with cardigans to match the predominant color of their skirts. Teens in giggling groups did their thing, pretending to not notice the gatherings of the opposite sex, but the attractions were obvious.

One teenage girl with a camera tried to get her friend to take her photograph next to a bunch of cute boys, as if she were with them, wiggling as close to the group as she could get without being noticed. The boys obliged and ignored her contortions, though everybody knew exactly what was going on. Handsome older Mexican couples strolled by, the men in pale suits and Panama hats, the women in dark dresses, heels and chunky silver jewelry.

One grouchy old U.S. couple told the boys with the purple spray to stop it right now, muttering, "What some parents will let their kids get away with." The kids were just being kids. In the States I didn't have experiences where entire multi-generational families just hung out and enjoyed themselves, not since the Schmidt family reunions in Detroit ended in the early '60s when most of us had scattered. To me the kids were exceptionally well behaved, probably because so many elders were around, lots of eyes watching them.

The family with the boys moved on but they'd left an irresistible mound of purple foam on a broad stone railing. All the young men who were kids at heart kept eyeing that foam, probably wanting to get their hands in it, wondering how to best slime somebody else with the stuff without losing their cool. Or so I imagined they were thinking. Maybe I just wanted to run my hands through the bubbles myself. The foam dissolved on its own, but what a temptation until it did.

Food stands plied their wares—hamburgers and shrimp *tostadas* and *chicharrónes* (fried pork rinds). The one that drew my eye sold steamed corn on the cob, smeared with unrefrigerated mayonnaise, then dipped in grated white cheese, and sprinkled with lime juice and chile powder. The cart attendant poured hot water over the ears every so often to keep them warm. Norma and I wouldn't dare eat any of it. Maybe some day I'll get used to local bacteria and take a chance.

Mexicans who visit the U.S. often get *turista*, too, from the change in flora and fauna. Norma had terrible food poisoning in Paris on her birthday one year. It's not just Montezuma's revenge.

In honor of my knee we took a cab the four blocks back to the apartment. Suddenly my mind went blank on the Spanish word for 60, and our address is 67. You should have seen me trying to tell the cab driver where to take us. The highest number I could remember was 30, so I said in Spanish, *"treinta y trienta y siete,"* 30 and 30 and 7. The driver was laughing so hard he couldn't see straight. But I got us there.

I tried to tell him it was only my second day out in San Miguel, second being *segundo*, but looking back, I think I said *"pregunto,"* or question. So I told him it was my question day here. He probably told his wife later, you should have heard these gringas I drove tonight.

But probably every night he can tell his wife how gringos speak such terrible Spanish, if they even try, and I bet he adds that they ought to try harder if they're going to live here.

I've read that's one of the main complaints by experienced travelers about San Miguel—it is too easy to get by speaking only English because there are something like 7,000 expats living here permanently on residency visas, and 11-12,000 here at any one time.

I feel much more sympathetic now to Mexicans who come to the U.S. with no English. I don't find everyone speaks English at all—a part of me wishes they did. But then that would be defeating the whole purpose of coming to a different country where even the differences in words and sounds reflect how others see the world differently.

This town has fireworks exploding and church bells ringing all the time. I can't find any pattern to the bells. We might wake up with 52 chimes at 7:04 A.M., or four chimes at 7:52. I've read that chimes ring out when someone dies, someone is born, someone gets married, someone is going on a journey, church services are coming up, or it's a holiday.

Fireworks can go off for the same reasons, or to scare the evil spirits who roam the earth at night away from the daylight hours. Fireworks are also supposed to make God hear prayers better. It is considered an honor to have someone pay for fireworks to awaken you at dawn in recognition of your birthday or some other special event.

We kept waiting for the lights on the Parroquia to go on at 9 P.M., which we read happened every night, but it's not happening now. Maybe the person who was supposed to turn on the lights forgot, or the city is saving on electricity, or the electricity is out, who knows. I have to give up trying to figure out why people are doing what they're doing, because I'm undoubtedly wrong.

One of my favorite novels is *Bedrock*, by Lisa Alther, about a New York photographer who moves to what appears in winter to be a picturesque Norman Rockwell small town. She writes home raving about the place, and the reader soon realizes she is wrong about everything she thinks she has figured out. There's a lesbian commune on one side of town, a Christian fundamentalist cult on the other side of town, and two of the teenaged children of the enemy camps are sneaking around for romantic trysts, bridging the gap between the foes. A straight hairdresser in *Bedrock* covets the beehive hairdo worn by the mayor's wife, as well as the wife.

When spring arrives, the solid foundation of the house the photographer bought in winter turns out to sit on a garbage landfill. I wonder how many of the guesses I'm making now will turn out to be wrong? I know we're in honeymoon stage right now, but we're sure enjoying it.

We're going to bed at 10:30 P.M. and getting up around 7, sleeping soundly (despite the fireworks and chimes). No insomnia. We took a cheaper equivalent of Benadryl, which has the same ingredient as Sominex, every night to fall asleep in Arizona. I woke from a dream that I had been a goldfish in a bowl of identical goldfish, all swimming round and round, fish police making sure everyone swam in perfect circles.

Suddenly I leapt out of the bowl and into the ocean where nobody paid any attention to me and I was free to turn into a wildly-colored tropical fish! Yes, I had to watch out for sharks but I could laugh at the clown loaches and jellyfish and starfish all doing their own thing. Nothing Freudian there! (I hadn't even seen *Finding Nemo* yet.)

The Mexican newspapers are far more critical of the U.S. government than the most liberal U.S. mainstream papers, and they print proportionately more international news, especially more news about Latin America than I have ever read before. Naturally, all news is local, and local media will always report local news first. My head expected that, but I was a journalism major who loves my familiar newspapers, so it is a bit disconcerting.

In the States I had to really search out different political views, while here they're in the paper each day. In Phoenix I got up late, spent hours on the internet searching for stimulating political commentary, looked forward to our one main meal out as the highlight of our day, and watched a whole lot of TV, dodging homeowner association members who were mad at either Norma for raising dues or me for something I'd written in the newsletter. That was our life. Five times a day we'd take the golf cart to the dog run on the other side of the park and the other retirees we met on their golf carts doing the same thing were our main social encounters. And half of those would be shunning us, driving by with noses high. The Amish have nothing on senior citizens in a snit.

Here, who knows what I'll do today? I hear there's an art teacher a few doors down on this very street, and I'll check him out today. Probably. No rush. This is Mexico. I can feel the slower pace seeping into me already.

承

Thursday afternoon we took a bus to the Gigante supermarket on the edge of town and bought a Teflon pan that actually has some Teflon and a knife that actually has an edge, compared to what comes with our "furnished" apartment. Prices are more expensive at Gigante than at the local storefronts, but not that much.

One difference I noticed between Gigante and a U.S. supermarket was the canned vegetables aisle—all kinds of *frijoles* (beans), corn, tomato puree, mushrooms and chiles. No beets, green beans, spinach, or the dozens of kinds of canned veggies I used to eat as low-cal filling snacks. Fewer varieties of frozen foods, too. But far more kinds of fresh fruit, many of which I can't identify. Nowhere near the number of more expensive "convenience" foods as in the States. I guess I'll be snacking on fresh veggies now and we'll be cooking more. That should save us money and calories as we worry about living on Social Security.

I didn't recognize very many brands at all. Nestlé products are on every aisle, though. Only a few of the Campbell's soup cans on display were varieties I recognized: no chicken gumbo or vegetable, pea soup or oyster stew, but plenty of cream of mushroom, corn, cheese, and tomato soups, chicken soup with tiny fine noodles called fideos, and others made from squash or from poblano chiles.

We planned homemade quesadillas for dinner tonight but saw a restaurant called Nirvana advertising fusion cuisine and we couldn't pass it up. We started with quesadillas filled with hibiscus flowers, which are also used in deep red Jamaica tea (pronounced ha-MY-ka tay). It took me a bit to make the connection between the flower I know as hibiscus, the island of Jamaica, and "ha-MY-ka tay.") The corn tortillas filled with the reconstituted dried hibiscus blossoms, probably sweetened, tasted like raspberry tarts.

Our entrees were a thin marinated flank steak called *arrachara*. Venison and ostrich were on the chalkboard menu. Never saw those at Applebee's. Prices were comparable to an Applebee's—not an everyday restaurant when you're on Social Security—but the food and ambience were far more upscale, and nobody rushed us. In Mexico you have to ask for the check, *"La cuenta, por favor,"* or you will be there all night. It's considered an insult for a waiter to bring a customer a check without being asked. Nobody is pushing you out.

Tonight we're seeing a movie called *Shanghai Triad* at the Biblioteca theater—no idea what it's about. The Biblioteca's Teatro Santa Ana has artsy movies almost every night.

We found out it is possible to get cable internet access even without a phone in our apartment, and we can get cable TV with the U.S. networks and HBO, too, but we might not bother. Too much to do! Like every night in the Jardin during International Brotherhood Week.

How to describe closing ceremonies for International Brotherhood Week tonight? Four-ring circus comes closest—four focal points, sometimes even five, totally unrelated to each other, all happening simultaneously in the center of the town at the Jardin.

On the stage was a procession of dancing acts from each of the regions of Mexico, alternating with a very strong-voiced male singer to allow time for costume changes. We got so we could see the differences between the regions—some dances and costumes seemed more traditionally Spanish, with flashing fans and whirling splashes of brilliant colors like flamenco dancers. That region's dances incorporated a kind of tap dance sequence almost as flirtatious as flamenco, but in more of a chorus line.

Another dance featured costumes that seemed like cream puff pastel bridesmaids' dresses, all frills and laces and bouffant sleeves. Another seemed more rustic—plainer skirts, unadorned blouses, and broader, less refined dance movements.

To my eye, tropical Jamaica, not Mexico, seemed the inspiration for the next act. The men wore white shirts that hung to their hips over white pants, multicolored scarves worn different ways and many kinds of straw hats. They differed on whether vests or boleros topped the shirts, and whether jewel-toned handkerchiefs were flashed. A border state's costumes of fringed buckskin and cowboy boots looked like the dancers had just come from a Texas rodeo.

I'm sure I'll eventually be able to tell regional costumes apart. Think Manhattan versus Miami versus Malibu versus Milwaukee clothing. What is "authentic" U.S. clothing anyway? (We already knew each region of Mexico has its own cuisine, and secretly prefer "California fresh" Mexican menus to anything truly "authentic.")

Comic routines interspersed among the serious dancers. A man dressed as a bull took on all comers, who tried many kinds of approaches to bullfighting. One drunken old female would-be bullfighter kept falling down and even landed on top of the bull. A woman substituted her swirling red skirt for a cape. The Devil waving a pitchfork still could not outdo the bull.

Finally came Death, a white skeleton painted on a black cat suit, wielding a scythe. All the bullfighters came on stage then, and Death won, to great applause.

Interrupting the most formal of dances was a man dressed as a pig that weaved and bowed among the women onstage. A rush of male dancers circled the pig, accompanied by much confusion and noise, and when the flurry stopped, the men marched off carrying the "pig" hung from a spit, ready for roasting.

In another comic routine, the Devil came back on stage and tried to look up the legs of the women as they twirled their long, super-full skirts. The male dancers used their straw hats to cool off the women's legs when they were really going full speed, kicking up their heels. This may have been a variation of the Mexican hat dance, but I'd never seen hats tossed and fanned like that in the States.

Meanwhile, small bands kept playing off and on at the kiosk farther back in the Jardin, and what appeared to be a high school band took off marching at a brisk pace. They weren't the Rockettes.

A riotous crowd of about 20 young men arrived, jumping around precariously on the back of pickups, waving yellow and navy flags and T-shirts which said "Coca Cola" on them but which also had a map of Central America with a big CA on the flags and shirts. We'd heard that the International World Cup Soccer competition starts Friday in Mexico City, and celebrating starts early. Or maybe it was a national win by Mexico in a preliminary, or maybe it was a high school victory—we never could tell.

So these young men and their growing number of followers jumped out of the trucks and began parading through the Brotherhood Week audience, splashing beer and yelling chants as loud as any I yelled in '60s demonstrations. Maybe they were chanting, "Two, four, six, eight, we just want to celebrate!" We jumped out of our seats at one point to avoid being splashed by beer and hit by flags.

Throughout all the commotion the singer and dancers on stage just kept on doing their thing, and the every-night social promenade of characters and families and lovers kept on circling the Jardin and the rotating bands in the kiosk played on.

Flashing lights and sirens announced the arrival of the police. The boys calmed down immediately and the main entertainment kept right on performing on stage. About this time fireworks began exploding behind the church. And the woman on our right selling corn on the cob kept right on coating the ears with mayonnaise, grated cheese, lime juice and chile powder, and the man on our left kept grilling thin hamburgers, overcooked hot dogs and greasy bacon for sandwiches.

He wiped dust off the Coke bottles with the same rag he used to wipe excess fat off the grill, handled money between food preparation, and piled the same ice into the soft drinks that had fallen off into the street and been walked on by street dogs. No, we are not eating from the carts, at least not that one.

A well-worn brown lab mix with nipples almost to the ground worked the crowds every night we've been to the Jardin, begging for food and attention. She grabbed a hamburger right out of a bawling toddler's fist and left only half a jalapeño on the sidewalk. Norma and I made bets on how long it would take someone to step on it.

Five people avoided it successfully before we picked it up and put it in the garbage, deciding we didn't want to find out if jalapeños hold the same danger as banana peels for unwary walkers.

The town is really very clean, especially considering the crowds and loose dogs. Monday morning all the sidewalks will be washed again by merchants and homeowners, and after big events sanitation department workers in orange jumpsuits flush and scrub the streets, often the last "float" in a parade.

Earlier in the evening a wedding party arrived in a horse-drawn carriage with red velvet seats. They had their photos taken in front of the Parroquia, which was finally lit for Brotherhood Week. The bride looked like a *Vogue* model in a Vera Wang-designed simple satin sheath. She oozed money. The couple spoke unaccented English and were probably from the U.S. They were yet another focal point. Truly a five-ring circus.

Someone new has moved into our apartment complex above Nancy, a woman named Sally who is here for a month's intensive Spanish classes at Instituto Allende. She already knows far more Spanish than we do and did some interpreting for us tonight when we could hear anything distinct over the chaos. We're pooling what we are all learning.

A husband and wife who rented the same apartment the week before Sally arrived considered themselves the world's greatest experts on San Miguel after one day. They hired their own driver for $100 U.S. a day who took them to nearby cities as well. They said he'd become their new best friend and had them over to his house for drinks their last night. For $700 I'll be your best friend and have you over for drinks, too.

The landlord wants us to move into his larger apartment that is like a greenhouse, and almost twice as expensive. The woman who is leaving says it gets too hot in April and May and too cold in December and January because of all the windows. It's right in the middle of the flower garden in the second courtyard. The landlord grows some veggies there and yelled at one of the departing woman's friends for allegedly stealing his green tomatoes.

The apartment is larger, and being surrounded by flowers was tempting, but we'll stick with our cozy place. Cozy meaning small. It may be a cave, but it's home. We think maybe we can make it work for full-time living if, no, when, we can sell our park model back in Phoenix.

We're going to buy our own sturdier bookshelves and rearrange things to make room for one of our big desktop computers, and we will definitely get cable TV and high speed internet. We'll probably have to hook up our cell phone, since it can take months or years to get a new phone line into a place. (Nancy shares a phone with whomever is in the apartment above her, and they shout back and forth to each other via the wrought iron curved stairwell that links their two front doors when one gets a call.)

We're almost used to the too-hard mattress, and we will buy our own comfy small sofa as well, though nothing can replace our soft teal green leather sofa back in Phoenix. That would never fit into this apartment; it would overhang into the kitchen and bedroom and block the aisles.

Nancy, Sally and I are going to a Bach concert Wednesday night, Bach not being high on Norma's list. When the new *Atención* comes out we'll figure out our next week's schedule. Nothing can top this week's International Brotherhood events but this isn't even one of the high seasons (July-August and November-April).

⚍

So far I can count on two fingers the instances of anger we've seen—the U.S. couple in the park angry at the young Mexican boys with the spray foam, and our landlord yelling at the woman who allegedly stole his green tomatoes. We've experienced no road rage in a city of 80,000 without a single traffic light. No nastiness among the teenaged boys, who will be boys—as someone who was very fat most of my life I keep expecting young males to crack some sort of insult as I pass by. Not here.

The closest to a scene was a disgruntled man our age at Harry's, who was upset because he specifically ordered his dressing on the side of his Cobb salad and it came mixed in. He and his partner, both tanned and in white suits, looked like Tom Wolfe dates George Hamilton—we're only assuming they were gay.

I tried cooking tonight. We'd bought something for an omelet that looked like chorizo sausage, but the label said it was *campestre ranchero*, a harder, coarser-ground red sausage with a strange (to me) taste. For a change, Norma liked something that I didn't. I wanted to mix in a few hot peppers to camouflage the disconcerting flavor but found that it is not true here that larger, lighter chiles are the mildest. The mildest ones we've found here so far are jalapeños, which I'd considered really hot before.

I roasted some big yellow chiles of unknown type I thought might be like the mild Hungarian chiles we'd grown in Michigan, but when I tried to peel them they were so hot they burned my fingers. I tossed them. I could only use half a jalapeño plus roasted onions, tomatoes and garlic, tossed in with the pseudo-chorizo. Norma gobbled her omelet, I threw mine out. Even the dog wouldn't touch it.

The landlord sold Nancy and me some of his goat cheese and honey. He has a ranch outside of town with goats and beehives. Norma wouldn't touch the cheese, though I assured her it tasted like spreadable feta. Nancy and I ate it all. Then the landlord said it wasn't pasteurized. Probably coincidentally, Nancy and I got turista while Norma was spared.

Nancy, who is into Wicca, is going to do a cleansing exorcism on her apartment, which has already witnessed three "deaths." Norma stomped on a centipede in Nancy's bathroom. Nancy swatted a bee that investigated her dishwater and didn't mean to kill it. And then she found a second bee drowned in the dishwater. She is crestfallen. (But I've seen her kill mosquitoes without a second thought.)

She missed some full moon ceremony someplace earlier tonight because the full moon never came out from the clouds. We didn't ask for details. She once celebrated Winter Solstice by casting a circle and doing some ritual while we were all camped near Hattiesburg, Mississippi. We'd cowered inside our RV hoping no one else at the campground would notice the woman in the black dress with the suns and moons design, waving a smoldering wand of sage twigs and chanting incantations. I think she'll find a few kindred souls here. Most art colonies harbor all kinds of free spirits.

After all the walking we do here, I sleep very well at night, despite firecrackers and chimes. I haven't fallen again but I notice that I watch my feet very carefully. Such a temptation to look all around rather than at the cobblestones. Have I mentioned I love this place?

We have our first new friend who actually lives here! Remember I described seeing Tom Wolfe meets George Hamilton at Harry's? The Tom Wolfe guy was at the Bach concert and introduced himself. (I'm going to call him Tom here, and change other names for privacy reasons.) Norma agreed to come just so she could see the inside of Teatro Angela Peralta.

Again Tom was all in white with a white straw Panama or fedora or some such snappy hat. I can't tell the difference between ear muffs and a beret. When I introduced him to Nancy he said I'd been flirting with him at Harry's, and Norma almost cracked her umbrella over his head. Well, yes, I had been staring at him, I was so glad to see someone so openly gay. That's a sign of an open and liberal community, like canaries in a mineshaft. No, he didn't have on a rainbow pin but I knew.

He's been in SMA ten years. He came down for a short vacation and also "fell in love with paradise," his words. He gave up his car years ago because buses and taxis are so cheap and plentiful. He told us that for the first two years he tried to get involved in all the activities but there are too many egos involved in the gringo community: big fishes in a small pond. He warned us that an Anglo will never be totally accepted in the Mexican community, not really, not even through intermarriage.

He also warned us of squabbling in most of the Anglo organizations. Too many expats move to SMA determined to "save" Mexicans and change the people and the country, which causes much bad feeling, he said.

We assured him we have no intentions of getting involved with anything resembling the homeowner's association we left in Phoenix. I will be very careful to not get involved in any political infighting or struggles. I've already learned that lesson. I keep telling myself that warning. Norma and I know we are guilty of having been the kind of people who want to take charge of a group and run it "right."

Our RV park was full of retirees who were used to giving orders in their professional lives and having underlings snap to and obey, and they had nothing else to do all day but drive around in their golf carts looking for rules violations to report at the next board meeting. In fact, our first night in San Miguel Norma jokingly tallied a dozen "rules infractions" that she'd have to report to the park manager! We are not here to change Mexico but to let Mexico change us. Please. I feel as if I have been under stress my entire life.

Tom said many who cross the border rewrite their resumés—the high school teacher becomes a former college dean, the small business owner's store was a multi-million-dollar chain. Norma said, "Oh, the border upgrade." We want to do a border downgrade and stay invisible nobodies. No stress.

Anyway, we're going to Tom's place for drinks soon to meet some people, and he gave us a 6" x 9" card with all sorts of names and phone numbers of recommended plumbers, handymen, doctors, etc. He's a lifesaver. *The Insider's Guide to San Miguel* is also a fantastic resource.

The Bach concert was in the Teatro Angela Peralta, built in 1873, like a classic European opera house. I've been told that the bullet holes were left in the façade to remember the revolution of 1910. Vickie Carr was one of the people who sponsored one renovation in the 1960s. The plush if worn red velvet seats are due for another. First level and side box seats went for $10 U.S., maybe 200 of those, then $7 and $5 for the second and third floor balconies, which probably held another 200.

Only about 100 attended the concert. A Mexican soprano soloist named Marta Silva seemed technically competent and quite expressive, to my musically untrained ear. Six men and five women made up the orchestra, all professional except for the third violinist. The young woman, about 18, kept rolling her eyes, scratching her head, and peering at her watch. Hope somebody will talk to her about stage presence.

The director was also the contrabassoonist and had studied at top schools in St. Petersburg, Russia, or so I think the Spanish-language program said. I didn't even have to jab Norma once to wake her during the concert.

We've tried another restaurant. El Palacio Chino had a good hot and sour soup, lighter and more like that served in LA Chinatown than the thick brown gravy we've gotten in some Phoenix restaurants. For $9 each we also had General Tsao's chicken, egg roll, rice and Coca Light, as Diet Coke is ordered here. Not everything was equally good. Norma and I had once talked about opening a California-style restaurant when we lived in rural Michigan, but she said my cooking wasn't consistent. I never follow a recipe exactly, and that's what diners expect in a restaurant.

I'm glad we never went ahead with that fantasy. Someone here joked that the way to make a small fortune in San Miguel is to start with a large fortune and open a restaurant. But they say that about every city. I first heard it said about Detroit fifty years ago.

We're still eating as we did in Phoenix to lose weight: one main meal and then small meals like cereal, fruit or yogurt during the rest of the day. But we're losing weight faster here than in Phoenix, undoubtedly because of walking a couple of miles a day, some of that uphill. Norma's T-shirts are hanging like maternity blouses. We're slightly too fat still for "L" sizes here, or, more accurately, "G" for *grande*. Mexican sizes seem smaller. We might have to resort to Querétaro Wal-Mart's large size department until we can fit in "L" or "G." Someplace has to sell large sizes.

Not all Mexicans are thin, though you don't see the number of fat people that you do in the States. The fact I'm tall at 5' 8" compared to most Mexican women is another problem. Looks like many blouses in the shop windows wouldn't cover my waist. I'm long past the age of exposed midriffs. Long sleeves would end above my wrists, slacks would be clam diggers.

I keep being surprised at how much international news we get here, and all the serious stuff from D.C., but sometimes I miss the fluff. You can really see the differences in the foreign currencies in Latin America by looking at the *Newsweek* and *Time* covers—in some South American countries the *Newsweek* price is $10,000 in their currencies.

At first I didn't miss U.S. television here but I'm starting to crave lighter shows. Okay, I'll admit it: I've watched *All My Children* since I was stuck in a hospital for a month in 1981 with nothing else to do but watch TV, and Norma has watched it even longer. What's going on with Erica, Erica Kane? I'm missing *The Sopranos* and *Six Feet Under* and *Nightline* and all the *Law and Order* shows. I can't wait to get cable TV next week so we can get the U.S. networks, PBS, CNN and HBO.

In Phoenix we joked about worshipping at St. Mesa, a gigantic swap meet, on Sunday mornings. Here we have Tuesday Market, about six small blocks of outdoor markets covered with red and blue tarps, next to Gigante supermarket on the outskirts of town.

New and used clothing was piled high on some tables, and Nancy said she'd spotted a silk skirt she liked that a Mexican woman was holding up for size. The woman asked the guy staffing the table how much the skirt was, and she was told 20 pesos, about $2 U.S. The woman put it down. Nancy swooped in and the guy said it was 25 pesos. Nancy raged but bought it. When she got home she found she'd purchased an Anne Klein II pure silk skirt that probably cost $200 in NY.

Most of the stalls sold fresh fruits and veggies, but I couldn't believe the number of booths selling plastic everything—ice cube trays and storage boxes and clothes hangers and dishes and combs and toys and three stacking bowls for a buck. Tables of bootleg DVDs of movies that were just out in the U.S. and CDs of both Mexican and U.S. singers were on display for one or two bucks.

The owners offered to play a sampling of any item throughout to show it was good quality. Bootleg movies often end abruptly in the middle when the person doing the taping is escorted out by perceptive ushers.

Mexican music blared, hawkers pitched everything from apples to zippers, caged canaries warbled, chicks peeped, puppies yipped, babies wailed, sample slices of mango or frosted cakes wafted in front of my nose, the aromas of roast pork *carnitas* and fresh pineapple tempted, and shoppers chattered indistinctly as background hum. Overdrive for all senses.

I couldn't help it, one stall fried fresh fish fillets, and it looked sanitary. The fish was firm and on ice, it went directly into batter and then into a huge kettle of sizzling oil, and then separate tongs were used to catch it in the oil and plop it onto a fresh paper plate. A ten-ounce slab of fish cost $1.50.

I said no to the accompanying salad in case the veggies hadn't been soaked in an anti-bacterial agent like Microdyn. We're very careful to purify our veggies. But then we think, produce from the same Mexican fields is trucked to U.S. supermarkets and no one soaks foods in any kind of disinfectant up there, so we wonder sometimes why we're doing it here. The fish was scrumptious. I felt so daring. May I live.

Down the aisle, full-grown live turkeys and ducklings strutted in wood pens, while the attendant fed tiny chicks with an eyedropper between bagging limes and chiles. Another stall offered rabbits and, gulp, guinea pigs. I was afraid the guinea pigs might be for eating, but I never saw any indication afterward that they were anything but pets.

One booth even had aquariums and tropical fish. My ex-husband worked in a tropical fish store in the '70s, and we had 17 tanks in our living room. Somehow I have no urge to ever have an aquarium again.

At the far end of the market men displayed used machetes, screwdrivers, bicycles, blenders, every tool or appliance you could need. You could furnish your house with hand-carved dark wood sofas, headboards, and dining room sets. A complete shoe store inventory hung from hooks against the temporary walls of several booths.

Other stalls sold underwear and socks of every kind. Flimsy thongs piled next to wool knee-highs. Bras clothes-pinned onto a rope, from 28AA to 44 DD, in laces, reds, florals and sturdy white, waved in the breeze. Bees swarmed around the honey stands, sniffing their relatives' output.

We spent maybe $10 on as much fruit and veggies as we could carry. Closer to home we picked up a rotisserie chicken with tortillas and salsa for $4—could we cook a meal that cheaply ourselves?

I checked out the art instructor on our block. He teaches oils, his former girlfriend shows how to do paper maché, and three other artists are on staff. He says he starts with basic drawing, and I have to demonstrate I know how to draw a sphere with highlight, light, shadow, core shadow, cast shadow and reflected light. No problem, I had five semesters of basic drawing and painting at Mesa Community College before we left.

What I want to learn most from Mexico is how to use color more freely, and his students' work showed they'd certainly learned how to do that.

The teacher is a character. He had in a display case two paper maché puppets done by students, and he watched me for my reaction. One puppet represented a beautiful woman, the other was a drag queen jerking off under his skirt. We laughed. The teacher said we'd fit in.

He said we looked very happy which would be a nice change. One of his students just got her divorce, and the other students insisted she stop painting men with arrows through their heads and crushed skulls. Some 25 years ago, right after my divorce from Michael, that's probably what I would have been painting, too.

Classes are M-W-F from 10 A.M. to 1 P.M., and the studio is open 24 hours for students to work. You get your own key, and you can store supplies and wet oil paintings there so I won't have cat fur landing on them. He charges $195 a month, which is less than the Institute Allende and more than Belles Artes. Sounds good. We'll budget for it. We need to find Spanish classes, too.

Paper maché is popular all over town. Nancy bought some kitsch, three little witches with big faces sitting on broomsticks when viewed from the front, and from the rear their skirts flip up to show their tushes. Not art, but cute. She has them hanging like kitchen witches for luck.

So that is where we are as of Wednesday night. Thursday and Friday nights we'll see two foreign films, *No Man's Land*, a war film about Boznia, and *Everybody's Famous*, advertised as a cult comedy. Most of the films the Biblioteca presents seem to be old Academy Award nominees or winners in the foreign film category. After the movie Thursday night we're heading for Mama Mia's, an Italian restaurant and bar that features salsa lessons and dancing.

Saturday we're going, don't laugh, on a chartered bus trip to the Wal-Mart in Querétaro, sponsored by Wal-Mart. It's $6 round trip fare on a first-class tourist bus, and there's plenty of room for purchases under the bus. (We've been told we don't even have to go into Wal-Mart—we can walk from there to Costco down the street, or take a cab back to Home Depot and Office Max, and return to the Wal-Mart lot for the bus ride home.) We have such funny stuff to buy—haven't seen a pancake turner here yet, for example, or a hand mirror, or Fixodent. (Unfortunately, Wal-Mart doesn't provide discount buses to Querétaro any more.)

Oh yes, we'll admit to some negatives. Our hot water heater isn't working tonight. It's probably out of propane. We have to wait until the landlord shows up tomorrow. And Nancy's water pump was off for several hours twice already. We need to buy some sort of tape or caulking to put around our screen windows to keep the mosquitoes out. We sleep with the fan blowing on us to keep them away.

I still have to watch the ground carefully to avoid falling, so I get lost a lot. But then I've always been directions-challenged. It feels as if we're walking the back streets of Spain, Italy, France or Portugal.

2

June

I'm surprised at the high quality of films we see in San Miguel. *No Man's Land* skewered Serbs, Muslims, the media and the United Nations equally on their rigidity. *Everybody's Famous* showed an unemployed Flemish father kidnapping the most famous singer of his country in an attempt to get a singing break for his talentless daughter.

The major U.S. first-run movies show in English with Spanish subtitles at the Gemelos, the twin theatres out by Gigante, but we'd seen everything current before we left Phoenix, so it may take six months before we can see a first-run movie here that we haven't already seen. Another small negative. But the artsy films more than make up for it.

Advertisements for Mama Mia restaurant say that if you haven't been to Mama Mia, you haven't been to San Miguel. So we had to go immediately for lunch, and the pizza was too thick and bland for us. If only our favorite pizza chain in Phoenix, Streets of New York, had a restaurant here. You may not move to Mexico for the pizza, but for us we need to have it every so often to live.

But we finally did get the San Miguel experience a la Mama Mia at salsa night Thursday. Sally from Dubuque came with us. We're still not comfortable with all this walking. Trying to keep up with Sally trotting ahead, we were huffing and holding on the walls as we walked to the restaurant, and we said we thought we'd walked a mile already.

Sally looked puzzled and said it was only three blocks, even if uphill. So maybe we haven't been walking as much as we thought.

It's been long enough we can't blame our breathlessness on the altitude any more. Let's face it, we're terribly out of shape. The 115° Phoenix summers aren't conducive to exercise. But any excuse would have worked for us back then.

Ads said the salsa started at 10 P.M., which is when we showed up. The waiter said wait until midnight, or maybe 11:30, or maybe 11. So we had nachos in the restaurant area while a lounge singer did old standards for a half dozen foreigners.

When we heard salsa music start at 11 we changed rooms, first going into one bar by mistake that had only bland rock music, and then finding the salsa room, which was really the rocking place. One show-off wore his glossy black hair below his shoulders. His black leather pants revealed all. A young woman danced by herself in the balcony, her skin-fitting blouse featuring a floral pattern that circled her abundant breasts. Dancers changed partners just about every song.

Three gringas came in alone and immediately they were dancing with Mexican men who appeared to be regulars. Our friend from Dubuque wanted badly to dance but no one asked her. Apparently we were an imposing group, while the other women came in alone and were approachable. And they'd probably come before. Or so we guessed. We're still guessing a lot.

Our landlords mentioned today they might be considering turning the complex into condos, and would we consider buying our apartment? It's too small, but if the price is right and our place in Phoenix sells...the thought is now out in the universe.

Wednesday I gathered up my Spanish to ask the maid when she was going to clean our apartment next. "*Hoy*," she said. Today. "*Bien*," I replied. "*Nuestros gatos estan en la juala.*" Our cats are in the cage. I don't know future tense, I meant I was going to put them in the pet carrier for her convenience, but I thought she would get the idea. Instead, she looked startled, then confused, then started to laugh.

When I got home I realized I'd probably said *gallos*, not *gatos*, and *toalla*, not *juala*. Our roosters are in the towel. I'd been so sure of myself.

⊘⊘⊘

Big news: we found a new place to live. On the Wal-Mart bus to Querétaro we met a couple who were moving into a new casa in Centro. They suggested we go by and see the place they'd been renting during the construction. They only got in because a previous tenant died.

We couldn't believe how big it was, for far less than anything similar would cost in Phoenix, and thousands less a month than it would rent for in someplace like San Francisco. Furnished, three bedrooms, two baths, 1,600 square feet, a big private roof patio, parking included. Plus, the price includes a housekeeper for an hour a day, six days a week.

We walked in and at first glance were turned off by the colors. The yellow walls have a hint of chartreuse to them, clashing with slate blue arches, green pillars decorated with rose cement flowers, wild painted flowers in the two blue alcoves in the dining room and kitchen, red-brown tile, royal blue hard-as-a-rock cushions on dark carved wood furniture, several red brick boveda arched ceilings, nice skylights, and a stained glass window of parrots (one piece of glass that was a pink flower petal has fallen out and has been stuffed with yellowed newspaper) in the hallway.

Bare hanging light bulbs. Narrow circular wrought iron staircase leading to the roof garden. Two plants in mineral-stained ceramic planters in the living room, one of them a scraggly, pathetic pothos vine that winds all the way round the living room on eye-level nails.

But the size of it, and the richness, and the skylights, and the colors, and the garden, and the courtyard below... *¡Grande! ¡Grande!* I kept exclaiming to the landlady who was showing us the place. I felt like dancing! "We'll take it!" I had to resort to my pocket dictionary: *¡Queremos esta!* We want this!

It's is the biggest place we've lived, except for the old country church in rural Michigan we once bought, with dreams of renovating it into a mansion. This casa is right downtown, not 90 miles from the nearest bookstore as that money pit was. We'd been trying to save money with that move, too.

The landlords let renters do anything we want, the neighbors told us, just so we don't bug them for minor repairs and complaints. Renters here are expected to pay for such stuff themselves. Whatever is missing, you replace yourself.

The last renter probably had to buy a new towel rack to replace the one the renter before took, so that renter took the towel rack as well, and now you need to buy your own towel rack, which you will take with you when you leave. You can't call a super for a leaking faucet, you hire your own plumber.

"Luckily" our present tiny apartment developed six leaks in the downpour Tuesday night, so we could be righteously indignant when we told our current landlord we were breaking our three-month lease and moving. We may even get our $500 deposit back.

This is the land of flat roofs. Leaks are not unusual. And you can expect rain will run in under your door. The cloth filled "snakes" we used to put in front of our doors in Michigan to keep out the drafts will be needed to absorb the water, if I can find them here.

The stuffed furniture is not at all comfortable—Mexican furniture usually isn't—so we'll be looking for a sofa and chairs when our Arizona home sells. The double bed (called a *matrimonial* in Mexico) has a hard mattress we hope we'll get used to. The headboard is dark wood carved into alcatraz lilies. (In English we call them Easter lilies). We want to put in some wrought iron chandeliers and ceiling fans, and we'll want to paint. Maybe a light terra cotta or peach, to blend with the red brick boveda ceilings and the floor tiles.

We met the guy I call Tom Wolfe at lunch at El Correo. Chicken enchiladas with green tomatillo sauce and scads of cheese, $5.

Tom came up with more info for us, including the best place to get mammograms. Now that's a guy being a true friend. We'll have ours done one last time in Phoenix in August when we go back to sell our park model. I'm getting really excited about making this move permanent. Our decision is starting to sink in.

We're sticking to Tom's advice: lie low, don't put your ego out there in competition because it can be a jungle of competing egos. We have absolutely no intention of doing so. Norma can't add, I can't write.

But we are helping a woman who lives in the apartment complex we are leaving who plans to decorate the children's rooms in the general hospital here. She couldn't find any picture ABC books in the Biblioteca for designs, so I'm drawing original art for her. Sure wish I had my desktop, design books, and software. A is not for apple, M is for *manzana*, a juicy red one. A is for *abuela*, grandmother.

珠

We went to a lecture at the Instituto Allende on Aztec law as it was written (drawn) in a book around 1521, shortly after Cortez arrived. The book was designed to be sent back to Spain so that the king could see what had been discovered and learn about the Aztec culture. The ships were highjacked and the book ended up in a British museum. We learned how archeologists read the Aztec picture writings and calendar. What a vicious culture! We knew about the human sacrifices, but even the kids were punished by being pricked with thorns instead of spanked. No simple "time outs" then.

The professor had pieces of obsidian that had been used as weapons, razor-sharp edges imbedded into clubs. He showed us one of the weapons that were used to gouge out the hearts of captured warriors as human sacrifices.

Our conversational Spanish classes in Phoenix had given us an overview of the capture of what is now Mexico City and the conquest of the Aztecs, but the books and weapons helped us see more clearly how and why that happened.

The Spaniards had killer dogs to supplement their handful of horses and soldiers who defeated the hundreds of thousands of Aztecs, but more importantly, they had the support of other small civilizations in the region that hated the Aztecs.

The Aztecs never totally conquered the other tribes, they kept them as enemies so that they could raid these communities for captured warlords to sacrifice. A warlord was a more important sacrifice than someone who belonged to your own group. So of course these communities did everything possible to help the few Spaniards overthrow the Aztecs.

(Later I read *Aztec* by Gary Jennings and learned that during droughts and famines it was very important that different tribes go to war so that the captured warriors who would be used in the sacrifices—and then eaten—would not be anyone you knew.)

Rainy season is definitely here. The bougainvillea is rippling in the brisk winds that churn just before each night's short storm. I thought we'd be in all night. But we heard music at dusk and had to climb to the roof to see where the party was.

I plowed up steep steps I couldn't have managed three weeks ago, though the maid scampers up and down them many times a day to hang and collect laundry. I'll have to shoot some photos from this roof before we move—fantastic views. We'll have a similar panoramic view of the city and mountains from our own private roof at the new place, however.

Feral cats are caterwauling outside and driving our three pets nuts. The wild cats roam from roof to roof. It's hard to tell whose roof is whose up there. All the properties seem to connect on high. I read a shocking statistic in *Atención* compiled by a group called Amigos de Animales, that this town of 80,000 has 45,000 dogs, 15,000 of them homeless. People who live here say that figure seems preposterously high. The group puts on free sterilization days several times a year for people who cannot afford to have a vet neuter their pets. Gringas with toy dogs dressed to the nines carry their pets with them everywhere, even into stores. You have the contrast of pampered pooches and starving curs.

Another of the major charities here is the Society for the Protection of Animals, SPA, similar to the SPCA in the States. Every year they save hundreds of dogs and cats for adoption and charge only $27 for sterilization.

They're always looking for volunteers to come spend a couple of hours at the shelter socializing pups and kittens so that they will be more adoptable. People we talk to say they could never volunteer, they'd be taking home a dozen kittens and puppies every visit. But then who will do it, people who hate animals? (I don't think we could do it, either.)

We encounter two or three beggars each day on our walks, usually very old women who sit on the sidewalks or curbs, legs tucked underneath, faces hidden in their scarves, only an outstretched hand showing. At one of the International Brotherhood programs a girl about nine simply approached everyone with one hand on her hip and the other jutting out as if to say, "You owe me." Her face and legs were smeared with dirt, her toes poked out of her tennis shoes. Nobody that we saw gave her even a peso.

Little boys sell small packets of chewing gum, which is common throughout many parts of the world. When we stop at an ice cream store for a frozen fruit bar, begging kids look up at us as we eat, wanting us to buy one for them. Overall, San Miguel seems to be a prosperous city with lots of active charities. But it's always uncomfortable for me to see a beggar.

I keep thinking of the men at the Phoenix freeway exits who looked as healthy and young as could be and who were at the same spots week after week, holding hand-lettered cardboard signs saying they are homeless and hungry. A couple of women in the RV park who worked as census takers in 2000 said they'd seen the nice homes some of these recurring "homeless" people actually lived in. They gave the really poor people who need help a bad name.

The problem doesn't seem to be as overwhelming here as in Los Angeles, where you could see people living under every freeway overpass and even on City Hall lawn. The poor people here are found more in the countryside, living in shacks and ruins, as far as I understand; only a few beggars come into the city. What is considered poverty here is far different than someone who is "poor" in the States.

I need to learn more about the Mexican economy if I am going to be a part of this country. I don't know how much to give and when to give to beggars here.

Someone I was talking to said she gives a two-peso coin, 20 cents, to the first five beggars she encounters each day. That sounds doable, $30 a month, even on Social Security. These ancient women sure don't look like fakers. I keep having the urge to empty my purse for every one. (Later: the local paper did interviews with many of the Centro beggars and they need the money, believe me.)

⁂

We're moving Monday! We talked again to the couple who had told us about the place and got the lowdown on water, maid service, cable, etc. Tom gave us more names of people who can help, starting with our immigration documents.

Norma got up her nerve to drive and we took the car out to Plaza Real del Conte mall that contains Gigante (the grocery store that we were delighted to discover also stocks Diet Pepsi) and the Immigration Office. I understand Immigration is going to move out past the major bus station on Canal soon.

Even if you get your FM3 *rentista* visa (the ones retirees usually come in on—there are other kinds of visas such as for those working here) in the States, you have to register it shortly after you settle in Mexico, basically recreating your FM3. More photos, more triplicate copies of everything including all the blank pages in passports, more financial verification that we make the minimum to qualify for a *rentista* FM3.

Currently that's $1,200 US a month, $600 for a spouse or dependent, or possibly half the monthly requirement if you own the

Mexican house where you live. If you can show you have a year's income requirement in a bank, $14,400, I understand that can be sufficient proof of solvency.

The amount changes yearly depending on a percentage of the Mexican minimum daily wage—which I was shocked to learn is around $4.50 U.S. a *day*. It varies slightly by region and by occupation. Each office can vary slightly in its requirements.

I'm not going to complain about the red tape. Just consider what Mexicans who want to move legally to the U.S. must go through.

ᗑᗑᗑ

The construction detour on the way to Gigante right now is about a mile of horrid rocky dirt road through a field. Today we had the added delight of floodwaters covering the road in two places. We followed the buses and made it okay, but then our car is a small SUV with high road clearance. Pity a loaded sedan trying to make it.

Norma did just fine on the traffic circles and speed bumps. No one stops at stop signs, even before entering a glorieta, unless you absolutely will hit someone. Otherwise, you'll be rear-ended by someone who didn't expect you to stop. Norma calls the traffic laws "suggested retail."

We discovered another nearby upscale restaurant today, Tio Lucas, which advertises that it has the best meats in town and live music every night after nine. The guacamole, chips, and salsa never stopped coming, and then they brought in the bread basket with herbed butter.

I heard that the French occupation of Mexico around the time of the U.S. civil war led to the custom of bread, not tortillas, being served many times at meals.

We should have stopped there, we were full. But no, I had garlic soup and Norma had Aztec soup, what is called chicken tortilla soup in Phoenix. Then I ordered baked spaghetti, remembering a childhood favorite. It tasted nothing like Mom's, too bland and mushy, so I piled on the salsa. Mom would not have understood.

Norma ordered Roquefort salad, made with a flourish by the waiter at the table, using cream and at least a cup of cheese. Nothing low calorie in that meal except the Romaine. Pineapple tonight.

We've changed internet cafés. This one charges less: $20 US for 10 hours. Those a few blocks out of Centro charge as little as $1 an hour. More of them seem to be springing up every day. Can't wait to get my desktop down here with high-speed internet. Today we walked four miles, much of it up and down steps. At least I think it was four miles—after our experience with Sally we're not quite sure. We don't have a scale here but I can tell I'm losing more weight from the way my clothes feel.

Our favorite walk is along Mesones from Hernandez Macias to the Civica Plaza, then north a block to Insurgentes, and back to Hernandez Macias, 13 blocks, probably a mile and a half the way we wander in and out of stores. Let me describe all the stores and restaurants we've discovered in just this walk alone.

On the corner of Mesones and Macias is the Teatro Angela Peralta on one side of the street, the opera house-style theater which often has small art shows in the lobby that is often open during the day, and a striking mural on one wall worth a visit all by itself.

Along that block on that side are the Galeria Izamal, a collective of a half-dozen artists and jewelers (love especially the free-flowing line drawings of bulls and other animals Britt Zeist paints on T-shirts), a money-changing store, a hotel and a condo complex behind deceivingly plain doors, and another couple of galleries and jewelry stores.

On the other side of that same block are Tio Lucas restaurant that specializes in excellent beef and live music each night after nine, Petit Four bakery that serves croissants and hot chocolate during the day while you drool at their pastries and chocolates, a fantastic restaurant called Nirvana which has the specialty arrachera (marinated grilled flank steak, a Mexican favorite) for $11, and a ceramics shop where we bought a bottled water dispenser for the bathroom.

We're eyeing their sets of brightly painted Mexican dinnerware to buy when the Arizona house sells.

On the same block is now a plain wood driveway door that once opened to a gay bar called 100 Angeles that closed around 2002, and later was replaced in 2005 by Proud, another gay bar that didn't last long.

On the next block of Mesones we've discovered a news stand that stays open until around 7 P.M. for when the Jardin newspaper sellers run out of *Atención* or *The Herald*, and a little burrito stand called Tortillas Harina de San Miguel that not only has something called *burritacos* (a small flour tortilla folded over a tablespoon of a dozen tasty choices of fillings for 35 cents), but the store sells the best flour tortillas in town for 50 cents a package of 10. You can get whole wheat, too.

I'm sure they're all made with lard—that's why they're so tasty. You can just point at whichever of the dozen fillings you want. I'm not sure which is which, but I can identify and pronounce the chicken in either red or green sauce (*pollo en mole roja o verde*), which are my favorites. We often have a $4 dinner there—eight burritacos and two Diet Cokes.

A dry cleaners, a plastics shop (think Tupperware but much cheaper), a cute little store with all kinds of gift wraps and children's animal costumes for parades, a Kodak camera supply store, El Tomate vegetarian restaurant, and an expat-owned greeting card shop with English and Spanish language cards are on the same block.

Duck into the courtyard housing El Palacio Chino Chinese restaurant and you'll pass an excellent jewelry stand, Border Crossings (one of at least three mail box services that utilize a Laredo, Texas, address for those who wish to keep a U.S. address), Sensual gourmet chocolates when you've got a ten-peso coin burning a hole in your pocket and you'd just as soon have one scrumptious truffle, and a clothing and hat shop. Several women's clothing stores are along this most favorite of all our "exercise" routes. We've only hit Sensual once so far.

Between Hidalgo and Relox on Mesones is Bonanza, the world's greatest small grocery shop, with probably 50 kinds of spices sold cheaply from bins; plastic bags of all kinds of bulk goodies we have yet to decipher; gourmet necessities like capers, sesame oil and tofu; and a sausages, cold cuts and cheese deli. (A tourist asked me last time I was there, "Where is the Scotch tape?" No, small grocery stores usually sell just groceries, a *papeleria* or paper store sells office supplies).

A few doors either way are shops selling sewing goods and fabrics, Apollo IX pork carnitas tacos, and a fresh veggies and fruit stand. You can get your watch repaired or buy a new one a few more doors down. (I'm sure I'm leaving out plenty of stores; these are just the ones we've noticed so far. We discover something new every day, and they come and go. Far more interesting than walking on a treadmill.)

Continuing on Mesones we pass a fresh chicken shop that gets in a truckload of fresh Bachoco brand chicken and eggs every morning, and by the afternoon they're gone. The eggs often are double yolked, they're so big. A kilo (2.2 pounds, about seven pieces) of boneless, skinless chicken breasts pounded flat to the size of a pie plate costs about $4.90. That means we get seven two-person meals of chicken for seventy cents a meal, our basic entrée at home. Norma can make hundreds of different kinds of meals from those chicken breasts.

Then we're at Plaza Civica, with its statue of Ignatio Allende on horseback, and stalls of books and foods lining the plaza. Balloon vendors are everywhere. Mexicans lounge on park benches or wait for a bus or head for the Oratorio church just past the plaza, behind and to the left.

Small restaurants and shops are tucked behind every doorway, including the highly recommended Café Colon with its cheap complete meals, called *comida* (also the word for lunch), for around $5, as you round the corner and head toward Insurgentes. (*Colon* is Columbus in Spanish, not a good name for a restaurant for English-speaking customers.)

We've discovered a cold cuts and cheeses store that sells a lean ham lunchmeat, *Jamon Americano Fud*, for $4.30 a kilo (about 35 calories a slice, a great high-protein snack); thick-sliced lean bacon which tastes much better than most U.S. ba-cons; and Oaxaca white string melting cheese that substitutes well for mozzarella.

One store owner cuts thin pork slices from a lean roast cooked like the lamb for Greek gyros and puts the meat into corn tortillas for *tacos al carbón*, 35 cents each.

Just behind Civica Plaza is Ramirez Market, the equivalent of Tuesday Market but it's open every day and under one roof, with probably 40 stalls selling mostly fresh fruits and veggies. One row is fresh flowers, especially on Thursdays.

If you keep winding your way out through the rear of Ramirez Market you come upon an area of shoe stores and an open air mar-ket with women sitting on folding chairs, their garden produce spread on a blanket or card table before them. Norma has noticed fresh mint, basil and other herbs for meals to come.

Sometimes a vendor has caged cardinals and canaries for sale, alongside too-small cages. I keep wanting to buy all the cardinals and set them free. We fed some almost-tame cardinals and squir-rels peanut butter crackers on our porch every summer day when I was a kid in Detroit in the '50s, and gradually they became rare. Our daily exercise walk brings up so many memories from how we did things as kids.

It's easy to get side tracked and wind down the Artisans' Alley between Loreto and Hidalgo, dozens more small tourist-oriented arts and crafts shops that close each night via folding aluminum walls that slide down to the sidewalk.

But we find our way back to Insurgentes, dipping into the crafts store inside the Biblioteca and usually renting a few more paper-backs, and passing lots more shoe shops, though nobody seems to carry women's shoes to fit our size 10s.

We're sure to stop at the fresh corn tortilla shop where you can see the thick masa dough going into a big machine and coming out the conveyer belt as six-inch-diameter tortillas, still warm, sold for 70 cents a kilo, a stack about six inches high. If you bring your own container instead of needing a sheet of newsprint tortilla paper, you can save a nickel.

Rotisserie chickens still on the spit can be had on this block for about $4 or $4.50, with corn tortillas, salsa and chiles thrown in. A Michoachan frozen paleta (fruit bar) shop is along the route, a tempting stop for a 100-calorie, 50-cent popsicle in familiar flavors like strawberry and chocolate, and also in mango with chile and chunks of fresh coconut meat. Often a whole frozen strawberry is imbedded on the Popsicle stick at the handle side.

This is where we turn back up Macias to return to the corner we started. If we keep walking west on Insurgentes we pass many more small Mexican grocery stores and bakeries, prices a few cents less even than Bonanza, though with much more limited choices.

We'd eventually wind around into San Juan Dios market, similar to Ramirez, a major covered marketplace with adjoining blocks of small shops. Every so often a stall is devoted to the Virgin of Guadalupe, a collection box out front to pay for the fresh flowers surrounding her statue.

Few foreigners seem to haunt these out-of-the-way Mexican areas, but these are our favorite walks. Who can get tired of walking several miles a day when we can enjoy looking and sniffing so much, not to mention people watch along the way?

It sure beats walking around and around Superstition Springs Mall in Mesa, which was our only real alternative for a walking program back in Phoenix. We just have to let our noses take in the food aromas rather than our taste buds, and to stick to only one main mid-afternoon meal a day. Somehow, we're still losing weight. I'm sure it's all the walking, however much we're doing.

We were celebrating our move to our new house with coconut shrimp and mango chutney at Nirvana when a friend, highly agitated, saw us through the window and rushed in to tell us the news she'd just heard from someone on the street. A terrorist was captured in the Sears Tower about to blow up a nuclear bomb.

We all panicked. Memories of 9/11 flooded over us. How could we find out the details? We wrapped the shrimp in napkins, shoved it in our purses, and headed for the closest internet café.

So it turned out that the guy already had been arrested a month earlier, and the planned attack was with a dirty bomb, not a nuclear bomb per se, and the attack was only in the planning stages, *abcnews.com* reassured us. Quite a relief. In fact, the major news story here is Mexico's success in the World Cup!

Is the massacre of 26 farmers in a land dispute near Oaxaca getting much media coverage there? Is the possible assassination of a woman political dissident who police insist committed suicide big news in the States?

How about the ongoing battle between the U.S. and Mexico over water along the Texas border? The Mexican government defaulted on a long-standing agreement to let water flow along the Rio Grande so that Texas farmers have enough for their crops. Now a repayment compromise cannot be reached. These are the page one stories in the daily English-language newspaper published out of Mexico City.

To accommodate its English-speaking readership, the *Herald* includes many U.S. columnists and editorials, along with my favorite comic strips such as *Doonesbury*. I occasionally check on the net how the *Phoenix Mercury* is doing in women's basketball. I'm really anticipating getting cable tomorrow, if it happens as promised.

We waited all morning for the start of new water delivery service. We've been told we can buy a five-gallon plastic bottle of purified water delivered upstairs to our new casa every Tuesday and Friday for $1.80 plus 20 cents tip. Our complex is in the Ciel delivery system, the water bottled by Coca Cola. Other areas are served by Santorini, Pepsi's product.

Our new neighbors said using reverse osmosis isn't enough to be sure drinking water is pure, you should have two kinds of water purification installed in your house, or use bottled water. They took pity on us and loaned us one of their empties to leave on the porch with the money underneath.

Can you believe leaving money out on your porch in the States? In rural Michigan, yes, but not in any city I've lived in. I feel so safe here, contrary to U.S. friends' warnings that we're about to be kidnapped and killed. We go out walking at night in Centro and feel totally free.

At least our new casa has plenty of electrical outlets throughout. One problem: you stick in a plug and it falls out. And the outlets are all the old two-hole kind. I understand that even if a three-prong outlet is installed here, very often it isn't grounded anyway. We'll need a lot of electrical work done.

The hanging bare light bulbs are annoying. You can expect to pay for a lot of renovations when you move into a Mexican-owned apartment. It's worth it if you plan to stay in the place a long time—in our case, we hope forever.

ᵍⁱ̈ː

What we do have is daily maid service included with the rent. We tower over almost everybody, including the maids, so nothing gets dusted above our shoulders, their eye level. Don't mention the top of the fridge, where I now store fresh fruits in a colorful bowl, once we scrubbed off a layer of crud.

Rather than put our "roosters in the towel," we decided to put our pets in one of the bedrooms while we are gone, with litter box and water, and to tape a notice over the door jamb so that the maids couldn't accidentally open the door without reading the notice.

And then our neighbor told us that illiteracy is high in Mexico and quite possibly the maids couldn't read the notice. I stayed home and consulted with my Spanish dictionary to make sure I told them accurately what we were doing.

We're thinking of asking that we not have daily maid service. We can't stand it. Norma's mother worked as a maid at one point, I have relatives who were hotel workers, and we're both too working class to be comfortable having someone doing what we *should* be doing. And we're washing the dishes and making the bed before they come. Our neighbors joke that we'll get over that soon enough.

Our kitchen looks like we hosted a Tupperware party. We loaded up on plastics at Tuesday Market and have every cupboard filled for $15. We found two giant if somewhat rough bath towels for $8 each. No towel racks yet, however.

We even found Hebrew National hot dogs, cheddar, and French's mustard at an expensive deli aimed at expats, though pickle relish is a no-show. All the Hellman's mayonnaise here has lime, *limon*, in it. Our neighbors say the States variety is available at Costco in huge jars.

We can't find sour cream except at a costly expat-oriented deli for $4 a carton, so we're getting used to *crema*. It has the same consistency but tastes like coffee cream. We discovered an egg crate mattress pad to improve our hard bed.

We found a painter, or rather, he found us, who will do our entire casa for $1,000. Not bad for two coats on 1,600 square feet, including the two-story utility room with circular stairs leading to the roof. He's done several of the hotels in town and we checked out his work.

A common wall treatment here is to do a base coat followed by a rag wash of a second color to give a rich, deep, mottled suede-like effect. Our park model in Phoenix has to sell first. *Septiembre*, we keep telling the painter when he arrives expectantly each morning, ready to paint. But somehow the colors here don't look as garish to us any more.

The 9' x 12' living room rug is deep red and looks vaguely Oriental, like one my folks had in the '50s. In fact, this one is so worn it very well might be the one my folks had in the '50s. It will be replaced when the Arizona house sells, too.

We won't get much out of the sale, but we're going to buy everything we need then, so that when our income drops to only Social Security, we can live on the smaller amount without feeling we're deprived of anything.

I finally ventured up the narrow wrought iron spiral staircase with see-through steps and no railings to the roof. What a sight!

A 360° panorama with church spires and domes all over the place, the pink wedding cake Parroquia the anchor. Cliff-hanging homes identify the wealthier areas.

Heavily flowered porches and rooftops dot the landscape, along with flapping drying laundry. Jacarandas, the lavender flowering trees I loved in Los Angeles, are near the end of their blooming cycle and the whole city is still purple. One of our neighbors keeps rabbits in hutches, while another has maybe 30 caged parrots and canaries on his patio.

We need to get a garden started on ours. It may be the only way we can get giant meaty Beefsteak tomatoes here. All we've seen are small Roma or plum tomatoes. (Later we found several sources for our favorite big tomatoes.) I don't know if tomatoes will grow on our patio. Someone said San Miguel is closest to a Zone Ten for what will grow here, but it doesn't fit into any one specific agricultural category.

Our cats are leaving puncture marks in the leaves of all the pothos plants throughout our house. Constantly we must shoo them away from drinking the water in the drip saucers beneath each plant. We call Calicat Old Moss Breath. In the end it's a lost cause. May they survive.

Sunday is a major festival, Day of the Locos. A huge parade will wind throughout town, everybody dancing in costume. Nancy plans to wear her witch's dress used in her Wicca ceremonies in the parade. All you need to join is a costume and a big bag of plastic-wrapped candies to toss to the kids watching from the sidewalks. We unexpectedly came upon what might have been a preview parade last Sunday at the Jardin. Or maybe it was another fiesta altogether.

At first glance I thought this parade was a giant game of teenaged cowboys and Indians, but I knew that couldn't be right. Or maybe it was. One side was in black military uniforms, waving machetes. The Indians, in fringed buckskin and face paint, also wielded machetes.

They crisscrossed the street like square dancers doing the do-se-do, slashing their machetes at each other. I do hope the blades were dulled. Wherever can I find out what this reenactment really means?

A second contingent seemed to be children dressed as devils. At least they all wore red, and a few had horns. Another group wore cartoon costumes. Disney could have made a mint on copyright violations. That's assuming anyone had any money to pay fines. I understand nobody sues anybody here because nobody can pay anyway, and if something goes wrong, God willed it.

A girl about thirteen in a flowing white dress sat on a float in front of a six-foot statue of the Madonna dressed in black. Or I think it was supposed to be the Madonna. I wouldn't have been surprised to see it was a skeleton. Grinning skeletons are a big deal here, all year round. We're thinking of buying a couple of *katrinas*, ceramic skeleton characters who are usually tarted up women in evening gowns showing bony cleavage, a thigh bone peeking through a slit in their skirt.

I'm looking forward to Day of the Dead celebrations November 2. I haven't been to my own mother's grave in Michigan in fifteen years but I'm going to visit other people's graves. Forgive me, Mom.

We also stumbled onto two funeral processions through the streets, six men carrying the caskets for miles. In these two instances, following the praying crowds were hearses that carried big silver candlesticks and bouquets, apparently for the cemetery ceremony. We think that's why men carried the caskets: the hearses were full. But we're guessing again. Mourners filled the streets for about a quarter block for each procession. Traffic followed slowly behind, no one honking in impatience.

While Norma waits for the cable box installer tomorrow I meet with the woman who is organizing the campaign to decorate the walls of the children's rooms in the general hospital. We're cutting out the designs tomorrow at her place.

Turns out that the project is under the sponsorship of the American Legion Women's Auxiliary, if anyone who knows me can believe I'm now part of what I always considered a very conservative organization.

I like the philosophy of the organizer: we want no credit what-soever, no names of any of us publicized, simply let the kids have a more pleasant place to stay in the hospital. Who was it who said that it's amazing what you can get accomplished if you don't care who gets the credit?

We must have a maid to ensure the unit is maintained proper-ly, the landlady has told us. But we were given as a trial another of the maids for this complex, a tiny tornado who whisked through our casa and found a huge amount of dust and fur on the floors from only one day.

She made a big fuss over how much she loves all animals, and please don't lock them away on her account. At least I think that's what she said. Calicat as usual threw herself all over the visitor. Lucyfurr disappeared into a closet and Lacey barked and peed on the tile, she was so scared of yet another new per-son in her life.

This maid said all animals love her, but nervous Lacey may be the exception. If only we could have her permanently. We're at the wishes of the landlord. Oh well, we'll enjoy her while we have her, our new philosophy of life.

Tomorrow we'll be gone when this maid comes so I think we'll lock up the animals anyway. She offered to do our laundry for free but I knew that was wrong, so I gave her 50 pesos, about $5 U.S., for a load, the same as we'd paid the other maid back at the other apartment. She did the load by hand and lugged it up the circular stairs to hang it on the roof to dry.

Norma pointed out to me that the load was much smaller than our usual, only three pairs of shorts, tees and underwear, and what if she expects $5 for every small load now? Oh, the problems of fair treatment of a Mexican maid. I hate it.

We'd better buy our own washing machine to solve the prob-lem. But what if she's hurt and thinks we think she didn't do a good enough job? I hate it. One of our new friends says he has two live-in houseboys; when he drops something he doesn't have time to realize it before one of them has picked it up. I hate it.

But some 7,000 permanent foreign residents probably means about 5,000 households with 5,000 maid jobs and 3,000 gardener jobs, so I guess we're an important part of the economy. Average wage the Legion women were paying is $3 an hour, though one woman "bragged" she paid only $2 US an hour. I wanted to kick her. The one time we had a housecleaning service for our Phoenix place for some special event, we paid something well over $10 an hour.

Discussion of fair treatment of housekeepers was a big part of the afternoon conversation at the American Legion work session. None of us is comfortable with it. What a stereotypical moment, a bunch of gringas trying to decide what is fair treatment of their maids.

I came out to the women right away, of course, and it didn't faze them. Three of the women were retired registered nurses who had volunteered at the general hospital but pretty much all they were allowed to do is to make beds. They want very much to bring improved medical practices here, but it has to be a long and gradual process of earning trust and respect. Doctors are kings far more than in the States, and they don't expect mere nurses to make suggestions, the women found.

We cut out and glued together 18 flowers of about three feet in height for one wall in the children's wards, and we started on the alphabet letters with items representing each letter. We'll have numbers one through ten on colorful balloons seeming to float on another wall.

We're using Foamy, a kind of stiff felt, in a myriad colors, sold at all the *papelerias*, or paper supply stores. It felt like what I imagined the old quilting bees were like, women gabbing away while we did something both pretty and practical. I don't think I ever saw anything like Foamy back in the States.

The organizer had piles of greens in many shades for anything leafy, all sorts of yellows to reds to purples to pick for the flowers, pastels for the balloons. It was fun digging through the piles all over the floor looking for exactly the right size and color for whatever pattern I was cutting out at the time. Snips of Foamy were everywhere, including in our hair. We sipped Jamaica tea or wine as we worked and chatted.

These American Legion women are not what I expected. I might as well have been in summer camp making log cabins out of Popsicle sticks with this crew. I would have never met them if we all lived in Phoenix or LA.

The Day of the Locos parade made me confront my own stereotypes and ignorance. We got a good vantage point for the parade by sitting on the cement retaining wall ledge of the lawn of the building between Belles Artes and the Hotel Sautto on Hernandez Macias. People crowding the sidewalk and street below us didn't get in our view, even when they put up umbrellas against the sun, and more people stood on the grass behind us. We found our seats at 10:45 A.M., none too soon, and waited two hours for the parade to arrive on its many-mile procession. Smart folks brought folding chairs for the other side of the street that remained in the shade all afternoon.

We'd heard estimates at least 7,000 people would march and I believe it. The parade took from 12:25 to 2:15 to pass us. I bet there were a thousand viewers at our intersection alone. In many ways it felt like an LA Gay Pride parade with all the crazy costumes, though not as organized or commercial.

The parade started two miles away and wound in and out to the Jardin, where a massive party is still going on late tonight, I can tell from the fireworks and music. But we're too pooped to check out the fiesta, even if we didn't march. We didn't get much sleep the day of the parade because fireworks woke us at 4 A.M. Fireworks are prayers, right.

Marchers wore the most elaborate and creative costumes I think I have ever seen in one spot. I took at least 50 photos, unfortunately stored in my digital computer until I can get my desktop here from Arizona. This is definitely a time when photos would be better than words, but I'll try.

Have to admit, I was horrified by the first marchers, a black-faced group in red and white polkadot Aunt Jemima dresses and turbans, many of the masks the worst stereotype of African Americans imaginable. Even the kids were in blackface. This contingent had a marching band playing sort of Dixieland swing, and the crowd loved it.

Another black-faced contingent enacted a jungle scene with cannibals boiling someone alive. Some of the natives swung bloody beef leg bones. No way would such groups be allowed in a U.S. parade of any kind today, unless the Klan rose again. I was dismayed. What had we done, deciding to move here?

Meanwhile, Norma perceived the first Aunt Jemima group as Caribbean dancers and the music as reggae. Their costumes were tied at the waists like Caribbean dancers. Some even had bongo drums, not likely to be found in a Dixieland group. Differences in perception. I hope she was right. I was so appalled I couldn't see straight.

And Norma brought up that Mexico had its own jungles and history of cannibalism and dark-skinned descendants from Africa, so I was wrong to automatically assume that African-Americans were being mocked. Even after years of anti-racism work and a background in the civil rights movement, I was still letting my own prejudices color what I saw.

I still do not know whether any particular marcher in black face was making fun of Mexico's own history or trying to be as outrageous as possible, the apparent goal of Day of the Locos.

Every group was ridiculed. Mustachioed banditos were everywhere. Fidel was a popular costume, as was Vicente Fox. I didn't see any Bush masks. All conceivable cartoon characters were well represented, copyright laws be damned. A whole herd of Smurfs ran amuck. Another popular mask was *The Scream*, but with a pump system so that "blood" streamed through the face, drained out, and recirculated.

Though the temperature was at least 85° F, marchers had on full regalia, including a troupe of Sumo wrestlers in full-body fat suits of foam. I've never seen such elaborate masks. I bet many would cost

$100 in U.S. costume stores. Spidermen were everywhere, but only on the ground. The Force was with Star Wars characters.

Not many floats were commercial, though we did see a Pepsi truck that did Norma's Pepsi-deprived heart good. Kids chanted the names of each of the floats as they passed, so we were surrounded by chants of "Pepsi! Pepsi!" Funnier was the Bimbo float—Bimbo is a Mexican bakery that owns Wonder Bread, I was told. "Bimbo! Bimbo!" the crowd roared.

Mainly the kids wanted candy from the marchers, and they shouted their demands for ¡*dulce*! I kept ducking as the wrapped hard candies flew. One very well-behaved boy about five sitting next to me the whole four hours filled his mother's big purse with sweets by the time the parade ended.

I gave him anything that landed on me in thanks for his putting up with my sun umbrella constantly hitting him the first two hours, until the sun moved enough that the trees could shade us. Paper sunshades were on sale for $2, regular umbrellas were $3. I still got a little sunburn on my thighs, unaccustomed as they were to exposure that high as my shorts hiked up all afternoon.

I told the boy's mother, ¡*Dos horas! Mucho bueno niño!*" So literally I said, "Two hours! Many good boy!" Have to get *muy* for very and *mucho* for many straight in my head. She didn't snicker. At least I didn't tell her the roosters are in the towel.

Lots of guys were in drag—definitely felt like a gay parade—and many women also wore tight dresses with balloon boobs. The upcoming World Cup soccer match between the U.S. and Mexico tonight around midnight was on many marchers' minds.

Funniest costume to me was a guy in a soccer outfit with a foam-made beer belly and a four-inch "outie" belly button hanging out at waistline level, complete with scruffy hair. At first I thought the "outie" was something else, but no, it was definitely a hairy protruding belly button.

Everything happened to Mexican dance music coming from the flatbed float trucks, with an occasional U.S. rock standard thrown in, and the paraders danced the whole route. I don't know where they got their energy to carry on for miles and hours.

Nancy had announced she would march the whole route, though we knew she'd never make it. She's in as bad shape as we are. She'd tried to get her daughter to send her witch costume through customs but the duty on used clothing of any kind is outrageous.

So she bought a Castro outfit, with full camouflage suit and a latex mask. She told us later she made it a block and a half in the heat.

She sat on the curb thinking she was having a heat stroke, waiting for a cab. But of course this was in the middle of the parade, and though there were medics with water all over, none saw her. She finally walked off the route to a restaurant that was closed but they saw her through the window and gave her a cold drink. She started to walk home. Uphill.

When she was only a block and a half from her apartment, the wrong way on the one-way street Quebrada, she sat on the curb and decided to sleep until dark when it would be cooler. I bet she really was having the first signs of heat stroke.

A cab finally came by. The driver couldn't believe she wanted a taxi for a block and a half. He had to wind through the tail of the parade to get to Quebrada going the right direction. Still a half block from her house, a broken-down truck blocked the street. Nancy would not leave the cab. The cab driver finally got out and helped the truck driver push his car out of the way so that he could get to her place. I hope Nancy gave him a good tip.

She carried a political sign urging Bush to recognize Cuba. As foreigners we are not allowed by the Mexican Constitution to take part in Mexican politics in any way without being deported, though a U.S. citizen criticizing the U.S. is okay. I didn't see any other political signs of any kind in the parade; Norma said she saw one that said, "Stop racist wars."

Nancy says the parade was late getting started because the priest who did the send-off blessing went on and on, he in comfort under a shady canopy, the thousands in weird costumes and in drag sweltering in the sun. What kind of blessing is appropriate for Day of the Locos—"Bless these smurfs, they know not what they do"?

One water company float had employees lobbing pint bottles of water out to the crowd, and one of the guys kept pretending he was going to throw a forty-pound, five-gallon water bottle at us. We all screamed appropriately.

Some pairs of dancers wore costumes that made them look like one big animal—think the traditional two-person horse costume in the States. Other individuals wore costumes that made it look as if they were two people, a second dummy person in their arms as a dance partner. Some somehow stayed aloft on stilts despite jostling crowds.

One boy never saw a bit of the parade. He was underfoot the whole time collecting candy that didn't get caught. Last I saw, he had a gallon bag full. One contingent of marchers carried extra candy in burlap sacks on two burros for easy refills. Generator-powered amplifiers kept the music coming. Before each float truck monitors walked ahead, pushing back the crowds spilling into the street. It's a wonder no feet were crushed.

To sit down on the ground with the least pain possible, left knee still sore from three weeks ago, I had to maneuver against a tree. At the end I had to scoot on my rear about ten feet across the grass to get to the stairwell where I could stand up easily. No one said a word. No one laughed. No one even looked at me funny. Elderly women and men had as much trouble as I did getting up from their seats on the thick stone walls.

To the very end of the parade the marchers were dancing with as much energy and enthusiasm as they had at the start. Conga lines inched back and forth across the packed streets, probably covering much more than the four or so miles of the parade route in actual steps taken.

After the parade passed us we went to Harry's for lunch. For some reason we felt like U.S. comfort food: meatloaf for me, thick pork chop for Norma, $25 with Cokes. An hour later when we emerged, the parade was approaching the Jardin, dancers still full of pep.

This is the first event we've experienced in San Miguel that draws so many tourists. Most seem to be Mexican tourists, though. Since San Miguel is an historical monument city, more Mexicans than U.S. and Canadian tourists visit here. We see some German, Japanese, and Chinese tour groups as well. But I've heard 90% of the visitors to San Miguel come from other parts of Mexico.

It's 11 P.M. and I still hear drums and fireworks. Parties will go on all night with the *futbol* game between the U.S. and Mexico at stake. Looking out our windows we can see all the churches lit up, glowing rose and gold in the night, occasional fireworks illuminating the night sky. Even the photos stored in my digital camera couldn't show how beautiful it is.

The next day I checked on the history of the Day of the Locos parade. According to a local magazine, *Punto de Vista*, Juárez Park once was surrounded by a pear orchard. A Franciscan monk named San Pasqual Bailon, who after his death became the patron saint of cooks, organized the religious processions for the Day of Corpus Christi.

Even when he left the pear orchards unguarded for the holy day celebrations, the legend says that the birds did not touch the fruit out of respect for the holy man. *Hortelanos*, men who tended the orchards long after the saint's death, would dance around a statue of San Pasqual as part of the holy day celebrations, and crowds would gather to watch the dancing.

Two men decided to shoo away the crowds and made costumes of flowers and put on masks for this task. They swatted the crowds with quince tree branches, and the people yelled, "*¡Los Locos! ¡Los Locos!*"

Through the years the festival around the Feast of San Pasqual overlapped with the Feast of San Felipe Neri and the Feast of San Antonio de Padua. The neighborhood that is still called San Antonio hosted amateur bullfights as part of its celebration, with bullfighters parading through its streets after the fights.

Through the years all the celebrations became one. Bullfighters pushing a paper maché bull ran into *hortelanos* from the Juárez

Park neighborhood who tossed pears to the crowds, and soon each neighborhood sponsored its own costumed parade participants in a competition.

Eventually the pear orchards were overtaken by new homes, but the parade continued, with candy replacing the pears tossed to the crowds. What a history this town has! *Punta de Vista* magazine is a beautiful glossy monthly with history articles I really appreciate.

Our Shih Tzu Lacey is running out of phenobarbitol for her seizures. Chelo, a bilingual pharmacy owner who helps gringos figure out how to get Mexican equivalents for their U.S. prescriptions (her pharmacy is at the corner of Hernandez Macias and Canal, and she will also give you shots and take out stitches), said that phenobarbitol only comes in small 100 mg. pills here. Lacey needs 8 mg twice a day. Can you imagine cutting a tiny pill into equal twelfths?

So we broke down and yesterday went to one of the most highly recommended vets, Dr. Edgardo Vasquez, who is also bilingual. Easy trip—two taxi rides with Lacey in her carrying cage. The office visit was only $20.

He did about the most thorough exam on Lacey she's ever had and recommended we take her off the pill to see if she still needs it. Phenobarbital has serious side effects with long-range use. No vet had mentioned that before. I don't know why I never did a net search on the drug; I check out every other medical question I have.

So now Lacey is meds-free, doing well, noticeably peppier. We're thrilled with the level of vet care we've found in San Miguel, taking care of yet another worry we'd had about retiring here.

The maid we liked so much broke her arm and we have another maid assigned by the landlord coming in now. We stuff the pets into the bedroom that will be Norma's quilt room, litter pan up on the desk so the dog can't get to it, sign on the door.

This maid is afraid of the vacuum cleaner and goes over the carpet with a damp mop instead. She changes the sheets on the two twin beds in the other bedroom every week even though it is clear they haven't been slept in, only the *matrimonial* is being used. She hasn't shown any emotions about the bed situation, and our Spanish is so bad we don't dare even bring up the subject. Probably best to not think about it—her motto and ours.

The maid we liked had noticed our old RV park lot sign in which I had painted Carol "heart" Norma, along with portraits of Lacey, Calicat and LucyFurr, and she had traced the heart with her fingertip.

"Are you sisters?" she asked in Spanish.

No, I answered, not quite sure what to say. "Very good friends."

"Very, very good friends," she'd smiled, and that was that. She always spoke of us as a couple after that. We miss her and hope her arm heals quickly. We may have to give into the landlady's subtle pressure that we should hire our maid independently, rather than take whomever she decides to assign to us that day.

We've started using a laundry service, which uses washing machines and dryers and charges $4 U.S. for an 8.8-pound load, using non-scented soap, pickup and delivery the same day included. Our clothes were not doing well with this maid's hand washing that involved rubbing our clothes against the rough concrete sink bottom. The maid is not happy. Our underwear was not happy.

Earlier this week we priced 100% wool rugs made here in town for future possible purchase. At first we were told $400 for a three-by-three rug and we gasped. But then we realized that was meters, not feet, and the price was for an almost ten-foot-square rug custom-made in whatever color and design we wanted.

The store owner's daughter who spoke perfect English was ready to drive herself over to our casa immediately and take exact measurements, but we said later, when we could sell our park model in Arizona. She could talk to our ever-hopeful would-be painter until then.

🌼

Last night was a bilingual presentation of *The Vagina Mono-*

logues but we were too tired to find it. The directions were unclear and the whole announcement we'd heard from a friend sounded iffy. Instead we saw *Lagaan*, a four-hour Bollywood film that I loved. Totally predictable, melodramatic, musical numbers sprang out of nowhere, and full of obvious messages.

In one scene an "untouchable," a man with a limp hand, is found to have a great curve ball, so he's recruited to join a newly created Indian cricket team that is playing a British team for high stakes. Team members get over their discomfort at having an untouchable on the team in about thirty seconds.

The village is immaculate, everyone is beautiful and well-dressed, the plot follows just so—but I still loved it. It was my first Bollywood film experience. I would have never gone to see it in Phoenix.

Turns out *The Vagina Monologues* was never scheduled for public viewing last night after all. Someone sent a notice to *Atención* as a joke with the contact phone number being that of the police. In reality it was presented for the opening of an international convention of midwives going on this week in SMA.

The woman who organized the presentation has performed in the Monologues on Broadway with Oprah and Glenn Close and has photos to prove it. But we missed it. A group is going to work on making a more Mexican adaptation with the experiences of Latinas included.

We got to meet another of the older lesbians in this town who has been here more than a dozen years but still keeps thinking about going back to her last U.S. home. She's from a Florida beach town that she says is also a real city designed for walking so you don't need a car. We love walking in SMA where we can see all kinds of people up close, living their lives. In a retirement community in the U.S., almost all white and middle class seniors, we felt isolated and segregated.

Norma and I have decided that humans were not made to live

segregated lives, by age, sex, race, religion, class, health or sexual orientation, even if the segregation is done willingly.

The woman from Florida signed me up for Scrabble every Monday morning at El Correo restaurant with her friends, at least until we leave here July 27 to go back to Phoenix to sell our house. *El Correo* means mail in Spanish, and the restaurant is across from the Mexican post office.

Everyone recommends that we sign up with one of the private mail services here (about $180 a year), with Laredo, Texas addresses, for the most reliable and rapid postal service. But a few others are very happy with the Mexican mail and have had no problems whatsoever.

We met our new friend for English fish and chips at Villa Jacaranda, a fancy hotel that also shows classic and artsy movies every night, a drink and popcorn included in the $7 admission.

Later we went to Nancy's place to see a videotape she'd bought on the roots and meaning of the major San Miguel festivals, which should help us figure out what is going on here all the time.

SMA has been called a party town for at least a century, I've learned. Decades ago the church ordered it to cut back on its six, count them, six major patron saints days, since nobody ever got any work done. A few U.S. citizens "discovered" 400-year-old San Miguel in the '30s, most notably a man named Stirling Dickinson who got off the train, took a burro-drawn cart ride into town, and announced he'd stay. He did so much for SMA through the years that there is a street and a park named for him.

The beats hung out here in the '50s, particularly at La Cucaracha bar that used to be right on the Jardin, where Banamex is now.

The first major influx of U.S. citizens came after WWII and the GI Bill, which allowed veterans and their families to live well here while studying art and Spanish at the Instituto Allende for recognized college credit.

Stirling Dickinson is probably the most responsible for earning San Miguel its reputation as an artists' colony by publicizing this possibility.

The original town was on the route for the transport of silver out of mines in this region. Nearby Guanajuato, now known as a university town, once produced 40% of the world's silver. Many wealthy Spanish families built sprawling haciendas outside town and mansions inside the city limits, giving SMA its colonial flavor.

Many of these mansions are now the foundation for complexes of apartments and condos inside gated walls, as well as the remaining massive private estates that look so plain from the outside.

It has been the Mexican way for richer people to not flaunt their wealth. Their poorer neighbors know full well the estates inside the walls are luxurious, but everyone has a plain front wall. That is why some natives resent the more ostentatious new gringo developments. Or so I have heard my first month here. I do not mean to be like the couple I criticized earlier who were instant experts on SMA in less than a week.

One legend is that dogs helped the first Spanish settlers here, particularly Fray Juan de San Miguel, discover the fresh water springs a few miles from the original church. Another is that Chichimeca Indians kept attacking the first Catholic church and settlement, and when it was safe to come out of hiding, the friar moved the church to a safer place.

SMA has changed names several times in its history and was once San Miguel the Grand. After its native son Ignacio Allende was a leader of the Mexican Revolution of 1810, the name was changed to San Miguel de Allende.

Today the springs still flow at El Charro, by Juárez Park, at a square where artists can show their paintings for free on weekends. We were expecting something huge from all the publicity about this weekly event but only a few artists had their paintings propped up against benches around the park.

When we walked through the park, a dozen Indian women were hand washing their families' clothing in cement washtubs into which the springs flow in El Charro, and they make it clear they do not like their pictures taken. Tourists were snapping them anyway.

It's 5:30 Saturday morning, and I got up an hour ago to use Benadryl cream for mosquito bites. We had the front door open so long last night for guests who couldn't get out the door that mosquitoes got in. We thought we had the mosquito problem solved by patching all the holes in the screens, taping the spaces under the screens where they squeeze in, and using a fan, but that wasn't enough last night. We hadn't been bothered since our first two nights here.

Mosquitoes love me. They ignore Norma right next to me and feast on any exposed inch of my hide. The small mosquitoes here are nothing like the jumbo jets we had on the farm in Michigan or in the jungle-like environment along Mexico's tropical coasts. But they can still chomp.

Somebody told us the best thing to try are the plug-in mosquito killers, made by Raid and Baygon, which have replaceable tablets to change every night for 12-hour relief.

So far it's been temperate here, a welcome relief from both Phoenix and Michigan. It's similar to Los Angeles, which has the closest thing to perfect weather, but we didn't realize it when we lived there. We've read that April and May are the hottest months, and occasionally it does go over 100°F for a few days in May, but you may still need a light jacket at night.

June through October is the rainy season, which usually means sunny weather all day and then a sudden thundershower rolls in around late afternoon or early evening for about an hour. Highs are in the low 80s, lows in the 60s.

In November it starts to cool off. December and January are the coolest months and some nights can dip below 32° while days are around 60°-70°.

February 2 is Candelaria day, the start of the spring planting frenzy, and temps rise slowly as April and May come around again. Sounds like my idea of perfect weather, a hint of seasons for variety but none of that white stuff, and no more 115° summers like Phoenix.

Supposedly San Miguel has scorpions and rattlesnakes like in Phoenix, especially in areas outside Centro, but we haven't seen any. We're still loving it here. I can't believe we've only been here a month.

A major barrier to our staying in San Miguel has been resolved. There is indeed halfway decent pizza here. A place called La Grotta is listed in *The Insider's Guide to San Miguel* as having the best pizza in town. The book's editor, Archie Dean, recommends having Roquefort and pepperoni—who would have thought of that combo?

The guy who does the Archie and Jughead comics left a drawing showing the cartoon characters exclaiming La Grotta has the best pizza in San Miguel, so it must be so.

But it's only halfway decent, the thin crust sometimes tasting more like piecrust. Norma says she's going to experiment with baking at a high altitude.

It's 5:30 A.M. and fireworks are in full force, welcoming the dawn. LucyFurr is hiding again. She gave us a scare by disappearing while the substitute maid was here yesterday, but after five hours she sauntered out of someplace. She hates this maid. All the pets hate this maid. This maid hates them.

Norma and I both expected that the city and people would be dirtier. So far she has encountered only one mentally ill street person, reeling down the street, muttering to himself, reeking. That's less than we would have seen in downtown LA in an hour.

Shop owners here are like Dutch or German storekeepers, washing down their sidewalks each morning before the stores open—I think it's the law. Deodorant is used pretty universally here compared to much of Europe when we last visited. I had to hold my nose as discreetly as I could on Roman buses. Kids seem so much better behaved here than in the States. I haven't seen a one with that slack-jawed sneer some "bored" U.S. teenagers put on when they can't get to their Gameboys. I don't live with that expectation that somebody is going to call me a fatso or lesbo or commie or dog or whatever.

Of course I'm 110 pounds thinner, and I'm losing even more rapidly down here. Most of my life I've come to expect nasty comments, especially from kids. Very fat people are certainly "the other." It was easy to identify with minorities in the civil rights movement and to expand my understanding of "minority" as the years went on.

Even at this weight we're still so much taller and heavier than the average Mexican adults that I think we'd probably be getting some insults if the people here were used to making them. But so far we've had nothing but respect. Not a fearful, cowering kind that someone who is feared gets, but ordinary human respect.

In one conversational Spanish lesson at Mesa Community College, the teacher said that *gordo*, or fat person, is not really an insult here, it's used as just another adjective or nickname. *Gordo* doesn't carry the hatefulness of the word "fat" as it is often used in the U.S.

Obesity is becoming recognized as a health problem in Mexico, especially among kids who are eating more junk food these days. Beans, rice, corn tortillas, fresh vegetables and fruit are a healthy diet. Sugar-laden soft drinks, chips, pork rinds and candy from the storefronts many Mexicans are opening off of their front rooms for extra income are not.

Class issues are involved as well. Originally fat people were more likely to be wealthy, living lives of leisure, and even among my older German relatives who were not at all wealthy it was considered healthy to put on a layer of fat in the summer to be ready for winter.

Then it became true that richer people were less likely to be fat, and obesity was a stigma of the poor, blamed on poor quality starchy and fatty food. It seems as if that might be true here, too.

I'm sure that anti-gringo comments are being made by some Mexicans, and some gringos say things that make me cringe. This is the time of year when "the Texans" come to SMA for relief from their hot summers, and I have indeed heard disparaging remarks from other expats about "the Texans." Even though I'm a Yankee, I have close Texan relatives so I'll take that personally.

I've heard some of the older U.S. men make slurs against older U.S. women, and some women throw all men into the same stereotype. The issues are so complex and interrelated. Here a whole bunch of new factors have entered into consideration.

One preconception we had was that young Mexican women would be loaded with perfume, and we were wrong. Norma is allergic to it, and after 23 years of living in her non-perfumed world, my eyes water at strong aromas. She has trouble breathing, a bit more serious. Only twice here has she been bothered by perfume, and that was on U.S. tourists dolled up for an evening out.

It's almost 7 A.M. and the fireworks are still exploding. Maybe I can get to sleep after writing so much, though. Another day, another parade, another fiesta, who knows?

One too-curious stray cat caused our entire apartment complex to be without electricity from 3 A.M. until 8 P.M. today. The sign up on a roof near the gate of the hotel parking lot says, *Peligro*, but the cat didn't know the word for danger. It is still on the roof, four legs straight up, the inside of its mouth all black, splayed against the electric coils and transformer. Norma had to say it: it looks like a *piñata*.

We need to have candles in stock at all times, we've been advised. We took our refrigerated food over to Nancy's and will have to cook up two pounds of defrosted hamburger and a pound of Kielbasa sausage tomorrow. Maybe we'll pretend we're back on the Atkins Diet and stuff ourselves with the fatty meats in a carnivorous feast. It's my German background; I can't throw anything out. But Norma can, thank heavens, even if she has to sneak stuff into the trash.

We were most concerned about our prized Costco-sized jar of rare non-limed Hellman's, the turkey lunch meat and muenster cheese which ended up costing $18 at the specialty deli when we weren't paying attention to prices, and the last of the Skippy peanut butter brought from Phoenix. I had made fresh salsa and guacamole, too. We had that as dinner.

This morning was my first Scrabble game at El Correo, and these people are sharks! I always get at least 200 points in four-person competitions back at the RV park, but I managed to rack up only 80 points the first game, 126 the second. The winner had more than that on one word—all seven tiles used and a well-placed Z on a triple-word space. We played using a small magnetic travel set and ate breakfast at the same time.

I've discovered *chilaquiles*: lightly fried corn tortilla triangles simmered in green salsa and light cream, topped with melted white Mexican cheese, slices of poached chicken breast, and slivers of onion. How could I have lived so long without *chilaquiles*? Salad tonight.

One of the onlookers was a very out gay Mexican man, the first I've seen here who absolutely could not be mistaken by anyone. Bowl haircut, kohl eye liner, such a flawless complexion it had to be from foundation, long white Indian tunic over white harem pants, and when we shook hands he had on so many bulky rings that it was like shaking hands with a metal robot. Necklaces included a genuine (I asked what kind of stone it was) blue quartz pendant four inches across. I do love blatant queens.

The Scrabble player I am replacing temporarily is moving to Thailand to be near her son. She said she couldn't wait to have servants fan her while a massage therapist started at her head and at her toes and concentrated somewhere on her middle.

The gay guy said, "That middle part, that is going to cost you plenty," as he twirled the massive blue quartz and rolled his kohl-lined eyes. Love it.

Tonight we saw Part 4 of the PBS *Jazz* series at the Biblioteca, and the volunteer coordinator of the Spanish/English conversations in the courtyard caught up to us and asked us to volunteer.

At least could we make up flash cards in English and Spanish with drawings or photos of each item? Surely such items exist already and aren't too expensive? When she found out we were going back to Phoenix to sell our house she begged us to bring back any kind of kids' games and books, in either English or Spanish.

We understand we will have to use a broker and prepare a *menaje de casa* list of everything in each box, in Spanish, in triplicate, for shipping. We each get a one-shot deal on a *menaje de casa* if we apply for one within six months after receiving our FM3, our visa to live here. Then we have three months to actually use the *menaje*. Married couples get only one shot, but for a change not being able to be legally married works in our favor, we could do two of them. The laws seem to change frequently and may be enforced differently from consulate to consulate, city to city. You have to verify everything at the consulate or office where you are.

I hate to pack anyway so we are dreading making out a *menaje de casa* especially in Spanish. Pages of "Miscellaneous" won't work, I don't suppose.

The new *Atención* came out today and we had to pick and choose to see as much as possible. Tonight is the continuing PBS series *Jazz*, tomorrow night is the film *Bread and Roses* after a day at Tuesday Market, Wednesday night is an Aztec Dance Troupe at 5 P.M. and a free classical ballet program at 7, and somehow we'd like to be able to sneak away for a lecture on *The Myths of Quetzalcoatl* in between.

Thursday is the movie *Lantana*, Friday is a lecture on "Mexican Magic and Mythology," Saturday is an all-day arts and crafts fair at the Instituto Allende and probably the biweekly $6 bus trip to Querétaro sponsored by Wal-Mart.

Sunday morning a new friend will speak to the Unitarian Universalists' meeting on changes she's seen in San Miguel since her arrival in 1980, followed by a garage sale benefiting the Society for the Protection of Animals.

Monday is another lecture, on Maximilian and Carlotta—somehow I never learned in school about the French ruling Mexico. Wednesday morning the American Legion Auxiliary women are cutting more decorations for the children's rooms of the general hospital. Thursday from 10 A.M. to 2 P.M. we're selling tickets for a production of *Cabaret*, and Monday morning is Scrabble again.

We need a date book, after vowing we would never have another. We're missing as much as we're scheduled to see.

And yet while we were reading our *Atención* in the Jardin, two women on park benches across from us closed their paper and sighed, "There's nothing much happening this week."

We've only driven the car 81 miles in 5 weeks, compared to 3,500 a month in Arizona and more in Michigan. Norma has to start it every few days to keep the battery running—and she missed a few days. Dead battery. A mechanic is outside with her now, working on it. He's gotten the alarm to work. Neighbors must love us.

I found green tomatoes! I haven't seen one since leaving Michigan in 1994. At Tuesday Market one produce stand had a box of forlorn tomatoes not quite ready for prime time, but perfect for me. So breakfast this morning was fried green tomatoes. Somehow I'm still losing weight. Must be all the walking. And no drive-thrus.

The lecture on the magic that underlies Mexican culture and religion helped me understand the historical underpinnings of this town. It is ironic that the decorative church details and support pillars for Catholic saints at churches are so often decorated with what I vaguely recognize as pagan symbols.

Dr. Marc Taylor, a local lecturer who is also a psychologist, presents an excellent lecture series each SMA high season on many aspects of Mexico few of us know when we get here. (Unfortunately, he received a job offer back in the States that he couldn't refuse. A new round of lecturers will come forward to replace him, as he replaced earlier lecturers who helped educate newcomers to San Miguel.) These are his ideas as I remember them.

Mexico is supposed to be one of the most Catholic of all countries, but the only reason Catholicism has "succeeded" here is because it firmly rests on magic and mythology. When the Spaniards insisted the conquered Indians put up altars to Christian saints, often the pillars and statues they built contained statues of their old gods inside. The Mexicans appeared to be worshipping the Christian symbols but in reality they were honoring their hidden traditional pagan gods.

Carlos Casteñada's books present these magical underpinnings of the culture and religion well, i.e., the shaman who goes on mystical journeys, often with the help of peyote, and whose discoveries are presented to the people via the priests. The rituals that are supposed to be ways to get to the magic end up being endowed with the magic themselves, in people's minds.

The power and prestige of Catholic priests here comes originally from that given to pagan priests. There is supposed to be a very strict separation of church and state in Mexico, and in fact there have been periods when the Catholic Church has been so suppressed that nuns and priests could not appear out of their homes in religious garb under penalty of death.

Through the years I've heard many people in the U.S. joke that they were raised Catholic with a touch of voodoo on the side. In reality that isn't far from the truth for many. My Catholic college education with a minor in theology and philosophy, taught by the Jesuits who are considered the intellectual leaders of Catholicism, makes me want a thoroughly grounded, intellectual understanding for religion. Others are content to get comfort. Others want justification for their existing attitudes. All I am sure of is that Catholicism as it is practiced here is not my mother's Catholicism.

We went to an Aztec dance presentation that turned out to be a dozen women in costumes of shiny gold, silver, and brilliant colors, performing what were once war dances and which are now dances performed in festival competitions between tribes.

Three of the women were pretty good, one put her whole heart into it, and two young ones in the back row weren't able to chew gum and dance at the same time. Literally. Their gum came first.

That same night we attended the semester finale for a dance school at Teatro Angela Peralta, packed with proud parents and with foreigners out for a free night's entertainment. First half was traditional ballet. Even the youngest and clumsiest were allowed to perform, with expected results. You know those long ribbon streamers used in rhythm gymnastics in the Olympics? Imagine kindergarteners creating a tangled mess with those same streamers. At least no one got hurt.

I remember attending one of my kid sister's tap dancing class recitals when she was about nine, and Norma went to more than her share of her kids' performances, but this time we didn't have to hold our breaths praying our particular kid performer didn't mess up. For those children who did, their parents caught it on tape. As many camcorders and camera flashbulbs illuminated the audience as at a similar recital in the States.

In the second half of our free night's entertainment, older kids did an excellent job with modern dance. The only boy performer of the night had his own preteen swooners in the audience.

It's the 130th anniversary of the Teatro Angelo Peralta, and all month they have been giving concerts of performers from throughout Mexico, free for the effort of picking up tickets the day before until they are gone. We got into a Flamenco show that was fabulous--I kept thinking of Lord of the Dance and of Sammy Davis Jr. as the man danced.

To me, one of the young women looked like Catherine Zeta Jones, another like Selma Hayak, and the third like Sara Michelle Gellar. Jones was a bigger woman with full power in her thrusts and wide-spread thighs when she jumped and leaped like a lion. Selma wore black, the full skirt lined in turquoise, and her dancing emphasized the flair of her skirt to flash that turquoise. Buffy was a waif with a white scarf tied around her hips, and all her flair was in the quick sway of those hips.

The guitarists and drummer behind the dancers were also excellent—the drummer used only a wooden box, not any kind of drum. He had white somethings on the ends of his fingers that at first I'd thought were painted white fingernails, and he kept building the rhythms on that box until the audience exploded. All of us were exhausted, not only the dancers.

Saturday morning we did the Wal-Mart bus trip again and are learning to appreciate Peter Pan peanut butter since Skippy can't be found, at least not now. Others tell me brands can be found here in cycles—next week it may be Skippy again. Same as in the States, where we never knew what the big box discount stores would have.

Still haven't found trivets, or sink stoppers, or a toilet paper roll holder bar sold separately from the entire holder. Once we found an elusive pancake turner, we started to see them everywhere.

We went to Costco to purchase a bathroom scale but I'd forgotten to look up the word for scale. I approached a stocker and acted out stepping onto a scale and looking aghast at the numbers—universal body language for women. But not this one.

She got someone who was supposed to be English speaking, a male, and he was even more confused. Norma finally said "kilograms" and he took us right to the scales. Same price and model as the ones at the Phoenix Costcos.

So now we really know what we weigh, and we've each lost 12 pounds in five weeks by walking and eating more fresh fruits and veggies. Our weight loss had slowed to almost nothing in the States but we jumpstarted it again here, as we'd hoped.

A friend from Arizona has arrived for a month. Though she'd confirmed her rental for today, it wasn't ready. On the internet she'd found a $700 a month one-bedroom apartment, Her whole apartment complex is like a lush tropical garden. You can hardly see anybody else as you walk the paths lined with rubber trees.

This morning we went to the Unitarian Universalists to hear another new friend speak about the changes in SMA since she arrived here in 1980 at the age of 31, having been a beach bum in Puerta Vallarta for years before that. She, too, was attracted to SMA's bohemian artsy reputation. It was even more of an art town then.

She said she sees too much of an influx today of rich people who treat SMA as their private preserve, out to change it to make it meet their resort expectations. Too many people are arriving to take money out of this town rather than to give back to the community, she believes.

It doesn't help that *Money Magazine* and the CNN website on hot retirement spots and many other media stories have played up how gorgeous and charming it is here, she said. Too many people are arriving on the wings of the latest fad, without having done any research into Mexico or having any understanding or appreciation of Mexican culture and people. She was pretty critical of the foreign community in San Miguel today.

At least Norma did six months' intensive research before we came, and she had traveled and camped extensively throughout Baja when she was raising her three kids. We did arrive prepared to appreciate and respect the diversity and to try to be as unobtrusive as possible, with few expectations.

Many of the people at the UU meeting were not at all pleased with any criticism of SMA, and our friend felt, as people surrounded her after her presentation, that some were downright hostile. We swept her out of there and on to our next destination, the garage sale benefit for the Society for the Protection of Animals held at St. Paul's Episcopal Church. Two churches in one day, I can't take it!

Not much on sale there, and what there was seemed overpriced for used stuff. But if anyone was searching for something that couldn't be found in SMA stores, brought here from the States, the prices were low compared to a trip back to the States.

Selling tickets to *Cabaret* in the Jardin was an experience. The first day we had a whole bunch of elderly expats crowding us on the shaded wrought iron benches facing the Parroquia, which apparently are the benches where many foreigners congregate. (I've heard one particular row of benches called "The Texas seats.")

All of them kept saying they did not want to be part of "the gringo benches," but there we were, making up "gringo benches" of our own. One woman about 80 who already had a snout full at 1 P.M. chatted nonstop at us for the whole four hours we sold tickets.

The second day a couple sat next to us, and I assumed they were native Mexicans. The guy stood up, looked over the all-English poster for *Cabaret*, shrugged, and sat down again. We got that a lot from Mexicans who passed by.

An expat approached and bought a ticket, and then engaged the guy in conversation in fluent Spanish. Eventually she asked him if his wife spoke any English, and he announced that she taught school in Texas, in English. So then his wife joined in. She was a U.S. citizen, and her husband wanted to show her their heritage.

They were on a ten-day crash course around Mexico, which was overwhelming her in its diversity. She loves San Miguel for its beauty and European feel. They live in McAllen, Texas, where he is a veterinarian. So much for my stereotypes. And hers.

Norma is on the great furniture hunt, looking for upholstered chairs and a sofa that are soft enough for U.S. tastes. At Icpalli she found two luscious Mexican barrel chairs with soft cushions, which require a month to be made to order, at $730 each. We were almost sold but at Costco we came across a leather sofa and two chairs for $1,800, not much more than what the two chairs alone would cost.

We do miss our teal leather sofa back in Phoenix, but we're selling that place furnished. To ship the sofa here would cost more than replacing it. If only our Phoenix place would sell, and fast. But then we haven't even put it up for sale yet.

The painter still keeps showing up many mornings ready to paint, apparently not understanding my Spanish that we have no money until our U.S. *casa* sells.

3
July

I lost both Scrabble games this week, as badly as last week. I am not used to losing. We went to another history lecture on Maximilian and Carlotta, who ruled from 1864 to 1867. I won't give the whole lecture as presented by Dr. Morton Stith (he also has since moved back to the States), but it is funny how a French emperor and empress could sit in power in Mexico at the same time Juárez was the duly elected president.

When European colonialists took over New World territory in the mid 1800's, France, which didn't get much in Africa, spotted Mexico. Just as Cortez's soldiers were the second and third sons of royalty with no jobs, Maximilian was the second son of the Hapsburg reigning king of Austria. Carlotta was the daughter of the Belgian King Leopold who ruled the Congo in the mid-1800's.

So Napoleon III decided they would be the ideal rulers for Mexico: high ranking, and unneeded in Europe.

Maximilian said he wouldn't go unless the people of Mexico really, really wanted him. Three million Mexican people were literate at that time and thus eligible to vote. Maximilian got seven million votes. He set out for Mexico with 15,000 French Foreign Legion soldiers.

Like Cortez, Maximilian was no Quetzalcoatl, the Feathered Serpent, even if he was also blond and blue-eyed and from the East as Mexican legends had predicted. He thought the Mexicans' cheers were for him.

Soon he and the Mexican people figured out the truth, and he retreated into expensive entertaining he could not afford. He wrote a book on etiquette. Mexicans made up mocking, dirty lyrics to the songs Carlotta sang to herself all day.

When Napoleon III called back the French Foreign Legion troops guarding Maximilian because Germany was uniting and expanding, Maximilian knew he was doomed. Carlotta returned to France to beg Napoleon for the troops' return but Napoleon hid from her and finally said no.

She went to the Pope, who had made Maximilian promise to get back all the church lands that had been seized in return for the Pope's blessing. The Pope pointed out Maximilian's failure and he, too, said no, even though there was no way Maximilian could have gotten back lands that long ago had been redistributed to the people.

Carlotta sank into madness. She was sent back to France where she died at an advanced age, for years rowing around in a moat believing she was rowing back to Mexico.

Maximilian was seized as a traitor and faced an execution squad in Querétaro, 45 miles from SMA. He had bribed the soldiers to not shoot him in his face, so that a death mask could be made for posterity. They complied, but Juárez didn't release the decomposing body for months.

The U.S. had a role in this overthrow as well, dumping the muskets and cannons used in the U.S. civil war into Juárez's army to enforce the Monroe Doctrine—no foreign power could invade this hemisphere. Fascinating information from Dr. Stith.

Surprise, July 4 is just another day in Mexico, though our Canadian neighbors put out a big U.S. flag on their porch, as they had displayed a big Canadian flag on July 1 for Canada Day. We're thinking of buying a Mexican flag to put out on our porch for Mexican holidays. To me, the Mexican flag stands for survival of the underdog and a perpetual fight for their own freedom, and I like that.

I used to enjoy the joint fireworks display put on by Detroit and Windsor on the river separating the two cities on a date between Canada Day and July 4. Here it's every day. When the church bells start chiming and fireworks exploding around 6 A.M. I tell myself:

someone died, someone was born, someone is getting married today, some church is reminding parishioners of early mass, or someone wants to keep the nightly evil spirits from entering the day. Fireworks are prayers. My sleep is irrelevant.

⊘⊘⊘⊘

We went to another history lecture—this is me, enjoying history—on how 550 Spaniards were able to defeat the Aztecs in 1541. Like Maximilian and Carlotta, these 550 were the useless, spoiled second and third in line royal sons. The Spanish Inquisition decreed that royal blood lines must have absolutely not a "drop" of Jewish blood going all the way back in history. This was, of course, ridiculous because Jews had been an integral part of Spanish life with considerable intermarriage for centuries.

But suddenly those who could somehow "prove" they were "pure" were required to carry with them at all times their letters of purity, so that they could be buried in Church cemeteries even if they died away from home.

The Inquisition also required that those of "pure" blood could not hold any job that Jews had traditionally held. That meant all banking, accounting, medical and teaching positions were closed, leaving mainly the military. Cortez's soldiers had failed in Cuba and saw Mexico as their last chance.

Mexican people were considered less than human, and even though Cortez promised all rivals of the Aztecs that he would let them live in peace after helping his army defeat the hated Aztecs, he had no such intentions.

Mexicans soon saw he was no peace-loving Quetzalcoatl. Even before his arrival the entire Mesoamerican world had been very violent. Tribes extinguished other tribes and entire civilizations were routinely wiped out. Aztecs were not the first to believe the sun would not rise in the morning without the daily sacrifice of a still-beating heart. Virgins were special sacrifices.

The Aztecs and other concurrent societies did not usually fight to the death in wars. They wanted to capture soldiers alive so that they could be sacrificed alive. The Indian generals were not leaders, they were referees to determine which soldier deserved recognition for each capture.

Their weapons were clubs imbedded with sharp obsidian shards, not long enough to kill, only to maim. Captured soldiers would be nursed back to health and then sacrificed, which was considered an honor.

Suddenly the Spaniards had weapons designed to kill, and they overwhelmed the native armies. They would also rape any woman they saw on the spot. Indian men could do nothing. (It could be that this powerlessness against the Spaniards turned into blaming the women as if it were their fault, a root cause of today's still-lingering machismo, though blaming victims is not unique to Mexico.)

Disease was an even bigger weapon for the Spaniards. Malaria and measles killed off entire civilizations with the arrival of Cortez. And the Mexican people were already in a state of despair, feeling that the gods had abandoned them, which made them even easier to conquer.

Cortez was extremely lucky. He landed during a celebration of the god Quetzalcoatl so that many Mexicans delayed any kind of wary response. He was able to find a Spaniard who had been shipwrecked earlier and who knew the Mayan language.

Then Cortez found a woman who became known as *La Malinche*, who knew both Mayan and Aztec languages. With these two translators he was able to make great inroads into the Aztec culture. He had her baptized and took her as his mistress. Without these two people he probably couldn't have succeeded.

Even today *La Malinche* is a controversial figure. Her name has become a word of insult describing any Mexican who is too identified with European or U.S. culture rather than remaining self-identified as a Mexican first. Feminists see her as a woman of great accomplishment, someone to be adulated; others see her as someone to be despised for abetting the conquest of her own people.

When the silver mines were developed by the Spaniards, the life of a Mexican was so devalued that the men were simply put to work in the mines until they died—which sometimes took only a few days. I had no idea of all of this history.

After selling tickets for *Cabaret*, I was eager to see the quality of this community theater. Most of the actors and production people had lots of medium-league experience and the show went like clockwork. Such an abundance of talented, artsy people here in all fields! I've always wanted to do some acting. But then I always wanted to be Joan Baez, too. Norma directed several shows back at the RV park. Maybe Norma and I will work on stage props or something someday.

But we've promised ourselves not to get overextended ever again. Nancy, meanwhile, has jumped in with feet and arms flailing and was a dresser for this play. She had a great time, saving the day by donating a button from her own blouse to replace one lost by a main character on a pivotal costume detail.

We leave here July 10 to get the Phoenix park model ready for sale and will return in a month.

4

August

So glad that ordeal is over. It felt like returning home to come back to San Miguel. The narrow cobble-stoned streets and rainbow house colors are so beautiful. The wedding cake Parroquia still takes my breath away every time I see it.

It's great to have our desktop computers up and running, brought back on our *menaje de casa*. When we finally sat down to do it, it wasn't that hard to prepare a list in Spanish of the contents of each of our 15 packing boxes purchased at OfficeMax. Only item that had me flummoxed was a sewing ham, a kind of overgrown pincushion used for ironing and sewing around curves. *Coser almohadilla*, I put, literally, to sew cushion. They could laugh at me, I didn't care, so long as they let us through.

No one asked a thing at customs; they looked over the list and waved us on. Lacey still didn't have time to get up a good bark at the guards. I'd heard opposite views on packing. Some say you will have a better chance of not being hassled if you look organized, others say it is better to have your packing look messy so that the guards don't want to deal with you. We went with well-organized. Worked this time.

We'd only been in San Miguel six weeks before we went back to Phoenix but we'd much improved our walking ability. Not walking for the past six weeks in Phoenix made us lose whatever strength we'd accomplished. I'm huffing again going up the 22 steps to our casa.

Not everything here is perfect, of course. We've had one lousy meal in the two months we've actually been present in San Miguel, and we experienced one lousy concert last night. It was billed as piano jazz, but the young man played a few piano bar standards like

"Misty" and one Scott Joplin rag before bringing out four accordions. Oh dear. My mother played the accordion. Badly.

Only about 20 of us had paid $10 for his solo performance, and half left at intermission, not wanting to be too rough on the poor guy. On our way home we wistfully glanced into a half dozen restaurant bars with better live music than that. Doris Rogers, an African-American jazz singer at Tio Lucas, sent haunting melodies out to us as we walked past the door.

Our phone has been out for 36 hours since lightning came very close to us Tuesday night. Norma was assembling a new computer desk from Office Max in Querétaro earlier that day when a bolt hit so close her chest felt as if a giant had thumped it. She was momentarily blinded.

All we lost was our phone. Luckily Norma had installed new voltage regulators on both computers and on the entertainment center and refrigerator. Surge protectors alone don't cut it here; brownouts and power failures are more common than power spikes.

Prices are jacked too high in SMA for us to even consider buying a house. Once in a while we hear someone has found a fixer upper for under $100,000, but budget houses are considered anything under $200,000, and so many are multi-million-dollar homes now.

Prices for real estate in the States continue to soar, too, at least in the "desirable" cities, same as in the most "desirable" discovered parts of Mexico, though occasionally there are signs the spurt in housing prices may be slowing. And the less popular areas of the U.S. have totally escaped the housing bubble, same as most of Mexico. If we hadn't had so many medical bills the past 30 years we might have enough saved for a down payment someplace. If, if.

Oh well, a whole lot of U.S. citizens are relying solely on Social Security these days. Though San Miguel and Mexico are nowhere near the bargain many U.S. citizens expect, we can still live better here on Social Security than anywhere in the States that we'd want to live.

And as our Spanish improves, we could move to a less popular area of Mexico or elsewhere in Latin America for an even cheaper standard of living. But I wouldn't want to live in a tiny town with nothing to do in rural Michigan again any more than I would want the same thing in Latin America. We're city culture folks.

The gardener our neighbors hired for our courtyard has been wonderful in helping us carry packages and grocery sacks up the stairs on shopping days. We paid him $10 to unload the car for us when we came back from Arizona, our car loaded to the rooftop with items on our *menaje de casa*. It took him half an hour.

But the next day he hit us with a sad story that I couldn't understand with my poor Spanish. It ended with *dinero para mi esposa enferma* (money for my sick wife). I said, I'm sorry, I don't have enough money now, and I felt badly all day.

By his standards I am indeed wealthy. I've mentioned that the Mexican minimum wage is around 55 cents an hour, and almost half of the population lives below the Mexican poverty line of $4 a day, $1,460 a year. Maids are considered well paid at $3 U.S. an hour, many earning far less. So there are low points to living here, too, but overall we are still as thrilled with the city as our first day.

After laundry pickup today we are driving to Dolores Hidalgo, a city of about 40,000 some 26 miles away that is renowned for its ceramics. Its artists are the keepers of the *talavera* style of bright glaze decorations that they brought from Spain. Several art centers feud over the legal use of the term *talavera*, which Dolores Hidalgo residents say belongs only to them

As soon as we can, we're taking a one-day bus tour sponsored by the Instituto Allende that will include the historical aspects of San Miguel, Atotonilco, Dolores Hidalgo, and Guanajuato, for $55. Everyone says it's really worth it to help understand this region of

Mexico's importance as the cradle of Mexican independence. But today we're concentrating on shopping.

We enjoyed the easy drive to Dolores Hidalgo, with all the ceramics stores and handmade carved wooden furniture stores lining the road into town. We drooled over a huge wood desk with hutch and keyboard rollout, at "only" $600 U.S. It would have cost at least $2,000 in the States. Our casa is big enough to hold such large furniture. I don't envy the delivery guys who will be bringing it up our stairs into our casa someday soon, I hope.

One store had well-carved wooden horse statues of all sizes, caught in every conceivable action pose, something else I coveted. Ceramics were both utilitarian and fun. I love frogs, and there were plenty of fanciful planters, soap dishes, washbasins, pitchers, etc. Some of the floral ceramic vases were big enough for an adult to hide in. Diego Rivera called himself Frog, the nickname for those from Guanajuato, known for being overrun with frogs during rainy seasons.

Styles and moods varied from store to store, some featuring blue and white tiny mosaic-like tile designs that looked Moroccan. (Spain was occupied by the Moors from the 700s until 1492, so they brought an Arabic influence to many aspects of Mexican life as well.) Others featured bright tropical fish designs, some subtle flowers, others religious themes. They're exported from this area to all over the world, the prices jumping at each destination farther away from this crafts headquarters.

The ride out was beautiful in itself, with rolling hills and rich farmlands and wealthy haciendas and hotels featuring natural thermal spas. Nancy and our neighbor go to water aerobics classes at one of the resorts Monday, Wednesday and Friday mornings. We're not morning people and can't make it up to be ready to face water and exercise at 8:30 A.M. They go to Taboada hot springs, Agua Magica, which has an Olympic-sized pool and several smaller pools.

They also like La Gruta, which has a series of three pools that are like underground caves connected by a tunnel, the deepest one very hot and lit only by a skylight. At both places they pay around $5 for the entire day and have lunch on the grounds. We hear you can rent La Gruta for evening private parties for up to ten for about $200 U.S., and even swim nude then.

Cornfields were in every stage, from sprouts a few inches high to stalks ready to harvest, high as the show tune's elephant's eye. When I first drove through Mexico in 1970 I remember being astounded at all the rough, dry terrain where sparse corn was being grown, on straight-up mountainsides in some places. This is a particularly rainy year, I've been told. The countryside is lush.

We want to explore all the renowned shopping towns nearby, like Leon, which is famous for its leather goods and shoes, and tour the beach resorts on both oceans. Mexico's Copper Canyon is supposed to be even larger than the Grand Canyon.

We ate at a hotel restaurant near Dolores Hidalgo's Jardín. Each of us had a kind of spinach fettucini pasta with chicken curry sauce. I had *queso* and *chipolte* soup (cheese and smoked jalapenos), while Norma had creamed corn soup, all excellent. A wooden wagon full of artificial flowers took up one of the parking spaces in front of the hotel so we'll know how to locate it next time. (Ha! Next time our landmark was gone and we never found it again.)

Norma is feeling more and more confident driving in new cities and in crowded streets while I strain to find the street names on the maps. The moment we think we've found the right street on the map, it turns out to be going the wrong direction.

We had a great time at our first luncheon meeting of the American Legion Women's Auxiliary. Only about 20 women showed up at Hecho en Mexico restaurant. Though our small group working on decorations for the children's rooms in the Hospital General had made it very clear we did not want any recognition for the work we'd done so far, we were still lauded. It felt good, I have to admit.

Tomorrow for the first time we get to put up the decorations, unless a child unexpectedly comes in as a patient. This is the first time the nurses have called to say no patients are scheduled to be in the ward. The children's care must come first, naturally.

Before we went back to Arizona I'd drawn designs for the nursery using clothes lines made of ribbon, hung with baby bottles, rattles, pacifiers, kimonos and such. Can't wait to see how the designs look.

🪰

Our neighbors who feed some stray cats went out of town for a few weeks, so we volunteered to feed the cats while they're gone. Our own pets were so jealous.

When our neighbors got back they told us the gardener did have a serious medical emergency for his wife the day he asked us for money, and now I feel even worse. The neighbors gave him $20, though, which apparently was enough for the doctor's home visit and medication. Really. Can you imagine a U.S. doctor making a house call for $20 and bringing meds as well?

Employees in Mexico are generally paid on Saturday afternoon for the past week's work, and they often run out of money by Thursday or Friday, I've learned. Mexican law is very much in favor of the employee and the renter. It's very hard to fire someone even for cause; you'll probably be sued and you will lose and have to pay considerable severance.

All employers, even for part-time help, are required to pay two weeks' pay as Christmas bonus by Dec. 20. There are strict rules on primary employers paying their permanent full-time employees' Mexican health insurance and vacations as well. The entire Mexican legal system has traditionally been based on Roman law and on the Napoleonic Code, i.e., you're guilty until proven innocent, which is the same legal foundation used by the state of Louisiana.

We've been told not to assume any Mexican laws are the same as in the States, even on something like libel and slander. You can be put in jail for "defamation" simply on someone's say-so, without any proof, until the lawyers sort it out. Truth is no defense, there are no jury trials, you may not even be able to testify before the judge in your own defense. And of course the Mexican Constitution forbids any foreigners to take part in Mexican politics or they can face deportation. We have much to learn and unlearn.

◈

Last night was an AIDS benefit, and the producers made a good attempt to balance Mexican and foreign entertainers. I enjoyed most of the Mexican acts better, particularly a father-daughter singing combo, except for a woman comedian who did no translations and I felt stupid for ten minutes while half the audience got the jokes.

Some of the young Indian women we'd seen perform Aztec dances at the Instituto Allende a few months ago this time did hip hop dances. No problems going between feathered headdresses and rap outfits.

One of the MCs did three readings of letters he had written which were supposedly from gringos new to San Miguel. The first was from a rich man who thought he was saving Mexico by his very presence. His idea of speaking Spanish was to add "o" to the end of every word.

That letter made me grimace. I'd recently had the experience of buying a mop at Espino's grocery story and then leaving it behind. When I came back for it, I kept telling the owner I'd left behind a *mapa*, which I pronounced as mop-ah.

I knew better. Beginning Spanish classes immediately point out the dangers of false cognates, words that look like English words but have very different meanings. *Sopa* is not soap, it's soup, and *ropa* is not rope, it's clothing. *Mapa* is not a mop, it's a map. A mop is *el trapeador*.

Finally the woman figured out what I meant, when I did some clumsy acting out of mopping, and she brought me my mop from behind the counter. *El trapeador*, she repeated slowly for me. I hit my head and said, *¡Estoy estupido!* I'm stupid!

Mexican people don't use the word stupid as easily as gringos do, but that's how I felt. I keep confusing *nombre*, which means name, with *numero*—"Doctor, there's a crazy gringa in the waiting room who insists her name is her phone number." So that letter at the AIDS benefit hit home.

The second letter by the MC portrayed a 40-year-old U.S. woman going through a divorce and finding herself among New Age "saviors" in San Miguel. She was about to be taken royally by a man who wanted her to give him all her money for investments promising 40% return.

In reality a few years ago investors could indeed make huge returns in Mexico, even 100% interest, after the last big devaluation in 1994-5. Now Mexican banks pay a few percent better than U.S. financial institutions but certainly not 40%. Same as in the States, real estate is the big investment boom now.

The third letter purported to be from a teenager who had no idea where he was or what he was doing in San Miguel with his parents, his U.S. arrogance and immaturity showing through his words to his friend back in Indiana. Any expat in the audience could have felt a bit guilty after hearing the three letters.

A closing performance was a space age fantasy dance seen through a billowing haze of dry ice smoke. The dry ice got out of hand and plumed into the audience so heavily that the first ten rows evacuated, including us. May it be under control for future performances.

Nowhere during the benefit was anything said actually relating to AIDS or gay issues or discrimination, or to the Mexican history of pretending the disease does not exist here. Shades of the U.S. in the early 1980s. The benefit coordinator sang two songs from *La Cage au Faux* on "being me" which gave no indication of their gay anthem meanings. Oh well, my friend Tom tells me there is now an AIDS specialist doctor in town who is prepared to help AIDS patients with an AZT drug regimen, something which he says was impossible here before now. HIV/AIDS patients can stay in town and get help here rather than having to either move to Mexico City or die.

Speaking of medical issues, we finally put up the decorations at the Hospital General children's and labor rooms. The barnyard scene has a horse, cow, burro, pig, goat, lamb and chicken peering over a fence, flowers and grass beneath the fence. They look cute as can be. Clowns of all kinds decorate the preemie room. The clothesline design looks great in the neonatal room. The nurses didn't want any baby bottles up—the hospital encourages breastfeeding.

We worked around two teensy preemies in incubators. The doctor gave us permission but I was not really comfortable being in the same room, even in hospital gowns, booties and hair coverings. Preemies always look so delicate, so tiny and wrinkled.

Nurses had left on a Mexican music radio station and I kept thinking to myself, "Why doesn't somebody turn that thing off? There's nobody here, let the poor babies sleep in peace."

And then one of the Legion women, a former nurse, said when a baby cried, "Hello, baby, it's good you're crying, it's good for your lungs. Do you hear us and the music? You need lots of sensory stimulation."

Aha, that was the reason for the music. And then one of the other former nurses said, "You should probably be talking to the babies in Spanish." So from then on whenever one of the babies cried, we all said, "*Hola, bebé.*" At least I could manage that much. I thought of a parrot. What if the babies' first words came out with a U.S. accent?

While I was waiting in the hospital lobby for the others to arrive, I took a seat along one of the three walls of folding chairs. Nobody sat down in any of the other empty chairs along my wall while I was there for the longest time, even though people were standing rather than having to sit next to me. Felt very strange. Not as if I felt it was wrong for me to be there, but I kept wondering if any of the patients thought I shouldn't be there.

Expats usually go to the private Hospital de la Fe, and richer Mexicans as well, I understand. Those who are on the Mexican health care system, IMSS, go first to IMSS clinics for referrals, and all medical visits and prescriptions are free. Non-Mexican citizens can buy into IMSS for yearly premiums less than most monthly premiums for U.S. medical insurance, but like most U.S. insurance programs, you can't get in with some pre-existing conditions. And, like U.S. medical care, some patients get excellent attention, others don't.

But I hear that the emergency room at the Hospital General includes U.S. doctors who are learning Spanish and Mexican culture in a hospital setting so that they can better serve their Mexican patients back to the States, and that the ER department is excellent. Some U.S. citizens say they would prefer to go to the ER at the Hospital General instead of de la Fe in a serious emergency.

There I sat alone on one wall of the waiting room, while Mexicans jammed the seats on the other three walls. I smiled; they stared or turned their heads. I tried to formulate a few words of compassion to say to the mothers of sick children, but I knew I didn't know enough to understand if someone answered me or asked me a question in return. I felt helpless and out of place.

Yes, I was there to "help," but what were my few pictures on the walls going to mean to these families anyway? Was the artwork even meaningful or relevant? Would some child some time in the future look around the pediatrics room and smile at the animals and feel maybe a teensy bit better? Would a mother in labor have her mind taken off her pain by looking at the peaceful scenes we'd put together?

And how much of what past colonialists and ugly Americans had done to Mexico were these people seeing in me? Did they even see me? And why should I be worrying about that? They were in a hospital, for heaven's sake, sick themselves or with someone who was sick. I was not on their minds.

I had absolutely no idea of what was going on in anyone's head but I kept imagining the worst, and then the best, and then I berated myself for my worries. Probably nobody in the room gave a damn about me except me. They were in a hospital. Still, I worried.

Then a bunch of boisterous teenaged boys came in with a sick friend, and they had no compunction about sitting in my row. And then others did, too, when the boys left.

This is the Hospital General on Reloj, and patients included what seemed to me to be poorer Indians from the rural areas, the campos, rather than from the city where many residents are more mixed Indian and Spanish (mexticos).

They were all much smaller than me, smaller than many within the city. Sometimes I feel like a giant here. Once the other Legion women came I felt fine, security in numbers. Will I ever grow up and stop worrying about what others may be thinking of me?

Yesterday was a day in which everything went right (until the plumes of dry ice smoke at the play engulfed us). Tel-Mex workers finally came to fix our lightning-struck phone wires outside. They asked Norma for our phone number and she was proud of herself to be able to give it to them in Spanish.

But when she bragged to me about what she had done, we realized she'd gotten the last digit wrong. We worried all day that our phone would now be messed up completely, but it was fixed right when we got home. Only took eight days.

Monday we had to leave before the laundry pickup guy arrived, and so we left our pillowcase full of dirty clothes on the porch. The maid also leaves trash on the porch. She assured us it was safe to leave both bags there, and both were gone when we got home later.

But then the laundry delivery guy did not come back for three days. We had visions of all our clothes being either stolen or thrown out with the trash. But he arrived with our clean clothes Thursday morning instead. "Oh, did you want them Monday night?" he asked so innocently. We'd thought the clothes would be picked up by 10 A.M. and delivered back by 6 P.M. as they had been in the past.

So both the trash and the laundry bags went to their right destinations. In LA both bags would have been gone through and the best items stolen within minutes of being placed outside, out of our sight. In rural Michigan we had to put a sign out, "Free—please take," on anything we put out on the road or it would be there forever.

In LA, we once had a brand new barbecue with chicken grilling on the rack, charcoal burning away, stolen right off our porch by guys with a pickup truck, the moment we went inside to get barbecue sauce!

We had agonized over the Spanish dictionary on how to ask the maid if she'd accidentally thrown out our clothes, or if she had specifically seen the laundry guy take them while we were gone. We especially did not want to give any implication to the maid that we were accusing her of taking our clothes. Like in English, "take" can mean "steal." She probably would have been highly offended and quit. That happened to a friend who tried to ask her maid what had happened to a dress that never came down from the roof after the maid washed it and hung it.

I have learned from reading that Mexican culture places far more emphasis on respect and honor. Any insinuation of something like stealing is considered a grave insult. I have so much to learn about what is appropriate or not. Sometimes I paralyze myself, not knowing what to do.

Luckily, the laundry showed up a day before the maid. Even the bottled water delivery arrived on Tuesday, only one day late. The $2 stayed on the porch under the empty jug untouched for 36 hours.

The big news is that we both now have our *rentista* FM3s (extended residency visas for those such as retirees who live in Mexico on independent income from elsewhere), signed and stamped everywhere they are supposed to be signed and stamped. (I hear it was the French occupation that got Mexicans into their love of stamping official documents.)

FM3 *rentista* visas allow you to bring in a U.S.-plated car permanently, so long as your FM3 is kept current, with an official hologram decal on the windshield. Tourists can come in on FMTs, tourist visas, as often as they want in a year, for up to six months at a time but they can only bring in a car once for six months.

Many gringos have come and gone every six months for years, reentering on new FMTs with their cars, but supposedly this is becoming less possible. Computers are talking to each other.

When you've had an FM3 renewed for five years (less if you're married to a Mexican citizen or were born in Mexico or have close relatives who are Mexican citizens), you can apply for dual citizenship. After five years you can also either renew your FM3 or apply for an FM2, the road to immigrant status. FM2s require a higher amount of verifiable money to qualify, and there are more restrictions on how often you can leave Mexico. You can no longer have a foreign-plated car, either.

We've been using a consultant who works in the same building with the official immigration office, and they refer people with problems to him. He tried calling us all week but our phone was out and he'd thought we'd left town. He even brought the FM3s to our casa one night when we were out. And now we're legal.

It took two weeks and $370 to make up for some guard's failure to stamp Norma's FM3 in the right place when we came over the border three months ago, and for our confusion over how long we had to register our FM3s obtained in Phoenix when we arrived at our permanent address. Somewhere we'd read we had three months, but it was 30 days. I don't know how anyone without a high level of education and bureaucracy navigation can manage the immigration procedures on either side of the border. I think everyone feels powerless and at the whim of those in charge at borders.

My Monday morning Scrabble game players were musing over such problems as the day's news about Zimbabwe government officials giving away white farmers' lands to their workers. Some of them were seeing it as reverse racism. I was finally comfortable talking a bit about my own beliefs. One Scrabble player said that the Mexican inefficiencies help keep more people employed, so that's a good thing. I don't know enough to be able to judge whether that is a racist statement when made by an outsider, or the truth, or both. The defiant me from the '60s would be aghast at this hesitant me, who is no longer sure of very much at all.

As the Legion nurses found when they tried to volunteer at the hospital, they have to move very slowly in suggesting what seems to them as "improvements." And the idea must seem to come from a Mexican man for it to have much chance of acceptance.

There are lots of telling stories about how "the American way" is not all that superior to "the Mexican way." One of my favorites is the U.S. businessman who sees a fisherman stopping work at noon because, as he explains, he's caught enough fish for the day, he's going home to his beautiful wife and wonderful children to enjoy the day.

The U.S. businessman tells the fisherman how he could work harder and make his business grow, and eventually he could build the business up to the point where he could expand and hire more boats and work harder and save up lots of money. It might take 15 years of very hard work and long hours, but he could become rich.

"What then?" the fisherman asked.

"Why, then you could retire and stay home with your beautiful wife and children and enjoy the day!"

So the businesses here do open pretty much on time, work does get done, life goes on fairly comfortably, most people work very hard, but there is a warmth and human component that can be missing when the main concern is getting the trains run on time. I'm here, not in New York City. These are some musings about the continual contradictions and petty annoyances of life in Mexico.

❦

Antonio Banderas is back in town, with Melanie Griffith, to start filming on the second recent major film to be set in this region. The first, *Once Upon a Time in Mexico*, was filmed last year and caused havoc in the town. Some folks couldn't get to their homes or businesses for days.

This time the film is about the 1910 revolutionary war hero Pancho Villa, who in real life worked with D.F. Griffiths on an autobiographical film of his life, selling the rights to make money for that revolution. *And Starring Pancho Villa, as Himself* is the rumored title. This one is supposedly going to be filmed mainly in the countryside, though the stars will reside in San Miguel. Maybe I'll catch a glimpse of Banderas this time, maybe not.

I loved seeing the occasional movie star when we lived in Los Angeles. Once I literally bumped into Charleton Heston in my ex-husband's tropical fish store and he said, "I beg your pardon" in a voice that could have rolled back the waters in the aquariums. I get as star struck as anybody, and I don't even like Heston. I hear Banderas and Griffin are staying at Casa Lisa B & B and that they're considering buying a vacation home here.

Tonight we'll see *Amelie*, a French art film we missed in Phoenix, and afterward have handmade ice cream at a new restaurant that opened nearby. Tomorrow is a concert by Indian children playing authentic pre-colonial instruments. So life goes on in San Miguel. I could be riding my golf cart to the dog run in Phoenix every day looking for park rules infractions.

We took a different bus to the Gigante supermarket last Tuesday and it didn't stop right in front of the market the way the usual bus we take does. This one kept on going, right on past the Plaza de Real Conte, the mostly-empty shopping mall that is dominated by Gigante and the Gemelos (*gemelos* are twins), the two movie theaters. Should we get out at the next stop and walk back? Should we wait for the return trip past the market?

We kept thinking the bus would turn around and go by the market again on its way back, but no, we ended up in a middle-class Mexican neighborhood on the outskirts that we didn't know existed. The bus driver was apparently due for lunch. He parked the bus on the shoulder of the road, up over a sidewalk, and took a paper sack lunch out from under his seat.

I scoured my pocket Spanish-English dictionary. Should I say *retorno* or *resume*? Didn't matter, he didn't know what I was talking about with either word. Later I learned *retorno* is used for the returns on highways and *regresa* was the word I should have used. The only word he said that I understood besides "no" was *otro*, or other, according to my dictionary. Still, he was very clear: we had to get off his bus.

So we could either wait outside until his lunch hour was over, and maybe it was the end of his shift and he wouldn't be driving again until tomorrow, or we could hoof it in hopes of finding an *otre* bus headed for the Centro district downtown or to Gigante. We walked.

We couldn't call a cab—no public phone, and we didn't know where we were to ask for a pickup anyway. Nice houses, neat lots, nobody apparently home in this bedroom community. Finally Norma spotted a bus a few blocks away and we found a bus stop and a bus came that was marked "Gigante." Another crisis averted. It was a relief to do our shopping. We took a $2 taxi home with our groceries.

That evening, the children's group, *Collar del Viento*, playing indigenous tunes on pre-colonial instruments at Teatro Angela Peralta was an enlightening experience. The songs really sounded from the earth when played on rocks and wood flutes and rough drums and turtle shells. Four girls and three boys aged from about eight to twelve made up the "orchestra." They wore simple Indian costumes of unbleached cotton with fine embroidery designs.

The two oldest girls performed historic tribal dances to some of the songs. They had gauze bandages around their ankles and the bottoms of their feet. Maybe the gauze was for traction, or maybe to prevent splinters from the wood floor, we could only guess.

One of the bandages started to unravel during the hot and heavy drum-accented dancing, and the whole audience and all the children could only watch this bandage come looser and looser. The growing tail threatened the balance of both of the interweaving dancers, the girl somehow managing to maneuver so that neither of them tripped on it on the small stage. Throughout an entire dance, all of us watched only the bandage.

Collectively we sighed in relief when that dance ended and she could sit down on the floor and take off the last twist of the bandage. In the Q & A period afterward one gringo asked if that number was called "The Ace Bandage Dance." The director didn't seem to think that was funny.

Two younger children, a boy and a girl, were in training, and they simply sat at opposite ends of the orchestra. The boy, about five, kept putting his head down, picking at his toenails, rolling his eyes, doing everything one doesn't do on stage no matter how bored, but he was forgiven, he was so cute.

Sunday was a Society for the Protection of Animals barbeque benefit. The SPA board expected about 300, at $10 a pop, and ran out of tickets but not of food. It was all you can eat for as much ribs, sausages and BBQ pork you wanted, plus a dozen sides, including homemade pickles. Mexico is not big on pickles or relish.

Everyone told the cook he should open his own restaurant. He donates so much to charities in town. (Barbeque Bob's is now a restaurant on Ancha San Antonio, even though Barbeque Bob himself died suddenly of a heart attack in 2005. His widow continued the restaurant and an adjoining organic veggies store.)

Part of the entertainment at the benefit was "stupid pet tricks," though few dogs actually performed as announced. One tiny poodle did jump through a hula hoop repeatedly, however, to great applause. She was such a ham, she must have been part pot-bellied pig.

My favorite was the mutt introduced as the world's greatest impersonator. Her first impression was of Whistler's Mother. She just sat there. When she laid down, head up, she became the Great Pyramid. When she rolled onto her back she was Anna Nicole Smith. Groan.

A stranger came up to us and said we sure looked happy. We said we were, we loved SMA. She said, "Look around, these are the same 500 people you're going to be seeing the rest of your life here." We could live with that. Actually we've only had a few real friends anyplace we've lived anyway. You only need a few.

Where have all the old hippies gone? A bunch of tie-dyed over-30 hippies were right here, alongside richer people in cruise ship casual. The intellectuals and politicos engaged in deep discussions across tables. I overheard exchanges of recipes and gossip, and lots were sharing remedies for various ailments. I remember being so bored as a kid when older relatives talked about health problems, and now I do it, too.

Purpose of the benefit was to raise enough money to build a separate area for sick cats, so they don't have to be housed with the healthy cats. Mission accomplished.

Speaking of cats, we're finding that the strays we're feeding for the neighbors are cleaning out four big soup bowls of Whiskas each morning and night. Such caterwauling when two show up at the same time for the same bowl! Our two indoor cats and our Shih Tzu are on high alert all day long, listening for strange cats at the door. I really like some of the cats, and a few let us pet them, so we think they had owners once and either ran away or were dumped. Several look like purebred Siamese and Siamese mixes.

⊘⁄⊘⁄⊘⁄

Our current maid assigned by the landlady is skipping days, without any apparent pattern or reason so far. So I rustled up a few questions using the Spanish dictionary to ask the landlady what had happened. And then I couldn't understand her lengthy and somewhat apologetic answer. I have no idea why we are getting erratic cleaning now.

It is becoming more and more clear that she would rather we hire Maria, the maid we liked so much, as our personal maid two or three afternoons a week at our own expense, once Maria's broken arm is healed, and it might be that we are being subtly maneuvered into doing that.

But so long as the other maid comes at least twice a week at the landlord's expense, why would we do that? Silly me—because the landlady wants the change. I didn't like having a maid, to be sure, but now we appreciate her. Friends had laughed at us that this would happen, and now we look forward to her coming.

Tuesday is the huge outdoor market and our weekly trip to Gigante next door as well, and the produce is always ripe. That means the pineapple, cantaloupe, mango and papaya must be soaked in Microdyn immediately, peeled and put into the fridge.

That means Tuesday afternoons we have a garbage can full of cores and peels and rinds and a syrupy floor. If the maid doesn't come we might have to pick up a mop and haul out the garbage ourselves! How quickly we got spoiled. Almost as quickly as Tuesday Market peelings rot. And we don't bother to make our own beds and wash the dishes before she comes any more, either.

We're looking forward to September's Independencia events, *Sanmiguelada* (a feeble imitation of Spain's Running of the Bulls), and the major feast day for St. Michael the Archangel. We've been warned that the Running of the Bulls is the best and worst of times, with thousands of drunken young men, mostly from nearby universities and Mexico City, acting like fools in the streets. But we should see it once, we've also been told.

I'd always wondered about the holes in the sidewalks in Centro, like someone put tin cans in place and then built the sidewalks around them. They're for crowd and traffic control, particularly needed during the Running of the Bulls. Metal fence posts fit into the holes, to keep the bulls and those running with the bulls in certain areas and the rest of us "safe."

Occasionally a bull will make it over the fences, though, so nothing in Centro is absolutely secure from the bulls. Old-timers stay inside or leave town for the weekend, we've been told. Our friend Tom said the very best place along the route for viewing is from El Pegaso restaurant because it has bathrooms. No way can most of us older folks last from 11 A.M. until around 2 P.M. without bathroom access.

So we checked out El Pegaso and found that the day's special is a *paella* feast, with raspberry pie for dessert and all the sangria you can drink, for only, only, $45 US each. The date is right between Norma's and my birthdays so I guess that will be our mutual present to each other.

We'd heard that San Miguel de Allende is the only Mexican town to have a Running of the Bulls, but later read about one that has been going on for 50 years in Tlaxcala, another town in central Mexico. They call theirs the Huamantlada, held annually in August on that town's commemoration of the "Virgin of the Flowers." In 2004 one person was killed; in 2005, 40 were injured, many as people jumped out of the bulls' path and over each other. Such insanity.

One of the casas here is about to become vacant, and we found a woman from San Antonio to take it. We happened to see an ad in *Atención* for a real estate pitch, and we decided to hear what the guy had to say. Right away we could tell we were out of our league—the others in the room looked as if they could easily afford the $500,000 and up homes he was pushing, except for one cute little Texan who looked to us as if she felt out of place as well.

The agent didn't have up-to-date information on a lot—he didn't even know that the immigration offices had moved from the Gigante mall to the extension of Canal Street last month.

Someone asked him if it were true that doctors here will not prescribe morphine or other powerful pain medication for cancer or similar serious conditions. He said that all you had to do was to ask around and buy a chunk of black tarry opium produced in many areas of the coast, and use a pinch in your tea as needed and you'd be fine.

As if the dozen wealthy people in the room and Norma and I and the new woman we'd spotted would risk life imprisonment in a Mexican jail to buy opium off of some stranger. No quality control on a hunk of opium, either.

While he was pushing houses in the half-million dollar and up range, including way up, the Texan woman drawled, "Do you have anything for under $60,000?"

After he stopped laughing Norma and I cornered her and told her about the casa in our complex that is about to come open. She will be our new neighbor when she gets her furniture from Texas and moves down.

⁂

Our troublesome gardener showed up this morning asking for his full week's salary (three days a week, $10 a day) even though on Monday he'd worked half a day, asked for $20 in advance from his Friday's pay, and then disappeared for the rest of Monday and didn't show up at all Wednesday.

Norma gave him his remaining $10 for the week, even though he'd only worked half of one day out of the three, and he promptly disappeared again. He "forgot" he'd gotten the advance. Our neighbors can straighten it out with him, assuming we ever see the gardener again.

I feel terrible paying someone only $10 a day, but that's the going rate that our neighbors pay. It's more than double the Mexican minimum wage. Maybe our maid's husband is working in a car wash someplace in Phoenix and sending home $30 a week. I hope so.

5

September

San Miguel and Mexico are in the throes of celebrations leading up to September 16th, Independence Day. Belles Artes is celebrating its 40th anniversary this month as well. I decided to take watercolor classes at Belles Artes rather than from the oil painting instructor, to try something entirely different.

I'd always feared watercolor as the most difficult medium, so why not tackle it now? I'm not out to become a great artist or to sell everything I paint, I'm here to learn and to experiment. With my personality, I hate to mess up, so this will be good for me.

Belles Artes hosted an anniversary fiesta one night and we encountered one of the traditions of SMA, paper maché giant heads and costumes, worn like Disneyland character costumes by dancers hidden inside, peeking out of holes in the costumes around where the dolls' navels would be. They're called *mojigangas*. I bet they stand ten feet high or more, the cartoon heads themselves four feet across.

A mariachi band provided dance music for the huge dolls to dance to. In the heat of the music, a neckline slipped—to reveal a fully detailed, rouged paper maché breast.

All the kids started giggling and their mothers were blushing and hiding the kids' heads in their skirts. Some people tried to cover up the breast of the doll as she danced and bobbed and hit her head against the chandeliers and knocked down the red, white and green ribbons festooning the halls. Silly stuff.

I am sure the exposé was planned, or why else would the breasts be rouged and in full detail if they were going to stay inside the dresses?

Some of the *mojigangas* were grinning red devils, some musta-chioed banditos, one couple was a bride and groom, and one was even Johnny Depp in his *Pirates of the Caribbean* costume.

One *mojiganga* was apparently a white-haired tourist holding a camera to her eye, so plenty of people took a photo of her taking a photo of them. A paper maché snake at least twenty feet long wound its way among the partygoers, reminding me of the Chinese New Year dragons operated by a half dozen people underneath.

At the start of the month, the Independence committees apparently hosted two competing beauty pageants. According to the paper, one had a minimum height requirement of about 5' 4", which would eliminate most of the shorter Indian women from the countryside, as far as I can tell. I hope I misunderstood the requirements. I'm never quite sure I'm reading Spanish correctly, even with diction-ary in hand. (And I never saw height requirements in future years' announcements—the joys of not being fluent and never being quite sure what is happening around you).

One of the contests was held inside the Teatro Angela Peralta, the architecturally ornate auditorium around the corner from our casa that is built like a European opera house. A horse-drawn car-riage awaited the winner that night, and the competition was also shown on a movie screen projected on the wall of the restaurant across from the theater, so that those who couldn't fit inside could see all the contestants. The winner of that contest, a cute little (dyed) blonde, had her photo in the paper.

I'm guessing that the official Independence beauty pageant was the one that happened last night in the Jardín, because the contestants looked taller to me. The woman who won was the tallest and thinnest, surprise, but she was indeed beautiful, both according to my standards for beauty shaped by U.S. media and according to the Mexican judges. The cute little (short) blonde was a darling, too.

The seven contestants, all with their contingents of adoring high school friends cheering from different sections of the packed garden and surrounding streets, first came out in native costumes with high flying feather headdresses.

It looked to me as if many of the costumes were cut tight on the bias, and the young women walked with that same hip-swinging style beauty contestants use in the Miss America and Miss Universe televised contests, not exactly fitting with the traditional Indian costumes.

Then they came out in revealing evening gowns and said a few words, little of which I understood, of course. They each picked an envelope containing a question to answer. One of the questions was something like, "What is the biggest problem facing women in the countryside?" That woman answered, "Machismo, same as everywhere else." She didn't win. But then she was shorter. (I don't know any of the real reasons behind any of this, I'm still guessing.)

I've learned that one reason so many people show up at the Jardín at night is that poorer families generally don't have living rooms in their houses. They often have a kitchen/eating area and a sleeping area, so the Jardín is the community living room. It's always a good evening's free entertainment to people-watch.

Between the beauty pageant acts, a boy around nine dressed in a mariachi costume sung his heart out. He sang far too long and emoted way over the top. But the crowd loved him.

Another act to kill time between the contestants' costume changes was a gorgeous male Indian dancer with a gold-colored metal breastplate and stunning headdress that could have given a Las Vegas showgirl a run. Throbbing drumbeats, pulsating spotlights, all that naked glistening skin…the beauty contestants had some real competition.

Six young men in tight red denim jeans and short black tops did a sort of lip sync version of *NSync, a kind of hip hop stripper act repeated to at least a dozen rock songs. Four would have been plenty, to me, but it was not my taste they were aiming at.

Finally a queen was chosen and the nine-year-old sang to her on bended knee, and a *castillo* (fireworks tower) that spun and sputtered and spewed sparks all over the crowd from a height of maybe 30' gave an appropriate send-off for the evening.

Every time I thought the top of the tower had been reached, a spark traveled up a cord to another level. All night long more fireworks kept going off all over town. Our Shih Tzu stands and trembles, LucyFurr ignores them, and Calicat still runs for the closet. Mostly we can sleep through them now.

We overheard one expat telling his friends that on the night called the Rain of Lights, the fireworks start at 4 A.M. and go on the rest of the night, and the tower will be even taller. "Bulls" made of wire holding small fireworks will run through the crowds, carried aloft by men. Everyone brings cardboard or a cheap hat to keep the sparks off, and lit pieces go careening off into the crowds. People are packed shoulder to shoulder for hours on end until dawn.

"Every year for twelve years I've seen the same thing," this guy told everyone listening to him. "Every year when that tower starts to throw off pieces the whole park freaks and people panic and get trampled and it can be really dangerous. It's like it never happened before, people forget and get right up under the tower, and when it goes off, they stampede."

He recommended, loud enough for all the eavesdroppers to hear, that we park ourselves in an area where there is space to move back into when the panic starts. He advised wearing a cheap hat and old clothes because we may be hit by sparks and something usually catches on fire.

This is Mexico, there are far fewer safety rules, though we see plenty of cops interspersed in the crowd looking for any trouble at all of these major events We also know enough to take safeguards against pick-pockets in any crowd anywhere. We can't wait.

What seems more unsafe to me is the Running of the Bulls. We learned that during a recent Running of the Bulls a 21-year-old Red Cross volunteer was killed, gored by a bull that got through a barricade. These same bulls are used later for bullfights, raised on special ranches for this purpose. I didn't ask any more about that.

We once went to see a bullfight in Portugal because we'd heard that the bulls aren't killed. They weren't, not right then, they were slaughtered afterward and the meat given to charities, which is supposed to make it all right. On the other hand, steers not raised for bullfighting are slaughtered, too, and we're not vegetarians.

In the Portugal bullfight brightly colored darts are still driven into the bulls' necks and backs so that they are bloodied—we'll never go to another bullfight. This Running of the Bulls is supposed to be much tamer.

Another truism everyone says: anyone taking an art class in San Miguel is supposed to paint the Parroquia church at least once, to prove you've been in SMA. I'm not ready to tackle that intricate stonework yet.

My first painting was of a small section of crumbling wall in the patio outside my classroom, with a dozen pigeons perched in the niches. It came out better than I expected, considering I was afraid of the watercolors. They've always seemed so much harder than oils or acrylics. Guess what, they are.

A guy we'd never seen before came into our watercolor class carrying rolled-up sheets of handmade paper, about 6' squares, for $40 each--thick textured stuff that would be fantastic for some kinds of artwork. He had worked some of the paper into smaller artwork himself, like weavings, all of natural tan paper he'd manipulated into patterns. He seemed so intense about his craft.

I keep wondering about him, where he learned his skills, whether he sells his artwork himself, whether he has to keep another job. He never came back to our class, and I never saw him again.

Later I learned that this paper craft is a tradition particularly from Oaxaca and several paper craftsmen sell their creations in San Miguel. I've since seen many of the quilt-sized paper artworks hanging simply as wall decorations.

The historic art centers, subsidized by Mexican taxes, that are designed to help Mexicans, seem to have more foreign students, though we pay much higher tuition. For classes three days a week, three hours a day, I pay about $100 a month. *Atención* lists at least thirty private teachers who offer various kinds of classes, so we have plenty of options.

One big disadvantage of my second-story Belles Artes class: 42 steps. That's after 21 steps at our second-story casa as well. My calves are starting to show muscles. I guess that's not really a disadvantage after all.

For my birthday dinner we were going to go to a Lebanese restaurant in town but it was closed that day so we went to our favorite Harry's for my fried oysters and jambalaya, and Norma always gets shrimp and tasso (Cajun sausage) fettuccini. Afterward we stopped by a bar to hear a '60s band.

Wednesday we're finally going to get high-speed internet again. Norma and I will be able to settle our million-dollar bets on the spot via Google. For twenty years we've been betting each other a million dollars when neither of us will admit we're wrong about something, Right now I owe her $41 million, down from $53 million. She lost a bet on our new phone number. Neither of us ever knows for sure what we think we know for sure.

At midnight Norma gave me another perfect birthday present. We found out for sure that our park model in Arizona has been rented until it sells, which gives us some extra money while we are supporting two households. Norma announced that she had found a jewelry shop owned by a woman who designs custom rings and the next day we would go to pick out our designs.

This is our third set of matching rings in 23 years together. The bands on our first set wore too thin and the stones fell out. Our second set was stolen in one of the five robberies and burglaries we experienced the last four years we lived in LA.

We had just moved into our first home together in Silver Lake in 1980 when we came home from work to find we'd lost almost everything. We had moved in together with two of everything—TVs, stereos, cameras, our wedding rings from our previous husbands, plus our wrapped Christmas presents for each other. In the presents were our new rings. The police said that many thieves target Christmas presents each year.

The thieves hadn't taken my Selectric typewriter, though—very heavy. And Norma got a feeling the next day that she should come home early to check on it.

She walked in the door and was knocked unconscious and slammed into a mirror on the hall closet that shattered and sliced her as she collapsed. She didn't get a glimpse of the robbers, which police said was just as well—they might have killed her if she could have identified them.

We lived on the same hill where the Hillside Stranglers had dumped one body in the '70s, and the Night Stalker was captured a mile from our house in the '80s. Whenever people warned us about moving to Mexico because of the supposed crime, we told them our LA tales.

After picking out our new rings the next day (large turquoise ovals set onto wide silver bands with design swirls of gold, very Mexican-looking), we returned to Harry's where it was two-for-one Margarita night. I drank way too much in my thirties and don't drink any more, but Norma's occasional Margaritas don't bother me. On these narrow sidewalks Norma usually leads (I'm directions-challenged), but this time she stopped at the door and said, "I can't make any decisions. You lead." I'm not going to let her forget that line.

For this entire month, each day there are about five Fiesta Patria (Native Land) events revolving around the 1810 Declaration of Revolution against Spain. On September 15, *charros* (horsemen from the countryside) rode into town in parades, then back out to the villages in commemoration of how the *charros* spread the word of the formation of the fledgling revolutionary army.

The *charros* in 1810 seized a lot of supplies from various *hacienda* owners for the army's needs, so we were told not everyone in

Mexico is thrilled with the *charros'* reenactment of their part of the war. But then not everyone is thrilled with the *hacienda* owners' role in history, either. Some *hacienda* owners ruled like kings over their castles, their workers practically slaves. As always, history is complex and not everyone sees it the same.

Motorcyclists roared into town and left again in another parade. Yes, they were on big fancy decorated Harleys. Veterans of various wars marched around town. Foot racers competed all over the region, not exactly in official marathons but the distance to Dolores Hidalgo is about 26 miles.

Sweating runners raced in, they raced out. Police cars escorted even the last ones, the "thunder thighs" as runners called the stragglers back in LA marathons. Native dress was everywhere. All sorts of entertainers performed every night in the Jardín, all for free.

Finally after yet another free concert in the Jardín Saturday night, September 15, the reenactment of Hidalgo's *El Grito* (the shout, the call for the revolution) went off as scheduled at 11 P.M. The Mayor read the words as the beauty queen (the taller one) looked on approvingly.

Both of them were on a small balcony of the building overlooking the Jardín, now the Allende Museum, where the revolutionaries actually plotted many times. Their meetings were concealed by noise of parties on the ground floor of the historic building. We're still going to go on that tour offered by the Instituto so that we can understand all of this history in context, viewing the actual locations where each major event occurred.

The crushing crowds Saturday night shouted "*¡Viva Mexico!*" and many other calls for freedom, and then the fireworks began. This time there were three 30' towers (I'm as bad on estimating heights as I am on directions, so please take all my figures as guesstimates) in front of the Parroquia.

We'd gotten there at 7 P.M. to get a good seat on one of the wrought iron park benches up front for *El Grito*, and had entertained ourselves chatting with a young couple from Mexico City who had driven in for the weekend.

They said they were staying in one of the more expensive hotels of SMA, which I know charges at least $150 a night. I was about to recommend some of the less expensive hotels when the guy mentioned he was a manager for a Coca Cola bottling plant, and she added that she was a computer engineer for Hewlett Packard. He bragged she was in charge of something or other for all of Latin American. They could afford it.

He'd gotten his business degree from San Jose State and had lived in Silicon Valley for years, so his English was perfect. Hers was close. And I'd assumed they'd prefer a cheaper hotel. Again, 90% of the tourism to San Miguel is from within Mexico.

They'd waited with us for *El Grito*, and as 11 P.M. approached, the crowds had gotten thicker and thicker, and we'd decided we'd better get out of there fast, but it was too late. We last saw the Mexico City couple standing up on one of the benches. He told us to stand up on our bench, too, but it was already too crowded for us to maneuver. The pandemonium quieted briefly while the actual *El Grito* was read, but immediately afterward when the fireworks started we were in trouble.

We were being carried off by the swaying of the crowds and we could no longer keep our seats. People were practically in our laps and our feet were getting trampled. The rain started again. I had my umbrella up, crushed shoulder to shoulder in the crowd, unable to move, when some young men growled at me in Spanish, "Thanks a lot." I realized that my umbrella was channeling the rain down their necks.

So I put down the umbrella with great difficulty and suffered the same downpour everyone else was experiencing, holding onto the umbrella for dear life with one hand and my camera in my pocket with the other. We'd bought our red umbrellas with "Bobby" police heads carved into the handles in London some 20 years ago and didn't want to lose them now.

We had each only brought two pesos for the public bathrooms if we had to use them (a little more money tucked into our bras), but the very thought of trying to make it across the packed Jardín was ludicrous.

We remembered the guy earlier telling everyone in hearing range about the Rain of Lights (also called *La Alborada*) later this month, when people panic and the crowds are too tight to run anywhere, and people really do fall. The fireworks kept getting louder and louder, more and more rockets shot into the sky, smoke hanging in the air.

The smell was making me woozy. I was terrified I'd faint or fall and be trampled to death. I kept thinking of the news stories of people being crushed in soccer matches in Latin America.

Young men waving huge Mexican flags danced round and round beneath the three towers as they erupted into fireworks and spewed sparks, but it was raining enough water that I doubt anything had a chance of catching fire. Everyone was yelling, "*¡Viva Mexico!*" Music blared from amps on platform trucks. Some historic movie was being shown on the wall of a building.

People were somehow up inside the Parroquia bell towers, waving flags, and everyone was singing. The same young men who had complained about my umbrella began to sway much harder. We were all hanging on as best we could when Norma saw the street cops plowing our way. She waved her arms to get their attention and yelled, "Help!" With the roar of the crowd, no one could hear her.

But the police were heading toward the rowdy guys anyway. The boys stopped swaying and somehow dissolved into the crowds and the crowd suddenly seemed thinner. Norma and I looked at each other and smiled. We'd survived. And had it really been that bad? I could get out my camera and start taking photos.

The fireworks were as spectacular as we'd hoped, each tower going off in turn, each level of each tower sparking off individually, until the finale when the very tips of each tower exploded and soared off into the air, afire. People ran when the fiery detritus drifted back to earth. It went on for hours and we could finally get out of the crowd and away from the Jardín.

We found ourselves at a bar and stumbled in to watch the Fiesta Patria celebrations from every major Mexican city repeated on television. Vicente Fox did the *El Grito* shout from Mexico City. We cooled off and let ourselves unwind until the streets outside looked more passable. And then we walked home, glad for the experience, as the fireworks lit the skies from other areas of the city for the rest of the night.

Coming up in two weeks are the celebrations around the feast day of St. Michael the Archangel, patron saint of San Miguel, which are supposed to be even more high-geared. Those parties and concerts are supposed to run all night long that whole weekend.

That's also the weekend in which the *Voladores* fly. I've heard so much about this ceremony and can't wait to see it in person. And of course this coming Saturday is the Running of the Bulls, which I will report on from my restaurant vantage point.

TV cameras from many stations are getting in place on many rooftops around the Jardín. We have been so tired from all of the events that we have passed on some of them. Next year we'll hit them all.

It's been an exhausting month so far. Tonight is another free concert, the only choice we're taking out of a dozen offerings today. Out by the open-air Tuesday Market on the edge of town, a fair is going on all month, with the usual amusement rides, booths, and entertainers we'd expect at a small U.S. county fair.

Of course we checked it all out and enjoyed tots on small trains and merry-go-rounds, older kids on ferris wheels, parents watching them with a beer or taco in hand.

We were thinking about what all this Mexican patriotism means and at one point Norma said, "I'm coming to the conclusion that the U.S. July 4th is understated." We recoil at all the flag-waving in the States, yet here the Mexican flags on every building and car seem okay, even fun.

It isn't a crass display of nationalism or jingoism, but a kind of self-defensive show of pride for a country that doesn't have any imperialism or colonialism in its own history, only as the colonized. The soldiers are right here at home, defending their own country, not in any other country. There's no fear Mexico is going to invade anybody or exploit anyone. It's hanging on, proud to have survived, to have defeated Spain, to have defeated France. It didn't do so well with the U.S. around 1847 when it lost half its territory, and no one here is celebrating that.

The younger Mexican students in my watercolor class haven't been showing up too regularly this week. The influx of college students from nearby Mexican universities has begun. The *Atención* ran a front-page editorial calling for gringos not to attack the concept of the Running of the Bulls: no bulls get hurt, and how traumatized can these half-ton bulls be to run around Centro for an hour or so while stupid young drunks fall over themselves and act like idiots? Could be the bulls are having a grand time. Uh huh.

One year the bulls acted in concert and outwitted the would-be matadors: they ran in a tight pack all along the streets where they were supposed to go and ran right back into the trucks which had brought them into town without any prodding. The crowds were really disappointed. Hurrah for the bulls.

The editorial warned that it always seems to be the foreigners who get hurt. Mexican youths seem to be able to dodge and avoid any real injuries, maybe from seeing bullfights all their lives. The editorial had an extremely negative attitude toward animal rights people, mostly gringas, who want to end the bull run each year. I have mixed feelings. (The next editor agreed with my views.)

Finally Saturday arrived and the Running of the Bulls was at hand. The first two years of the event they used only cows, to see how it would go. Even now the bulls are not the huge ones, though they look gigantic when they're running right at you.

This event is not as dangerous as the one at Pamplonada in Spain where each day the bulls head down one narrow street at full barrel, just behind the runners, on their way to the bull ring, and the whole thing is over in a few minutes.

Here the bulls are loose for an hour (reduced to only a half hour in 2005), and they roam around the four streets surrounding the Jardín and another four blocks nearby at their pleasure.

Their release is staggered now, so that the bulls can't pull a repeat of the year when they ran in a tight pack right back to their truck. The bulls are fresh and feisty when they roar out of the trucks. After a bit they slow down and look around and wonder what the heck is going on, and walk leisurely back to the truck. Staggering their release means that there is a fresh bull every few minutes.

I heard that one year a bull somehow got over the barriers at the Jardín and scared the hundreds of people who thought they were safe behind steel. This town routes traffic and pedestrians all the time, using pickups to move small trees in huge cement pots as movable street barriers.

My art teacher also told me of her experience at her first *Sanmiguelada*, as the Running of the Bulls is also called. A bull spotted a red VW and creamed it, the crowd yelling, "*¡Toro! ¡Toro!*" at every impact of horns against accordion-pleating metal.

We left our casa early and still found we were among throngs working their way toward the Jardín. We had to squeeze through a small space between the barriers at two points, to get into the area where the bulls were to run and then to get out again at the restaurant's corner. Two years ago before I started to lose weight I couldn't have made it through the spaces.

We were the first to arrive at El Pegaso and the waiter proudly escorted us to the best seat in the house, next to a window where he assured us we could see everything. Then he started pouring the sangria.

The city made a decision several years ago to stop selling alcohol at 6 P.M. the day before the run, and to not resume alcohol sales until 2:30 P.M. after the run, though restaurants and bars could continue to serve drinks with meals. Plenty of people were visibly intoxicated anyway, and I saw ice chests in some cars. The restaurant's sangria was pretty weak, Norma says. I had Jamaica tea.

The *paella* was topped with a half a mushy crab that had obviously been frozen. SMA is not exactly a beach town. The clams, mussels, shrimp, chicken and sausage in the rice were excellent, though.

And I can see why the restaurant is proud of its raspberry pie. When we lived in Michigan we would go to the pick-your-own fruit farms and make 10" pies loaded with half a gallon of fresh raspberries. This one wasn't quite that good. SMA is not raspberry country, either. (El Pegaso is the only place in town I know of that also sells pastrami on rye. Hecho en Mexico sells corned beef sandwiches. Neither place is the New York Stage Deli, but they have to do.)

As we finished eating around 12:30 we heard the firecrackers that meant the first bulls were let loose from the trucks. Nothing happened on our street for quite a while. We watched the action at the Jardín on the restaurant's TV. Most of the bulls were fighting only with each other. The people in the restaurant were groaning, they said it was so dull. The waiters kept saying the bulls looked bored.

Suddenly the first black bull wandered into our street and the kids jumped up on all the windows, hanging on tight to the metal security bars. All we had looking out our prized window were crotch shots of boys' jeans. So much for our excellent view. So we pushed outside to join the crowds behind the steel fences.

Every time that bull turned his head, people screamed. But that bull could not be tempted by anyone into charging, though plenty tried. All the shops had sold red *Sanmiguelada* scarves and T-shirts the weeks before the running. The young men used both the scarves and T-shirts as capes. The bull wasn't interested.

Then a whole slew of bulls came running the wrong way from the route they were supposed to take, which caught everyone off guard. More window scrambling, more cape waving. The bulls ran right past.

A few bulls meandered our way later, and some of the young men were obnoxious, pulling the bulls' tails and slapping at them. I was disgusted. A few young women, Mexican and foreign, put themselves right in the middle of the "action."

Luckily I am tall and could get some good photos. With my zoom lens, one shot looks as if the bull is racing right at me. The metal barrier doesn't show up in the shot.

Nancy stood around looking at the backs of the crowd and got frustrated. She held her camera up as high over her head as she could and aimed in the general direction of the noise when a bull charged somebody.

I don't know if that technique resulted in any good photos or not. I'm convinced that, for me, most good shots are a matter of luck and persistence, anyway—take a hundred photos and two or three will be good.

Around 1:30 P.M. the firecrackers went off again and a few workers came by to round up the last of the stragglers and get them into the trucks. I don't think there were even a dozen bulls total. The whole thing was highly over-blown, but admittedly a bit of fun with moments of excitement.

I probably would have felt differently if I had been near the one person who was seriously injured this time, a woman who was gored and taken away by ambulance. Ambulances were at every corner of Centro at the ready.

Once the bulls were back in the trucks everyone cheered and the barricades came down and those who had smuggled in beer passed it around freely. The bars still didn't reopen until 2:30, another half hour, so there were crowds waiting in front of some establishments.

One bar had set up a mechanical bull out in the street—it gave the most action of the day.

It was like Daytona Beach Spring Break, or Rocky Point Spring Break, or homecoming weekend at any football college town. So many enthusiastic young men. Most looked pretty clean cut, your average Mexican college students.

But by 7 P.M. when we tried to go out again by car, everyone on the streets seemed to be drunk and the town was one huge party. We had thought we would experience the Full Moon Ceremony with Nancy that night out in the Botanical Gardens. The site would be more easily reached by car since the taxis were pretty well occupied, and we figured we couldn't count on cabs sticking around or coming back as promised to pick us up a few hours later.

As soon as we hit the crowds outside the parking lot we wanted to turn around. But Nancy insisted we drive her out to the Botanical Gardens as promised, and she'd get a ride home with someone else. The main street out of town was so jammed we could hardly move.

At one point some guy jumped on the back of our car and began bouncing up and down, jarring us inside.

The first road rage we've experienced in SMA and it was me: I started to jump out of the car, screaming, "Get the f--- off my car!" Norma grabbed at me and hissed to get back in, don't make the situation worse, we'd be the ones arrested for causing a disturbance, and maybe even profanity in public, who knows the laws here.

I shut up and got back in the car, muttering under my breath. We waited. I clenched my fists to my side and forced my mouth to stay locked.

After a long minute the guy got off the rear of the car and stumbled to the front window on Norma's side and stared deep into her face all bleary-eyed, as if he were proposing. She rolled up the window and drove off. It was a wee bit unsettling.

Frequently kids will jump on the back of a slow-moving pickup going by and hitch a ride for a few blocks before jumping off again, so I don't think this guy meant anything by his jumping on our car. It still made me angry. This German's personal space had been invaded. And it was scary. He was too drunk to do a carjacking, and I haven't heard of such a thing in San Miguel anyway.

We dropped Nancy off at a parking lot where a dozen others were unloading drums from their cars and we took off. This time we tried to go a different route, but that street was blocked and we were back on Ancha San Antonio, hoping the car-jumping guy was far away by now. We followed a local-plated car through a parking lot shortcut to evade one roadblock and made it back.

The police had apparently done a road sweep and it wasn't really that bad. I've been in far worse mob scenes—massive antiwar demonstrations in D.C., Chicago and New York, for example—when I was scared of the police clearing the streets where I was marching. This time I was glad for the police sweep.

The next morning the kids and tourists poured out of town and the city quieted down to normal. The sanitation department women in orange jumpsuits mopped down all the streets with water brought in on city trucks. Like day and night, who would have known it was the same city 24 hours later?

The festivities weren't over, though. That night we went out for a walk and came across a parade of what looked like Day of the Locos dancers around Plaza Civica. We heard drums and walked that way and came across another parade, this one starting with a small brass band and drummers, beating on old oil barrels carried by helpers.

Now I knew the origins of the battles that I thought had been "Cowboys and Indians." Some featuring children with machetes fighting soldiers were reenactments of the historic battle of the children, in which a handful of motivated children held off a much larger number of invading French soldiers. This is the same battle that is the origin of the Cinco de Mayo holiday, celebrated more in the U.S. than in Mexico. (The French returned a few days later with more troops and defeated Mexico, leading to the rule of Maximilian and Carlotta.)

Some of the parade battle scenes were Indians against the Conquistadors, some were simply good versus evil, "evil" depicted via red satan suits and horns.

Then the Conchero dancers appeared, first the women in indigenous dress, then the half-naked men in fabulous body paints and breastplates and peacock feather headdresses. Dressed-up toddler Concheros in training clung to their parents' hands, not quite in step.

Next came a procession of four young girls in white with gold wings, carrying on their shoulders a wood platform displaying a glass-enclosed St. Michael the Archangel statue. The float is making the rounds of all the churches and neighborhoods before next week's feast day.

Behind the saint at a respectful distance were three of the *mojigangas*, the giant paper maché puppets with men inside them, making the dolls bob and bow and dance wildly to another band behind them. Again one of the dolls was a bride, though a different one than we'd seen at the Belles Artes anniversary party. No breasts accidentally slipped out of the doll dresses this time. Just another ordinary parade in SMA.

From there we walked back to the Jardín where an apparently famous female singer had performed moments before and was being whisked out of town in a huge motor bus. We couldn't believe that bus could back down the narrow streets and around a tight corner, but it did and she was gone and the street was closed again.

Four men on glistening horses with embossed and silver-trimmed saddles trotted down the sidewalk as we were walking home, and when a space opened in traffic they moved into the street. The four horses took up the equivalent of one car space and they clip-clopped out of town as if they did this every day.

᷾

I read in one of my watercolor teacher's art books depicting fi-esta scenes that many Mexican men, especially from the rural ar-eas, hang back in church all year, feeling out of it, unable to show their emotions, letting the women control the scene and the family participation in religious rituals. But when it comes to fiestas the men are able to use the anonymity of costumes and masks to show their emotions, to take charge, to have some control over their lives when usually so little is in their control.

The dates of the fiestas are known years in advance, people can prepare for them, they are settled events. The art book said that the poorest towns often have the most intense celebrations and do the most preparation for them, using corn husks and homemade ma-terials to make their costumes and floats with devout fervor. The book said that it is this obvious religious and cultural significance to these festivals that make tourists flock to them, searching for that kind of meaning and honesty so rare in city festivities.

Although both men and women can be Conchero dancers, only men carry the big drums, and from the apparent weight of them, I can see why. Many of the drums are deeply hand-carved wooden instruments, though some neighborhoods opt for the oil drums and lighter weight commercial drums.

I keep thinking about the text in that art book—is all this ceremony an outlet for machismo? I don't know, but I find it exciting to see men being so open and emotional and intense in their anonymous costumes, dancing proud and free.

I read that more women are starting to encroach into traditionally male roles, such as the young girls who did drumming in the children's band using pre-colonial instruments I wrote about earlier. It's none of my business, I'm a spectator. I've read many places that the Mexicans taking part in all of these festivities are doing it for themselves, not for tourists. They were doing the same celebrations long before all of us arrived.

One problem is that some colonias which once had lots of participants, who shared the costs and responsibilities, now have so many foreigners owning homes that there are fewer Mexicans to carry the load any more; their new gringo neighbors don't take up the slack. Mexico will change on its own pace and not everything should be changed that will change.

I'll quote the schedule for the Fiesta Patrias events from Atención (website *www.atencionsanmiguel.org* for the latest SMA news) so you can see what all is going on this week, not all of which we attended or plan to attend:

"Friday, 10:30 A.M., Anniversary of the end of the fight for Mexican Independence from Spain, Plaza Civica, and offering of Museo Allende at the Jardín;

8 P.M. Grand Fiesta Dance, Recreo 4, and music and food to celebrate San Miguel Archangel, preliminary to collecting the fireworks from the neighborhoods, at Colonia Aurora playing fields.

Saturday, 1 A.M., Musical bands and collection of fireworks, Jardín to Valle de Maiz.

2 A.M. Collection of fireworks, Colonia Aurora to Jardín.

2:30 A.M. Bringing the fireworks to the Jardín.

3 A.M. Parade of Stars, Mojigangas, musical bands.

4 A.M. Traditional Rain of Lights and celebrations for San Miguel de Archangel, Jardín.

9-11 A.M. Music in the Jardín kiosk.

10:30 A.M. Anniversary celebration of the capture of the Alhondiga de Granaditas, Jardín.

11 A.M. Arrival of the horsemen of San Martin Caballero, Jardín.

1 P.M. Voladores de Papantia, Jardín.

3 P.M. Indigenous community celebrates the encounter of crosses and souls and blesses the new clothing for Archangel San Miguel [the statue displayed in the Parroquia].

4 P.M. Dance and Xuchiles, Plazoleta de la Caldada.

5 P.M. Voladores, Xuchiles, regional national dancers, musical bands, Mojigangas, and decorated floats.

8-10 P.M. Popular and traditional dances, Jardín and central streets.

9 P.M. Fireworks

Sunday, 9-11 A.M. Music in the Jardín kiosk.

11 A.M. Parade of traditional dancers, musical bands, decorated floats, Centro Streets.

1 P.M. and 5 P.M. Voladores.

9 P.M. Fireworks."

No way could we attend all these events! So this is what we actually went to during the weekend.

We knew we couldn't miss the Rain of Lights, even though it would be at 4 A.M. We took sleeping pills at 6 P.M. Friday so that we would have a full night's sleep before the 3 A.M. parade. But we couldn't sleep anyway and dragged our drugged selves down to the Jardín at 2:30 A.M.

It wasn't as packed as the night of *El Grito*, but this time we knew not to try to find a place on the benches or where the crush was last time. So we found a spot on the steps around the statue of Fra. Juan de San Miguel in front of the Parroquia and wondered why the spot was otherwise empty.

Neighborhoods arrived in their own parades bringing their collections of fireworks to add to the night, accompanied by their own bands and dancers. The tall *mojigangas* puppets wound their way through the crowds, visible from anywhere in the Jardín. Three towers were again set up with fireworks in pinwheel designs.

We were aware this time that at the very end of each tower's display a foot-wide disk would be launched, soaring ablaze a hundred feet high and sometimes landing back in the crowds, people ducking every which way. Nothing like that would be allowed in the U.S.

So the fireworks started, and they came from two places, the big traditional ones set off behind the Jardín so that they exploded high overhead, reds and greens and yellows, and those screaming bomber ones that blow up in silvery blasts. Someone somewhere from the side occasionally launched rockets of some sort that whirled and twisted in flaming paths and bounced off of walls and landed on the crowds, particularly in our area.

I got hit on the cheek by something and panicked, but there wasn't even a mark to show for it later to proclaim my bravery, or stupidity. Now we knew why no one else had chosen to sit on the steps—the area was in the middle of a firing zone!

The stage next to us was also a primary target for the bouncing remnants, and the backdrop screens got knocked over. People scrambled under the wooden stage for safety. Kids were giggling and screaming simultaneously.

Something hit my scalp and sizzled for a second. Those of us around the statue of Fra. Juan finally got the message and ran around the corner behind a stone wall. We'd peek out and a streaming blast would drive us back out of sight.

The gorgeous display went on for more than two hours. I think it was even bigger than the joint Detroit-Windsor fireworks on the Ambassador Bridge of my childhood, and the stylized, so-professional July 4th fireworks set off at the beach around Santa Monica I remembered from the '70s. I can't vouch for my memory any more, however.

One thing the SMA celebration had that I'd never seen before was the launching of paper bags with flames inside them, probably from candles, that floated above like miniature hot air balloons on fire until each paper bag caught fire and floated to earth. Usually the fire was out by the time the bags landed, but not always.

At Christmastime Mexican neighborhoods often use lit candles inside paper bags anchored with sand to line stairwells and sidewalks. I always loved the looks of those gleaming paper bags on the ground—but it is quite another thing to have them floating down toward your head.

It was one of the most incredible experiences of my life to be with so many happy people, all in awe, infants and elderly alike awake to greet the dawn and hurry it on its way.

Saturday afternoon, after a short nap, we returned to the Jardín for yet another parade and the bringing of the Xuchiles floats, which are tall bamboo altars decorated mostly with golden marigolds. The altars are leaned up against the walls and fences around the Parroquia in an impressive display.

I've learned that the *Voladores* are performing no circus act but a religious one, and that these are five average guys, not trained acrobats, who perform for their own spiritual improvement. Four men let themselves fall backwards off of the tiny platform, connected only by a rope tied around one ankle.

The landing on the top of the post from which they drop represents not only the center of each human being but as high and as deep as it is possible to exist, taking in the entire universe and all its gods. One man stays behind on top of the platform, playing ancient songs on his flute to call to the spirits from the four corners of the earth. Slowly the men make 13 slow arcs to the ground as they drop.

Together they represent an Aztec sheaf of 52 years of 13 months each from the Aztec calendar, though the Mayan and Aztec calendars are highly complex and involve the interplay of both civic and ritual calendars and days of atonement. (The Mayan calendar reflected the exact amount of time it takes the earth to circle the sun more accurately than European calendars. According to the Mayan calendar, on Winter Solstice Dec. 23, 2012, a remarkable convergence of calendars comes to an end and a major new earth cycle will begin. Some fear it will be the end of the earth.) The four *Voladores* make the motions of a swooping bird as they alight, further tying the ceremony into the gods of all of nature.

One of the *Voladores* is the same man we've bought vanilla beans from on the street—he sells the beans for $3 each. He also has bottled pure vanilla and carries a dozen embroidered shirts for sale as well. The area where the *Voladores* ceremony originated is also known for its vanilla. I would have never dreamed this little street vendor was capable of such majesty.

The Xuchiles altars covered with marigolds are a reminder of a 40-day war between Chichimeca Indian tribes, who finally halted the fighting when a cross appeared in the sky to tell them to stop. The altars represent their funeral biers, the flowers of mourning tied to bamboo structures.

The Indian word for marigold means flower of 400 lives. Deceased Chichimecas traditionally were placed in caves on such altars rather than buried in the ground. These altars and the *Voladores* and many other floats and native dancers appeared both Saturday and Sunday, until everyone was in a dancing fury of passion.

Conchero dancers, also called *Danzantes*, wear costumes identifying their home state. *Huesaras*, tree seeds representing the earth, looking like hollow acorns strung on cords, decorate their ankles and make a rustling sound as they dance, as if they are running through autumn leaves. Their costumes are covered with pre-colonial pagan symbols.

Their giant headdresses of peacock feathers and many other kinds of feathers are unlike the heavy, hanging headdresses I think of for U.S. Indian headdresses. These go up and out like a peacock's tail.

Often the headdresses incorporate a realistic carving of a bird or animal coming down over the wearer's face, such as a fierce jaguar or eagle mask. The dancers are supposed to be a channel of energy between man and the gods. Each dancer performs as part of a personal spiritual quest. (When I asked one dancer for permission to take his photo, he agreed, posed, and afterward asked for $5. I laughed and walked away fast.)

Each colonia sends its own dancers to the major parades, the neighborhoods announced by banners carried by two young people walking in front of each contingent. Of course the neighborhoods and families compete for the best costumes and the most enthusiasm. This weekend is considered to be for the local people, not for the tourists who are the primary focus of the Running of the Bulls weekend.

Being in sleep deprivation when we started, we only narrowly survived the weekend but had a fantastic time. Things are back to normal for a few weeks now, until Day of the Dead November 2-3. I'm not sure I'm ready for a weekend celebrating the dead walking among us. And the more I read, the more Day of the Dead seems like a very private celebration among families, and I don't want to intrude.

Finally we took that $55 Instituto Allende tour of Atotonilco, Dolores Hidalgo and Guanajuato to put all of these bits of history into some sort of context. A former high school principal named J. César del Rio Garcia, lawyer and teacher, is the guide, and it's apparent he loves his job. The bus took us to Atotonilco first, the name an Indian word for a place of hot waters, and several thermal spa resorts open to the public are nearby.

The sanctuary was built in the mid-1700s after Father Alfaro had a vision that a church should be built at that spot, dedicated to Jesus of Nazareth. The walls of the church are covered with restored paintings and wood carvings depicting biblical history, and it is listed as a World Heritage Site by the United Nations.

Cesár recounted tales of his own baptism there, and of times when people would dress up as Satan and terrorize little kids into repenting of their sins. After one such ghostly performance, crowds chased the Satan impersonator and beat him to death. That was the end of that custom.

Allende was also married in the historic church. Stalls outside the sanctuary sold rosaries, crosses, and other religious icons, along with tacos and gorditas. Pilgrims depart on foot from Atotonilco for San Miguel seven miles away for various religious holidays.

The sanctuary was known for its beautiful large banner of the image of the Virgin of Guadalupe, Mexico's patron saint. The story of how the Virgin Mary appeared to a poor Indian, Juan Diego, in 1541 is a basic truth for most Mexicans. Juan Diego was supposed to have walked 15 miles each day to attend Daily Mass in what is now Mexico City.

One day on Tepayac Hill, the Virgin Mary appeared to him dressed as an Aztec princess. She told him she wanted a church to be built in Mexico City, and he was to tell the Bishop of her request. The Bishop asked for proof it was the Virgin Mary.

Juan had to miss his next meeting with the Virgin because his uncle was dying, but on his way to his uncle's bedside the Virgin appeared to him on the road to say his uncle was cured and to go back to Tepayac Hill. There he found roses growing in the frozen earth—Castilian roses not grown in Mexico. He gathered them up in his cloak for the Bishop.

When he laid the cape down for the Bishop, his cloak was emblazoned with the image of the Virgin Mary with a dark complexion, the rays of the sun radiating out from around her. The church was built in her honor, and Our Lady of Guadalupe was declared the patroness of the Americas.

Pope John Paul II made Juan Diego a saint in 2002, though there is some criticism by religious scholars that Juan Diego never existed. But St. Juan Diego and the Virgin of Guadalupe are much beloved in Mexico, legend or not. The poor farmers the rag tag revolutionary army passed by in 1810 would follow any army carrying that flag.

I mentioned earlier that Father Miguel Hidalgo and Ignacio Allende used to meet in Allende's home, now the Allende museum adjoining the San Miguel Jardín, to plot the revolution against Spain in 1810. They'd meet while parties were going on downstairs to camouflage the comings and goings.

The same way that the U.S. founding fathers argued whether the proposed country should be a true democracy or a representative republic, with white male property owners gaining the vote while slaves and women did not, the Mexican revolutionaries faced the same kinds of philosophical decisions.

The upper class Spaniards born in Spain looked down upon pure-blooded Spaniards born in Mexico, who were called *criollos*. They in turn called the Spanish-born *guachupines*, or spurs, because of the way the Spanish-born treated those born in Mexico. Those of mixed blood were called *mestizos*, and the lowest class, those of pure Indian descent, were the *indigenas*. Some *criollos* wanted power only for themselves, while others plotting the revolution wanted freedom for all.

Allende and Hidalgo also had such discussions as prominent members of a "literary society" that met in the home of Josefa Ortiz de Dominguez (who later was called *La Corregidora*), and her husband Miguel Dominguez, the government official representing Spain in Querétaro. It was that house which was searched first when Spanish authorities heard there was plotting going on.

She got wind of the suspicions against the plotters and warned Hidalgo and Allende so that they were able to escape. They were forced to start the revolution prematurely. *La Corregidora* was later arrested, tried, and convicted. She spent years as a prisoner in various convents.

On the steps of the church in what later became known as Dolores Hidalgo, in honor of the priest who is considered the father of Mexico, Hidalgo issued *El Grito*, the cry for independence, gathering the first of their amateur army. It was late September 15, 1810. They rode to Atotonilco to pick up the Virgin of Guadalupe banner so that the Indians would choose to follow them. Then it was on to San Miguel, an easy victory, before they would aim for Guanajuato.

We stood before the church in Dolores and imagined Hidalgo rallying his troops with *El Grito*. In the fifth year of his six-year term every President of Mexico is supposed to visit this church Sept. 15 to proclaim *El Grito* on the same footsteps, while the original bell chimes overhead. Vincente Fox didn't. Between these Presidential visits the historic bell is kept in a Mexico City museum, like our Liberty Bell in Philadelphia. Dolores Hidalgo wants its bell back permanently.

While we were in Dolores, our busload of tourists had to try the city's famous ice cream stands in the Jardín in front of the church. Cesár warned us there would be flavors like shrimp (a frozen icy shrimp cocktail, no milk at all), tequila, beer, avocado, corn and prune (whole dried prunes complete with pits).

Most of our busload stayed with traditional fruit flavors while I had the shrimp cocktail ice cream and Norma had a combination of pine nuts, coconut and those whole prunes in a vanilla base. Delicious, if disconcerting to bite down on a prune pit.

⁂

The tour stopped for lunch in Santa Rosa, a town at 10,000 feet altitude, as we wound our way through the mountains into Guanajuato. The meal and shots of mescal were included. We selected the lightest, tastiest, non-greasy chile rellenos we've ever had. Everybody else on the bus was a visitor to San Miguel. We were told repeatedly how lucky we are to actually live in SMA. And we know it.

On to Guanajuato, a city about the same size as San Miguel and at about the same elevation.

We learned that more than half of the silver the Spaniards ripped from this country came from Guanajuato, and it was used to finance the wars, colonialism, and extravagant living of European rulers of the 16th and 17th centuries. The area is still a major producer of silver, though supposedly the main vein has never been found. Today's silver mainly goes to Japan for electronic components.

An underground river used to run through the city until a dam broke in 1905, and the city was trashed. City leaders moved the river and used the underground passages for streets.

The major way into the town is through a 1.5-mile tunnel, very dark and eerie. Our bus probably wouldn't fit—we stopped first on top of the city at the mountainside statue of *El pípila* and then took the new funicular cable car ride down the hill to the main square of the town.

El pípila, full name Juan Jose de los Reyes Martinez, was a miner whose nickname means turkey. Turkey eggs are spotted, and freckled people in Mexico often are nicknamed *El pípila*.

Hidalgo, Allende, and two other leaders, Aldama and Jiminez, had rounded up 20,000 soldiers on their way into Guanajuato. The Spaniards were holed up in the granary, Alhóndiga de Granditas, which even today is an impressive-looking gray boxy structure with tiny windows lining the top floor. It was a seed and grain warehouse built in 1789 and had also been used as a prison, being pretty impenetrable from inside or out. At that time, miners often put stone slabs on their backs to protect themselves from falling rocks. *El pípila* was asked by Hidalgo to put a stone slab on his back and make his way to the door of the fortress to set it ablaze, despite bullets and fire raining down on the army from above that had kept the revolutionaries from entering the granary. His bravery made this crucial victory possible.

Cesár told us that for years historians were not sure *El pípila* even existed, but Cesár was principal of a high school named after the hero. There was talk that officially *El pípila* would be declared a myth and the school would have to be renamed.

Cesár and others did some research to find that not only had the miner existed, he had been born in San Miguel, not Guanajuato! So SMA put up a big statue of the man with a slab on his back at one of the two main glorietas into town to celebrate their new-found hero, and *El pípila*'s place in history as a genuine person was guaranteed.

His 30-foot-tall statue in Guanjuato has more European features, while the more recent SMA statue shows more of his Indian ancestry, Cesár pointed out.

From the funicular down the Guanajuato mountainside we walked to Teatro Juarez, one of hundreds of impressive buildings and monuments erected by President Porfirio Díaz throughout Mexico to commemorate the 100-year anniversary of the 1810 War of Independence. Díaz was a dictator whose reign led to the 1910 second war of Mexican independence, this time from its native born dictator.

But while Díaz was in power his last years he made Mexico beautiful with thousands of tributes. The monuments were meant to reflect his own glory as much as they celebrated Mexico's history.

The columned four-story Teatro Juárez is indeed impressive. Dramatic statues of the Greek muses line the roof. A just-married couple was having wedding pictures taken on the steps as we watched, the bride's carefully arranged white gown and train flowing in a cascade down the stairs. I took her picture, too.

We walked past the granary and saw the metal hooks at each corner of the building where the heads of the four captured leaders were hung in cages the following year, the rotting carcasses meant to discourage Mexicans from continuing the battle that waged another 10 years before independence was achieved. The remains of the four heroes are now in Mexico City.

At the Basilica of our Lady of Guanajuato, we saw the 40-pound square of blackened silver that forms the pedestal of the saint. Cesár said it is considered the oldest surviving piece of Christian art in all of Mexico; the church's façade dates from 1671. So much money was raised for the church that what was left over after it was built was put into the silver cube pedestal.

From there we went to Museo Diego Rivera where the muralist was born in 1886 and lived for seven years. His house felt like my grandparents' old farmhouse, with heavy carved dark wood furniture and aging intricate wallpaper throughout. Artwork hung in the upper floors.

We didn't have time to visit Mercado Hidalgo ten minutes away, a two-level outdoor market designed like a French train station in 1910, but we could see the majestic dome. Cesár didn't make us see the Mummy Museum on the outskirts of town next to the city cemetery, where some 100 corpses of men, women and children, some with skin, hair and clothes still intact, are on display.

※

We did get to see the prestigious University of Guanajuato, known for its law and its dance and music schools, founded by the

Jesuits in 1732. The hundreds of stone steps up to the law school are the site of an annual second "entrance exam" administered by older students for incoming would-be lawyers, who must run up and down the steps ten times without stopping to ensure that they will finish their law studies in the prescribed years.

Guanajuato is the city where *Las Tunas* originated in Mexico, the custom of strolling bands of musicians dressed in 16th century velvet costumes brought over from Italy and Spain. The *Estudiantinas* were founded in 1963 and are now replicated throughout Latin America, including in San Miguel, Cesár told us. We're looking forward to seeing them in SMA some day.

Guanajuato is also internationally known for its Festival Internacional Cervantino, started in 1972, a two-week music, dance and theater festival featuring acts from around the world, held in late October each year. Some of the performances are for free in the city's outdoor stages.

Originally it was a sort of street fair by hippies, and it grew in professionalism to become the Cervantino Festival. The street fair events still go on simultaneously, sometimes the two audiences bumping into each other with less than pleasant encounters.

But one year the official poster for the festival incorporated both elements—a bare-chested multi-pierced young man in a Mohawk haircut holding a Shakespearean-looking plumed pen was featured on the poster, which some businesses refused to hang.

Cesár said the entire town becomes one huge party during the festival. Legendary Hugh Masekela, father of African jazz, brought to the U.S. by Harry Belafonte, was one of the headliner acts the year South Africa was the featured country. We're going to get to Cervantino someday.

⌘

We were able to experience firsthand those underground Guanajuato streets, which follow the riverbed of the Rio Guanajuato that used to flood the city before it was diverted. During heavy rains the tunnels now used for roads still may become impassable, Cesár said. He took our group on a walk through a part of the tunnels, which seemed full of car pollutants to me. I wouldn't want to spend much commuting time in those tunnels.

The tunnels were lined with bricks and heavily enforced buttresses and arches, and the stone glowed an orange-rose under the glare-resistant lights. The aboveground city is so congested that cars are not permitted in most of it, much of the traffic being carried beneath the city in the bricked and reinforced tunnels.

Houses perched on high hills must be very tiring to reach at the end of a long work day. The only way you can get home is by climbing up a steep and narrow alleyway.

Seeing the route of the revolutionaries of 1810 was a wonderful experience, as thrilling as seeing the Liberty Bell in Philadelphia when I was in school. I would go on any tour the Instituto Allende offers.

Music students from Guanajuato often perform in the Sala of the SMA Biblioteca for their required public performances, and we were able to see one of these young pianists when we got home. She seemed so surprised people actually applauded for her. It was a nice way to spend an early evening.

6

October

History was never my favorite subject in school, but I enjoy the frequent lectures here on Mexico's past. Did Mexico embrace Catholicism so quickly and thoroughly when Cortez arrived because there was no "love" archetype in Mexican culture before the concept of Jesus was introduced? That's the fascinating thesis being developed by Dr. Marc Taylor (the lecturer who has now gone back to the States).

This lecture started with an analysis of all of the pagan gods from when the goddesses were displaced (around 2800 BCE) up to the present. The theology behind all of these pagan gods emphasized that the power of the gods was derived from the sacrifices and rituals of humans. This is the opposite of what Christianity preaches, that it is the people who are empowered from the sacrifice of Jesus for their sins.

The Aztecs in particular and many of the other Mesoamerican civilizations sacrificed humans alive to offer up their blood and their still-beating hearts so that the sun would come up each morning. They used small bleeding sacrifices throughout the day to ensure that the world would continue on schedule.

Imagine the Mexican natives' shock to take part in a Mass in which it is proclaimed that Jesus's body and blood are being offered up—for them! And Jesus did it out of love, and they were to love one another as Jesus loved them.

This was a major upheaval in thinking of the entire 12,000 years of Mesoamerican history, Dr. Taylor said, and it happened so quickly because of human beings' innate, archetypal yearning for love. Quite a revolutionary theory.

Shamans were different from Catholicism's priests in that in times of crisis, they left the community to be directly with the gods, often with the help of peyote, and they returned to tell the people what they had learned from the gods about solving a current community problem. Shamanism continues up until today in Mesoamerica, never disappearing even as Catholicism spread.

I have been told by several long-time residents that there are practicing witches alive today who are greatly feared and respected by many Mexicans. You do not make fun of witches. Nancy showed her kitchen witches to her gardener who was visibly upset at her for hanging the cartoon figures.

The lecturer believes that instead of the commonly accepted belief that Catholicism spread among pagan worlds by picking and choosing among pagan rituals and incorporating them into Catholicism so that people would be fooled into converting, the exact opposite is true. Paganism widened to encompass Catholicism, and accepted what it would, and ignored the rest.

Paganism is the foundation upon which Catholicism was welcomed into Mesoamerica as one more alternative view, an expansion of thinking. Paganism swallowed Catholicism and allowed it to continue rather than Catholicism swallowing paganism and killing it. This was certainly a whole new way of viewing the Mexican culture.

When the Catholic priests ordered that Catholic churches be built on top of pagan sacred land, obliterating the former holy structures and practices, and that the newly Baptized Catholics must destroy their statues of pagan gods and replace them with Catholic saints and symbols, the pagan symbols were simply hidden inside the new, or made a part of the foundation. The pagan gods continued to be worshipped.

Did the priests not recognize the pagan symbols incorporated into the churches, or did they figure they'd better be happy with whatever they could get? I'm still guessing, again.

We saw a slide of a statue at a nearby church of St. John, whose gospel begins, "In the beginning was the Word." The statue of St. John rests upon a mask of the Green God, who was called the speaker of the word in paganism. Coincidence?

Mexico is considered by many as the most Catholic of all countries, yet in many ways it is not Catholic at all. Mexico is considered by many as closely related to the U.S., and yet I have heard that it is the most foreign of all countries to us. The friendliness and apparent similarities are purely superficial, and some inherent fundamental differences are irreconcilable.

I have no idea whether any of this is true. I don't feel any of that strangeness or alienation, I feel a genuine warmth from the people. Or is it because I want to feel it? With poor Spanish, I'm in no position to take part in customs or to understand what people are really saying anyway.

Someone asked me if there is anything I don't like about Mexico, since I talk of it so idealistically. Not knowing the language enough to understand what is going on is a biggie, of course, but that's not the fault of Mexico.

Dog poop on the sidewalk before it gets cleaned up the next day bothers me, but then our old RV park trained us well to pick up all droppings instantly or be fined. We seldom see anyone else carrying sandwich bags whenever we walk Lacey. It can seem ridiculous to pick up her mess when it is among other dogs' messes we ignore, but we don't want to spend our lives picking up the droppings of all the dogs in San Miguel.

I keep wanting to take home every stray dog and cat I see, not to mention the beggars and the kids selling gum. Beggars here are inches from me, I can see their eyes.

I'm conflicted about how to respond to poverty. That early Catholic upbringing told me to sell all I have and join the beggars. I was a "Sermon on the Mount" Christian, not a Ten Commandments one. When Dorothy Day, founder of the Catholic Worker movement which organized soup lines and communal farms throughout the U.S., came to speak at Marygrove College and told us to give away all our sweaters and blouses except two, I may have been the only student who took her seriously. I volunteered at their soup kitchen in downtown Detroit on weekends until I had to get a second job to pay for college.

I keep having this urge to give away all the money in my purse to whatever beggar seems to be in need, but of course I can't. We may be seen as rich gringas, but we have to live on basic Social Security.

Norma and I got scammed a lot back in LA by people who said they needed gas money to get home, and then we'd see the same people still asking for gas money hours later when we'd already given them enough to easily get home. We never learned. So my discomfort cannot be blamed on Mexico.

We chose to live in a tourist town, so we can't exactly complain on days when the tourists are here in force, from other parts of Mexico and throughout the world, not just the U.S.

We don't come in contact with the richer expats who live in a different world from us. They do seem to be renovating more and more homes and ruins into mansions, however. The real estate frenzy and housing bubble are hitting San Miguel hard. New real estate offices keep popping up all over town, photos of million-dollar homes in their windows. That's all I can think of so far when asked what I don't like about living here.

Enough talk about what I don't like about Mexico and more about what I do like. Saturday evening we went to a free concert by seven Italian classical guitarists touring the world. They looked as if they were in their early 20s at most. They were joined by harpsichord, violin and cello players for two numbers. The lead guitarist then sang what seemed to be a sweet song to San Miguel as the closing number, and, looking beyond our inability to understand all the Spanish lyrics, his genuine love for SMA could be felt.

Then it came out in the translated closing remarks that the lead guitarist had been a scholarship recipient from the Biblioteca scholarship fund years before, and the grant had made his future possible.

Each year the Biblioteca scholarship committee helps more than a hundred young people to either finish high school or go to college, from donations and the profits from the *Atención* newspaper, the House and Gardens tours, and the art films. The program is even putting fledgling doctors through medical school. Tuition is much cheaper here. Sometimes scholarships for schoolbooks and bus fares alone are what allow kids to go on with their education.

So that whole experience, the free concert, and seeing one of the San Miguel scholarship kids go on to become an international music figure, organizing a small orchestra and touring the world at a young age, made me thrilled to be living here.

As we left the small theater in the library, we came across a street blocked by traffic, where only a few cars honked occasionally, a kind of street theater apparently underway at the next intersection. Finally we were close enough to see a group of musicians in black velvet medieval-looking costumes with lots of gold embroidery and braiding. They had the intersection blocked all four ways for at least fifteen minutes before they moved on.

We followed right along with the revelers, singing, swaying, swigging wine from plastic glasses handed out by one man in the same kind of velvet costume. At the Jardin they stopped before one of the restaurant bars which swung open its doors. More wine was passed through the crowd, while the music continued.

I think someone was collecting donations for the wine, and probably for the group. We left only when we had to go to the public restrooms. I gave two pesos to a kid who looked desperate and didn't have any money. "*¡Muchas gracias!*" he yelled as he rushed inside.

When we rejoined the procession we met two women vacationing from San Francisco who asked us what the medieval costumed-group was all about. We didn't know. A bystander overheard us and said they were *Las Tunas*, one of three similar SMA groups of musicians in medieval costumes that play in the Jardin weekend nights.

Aha! These were the same groups we'd learned about that started in Guanajuato! We followed them for several blocks until they reached Ancha San Antonio leading out of town.

Lots of people were in the streets, the air was crisp, the night taco stands were sending out aromas of sausages…we weren't in the States any more. I'd said to the San Francisco women that maybe we would live in SF if we could afford it, but SMA was second best. One replied that she was beginning to think that maybe SMA wasn't second behind SF after all!

The more I think about what I said, the more I think she's right. In fact, later that night I decided that if we were given this exact same perfect rental casa in the form of a paid-for condo in San Francisco, we'd sell it for a million bucks, move back to San Miguel, and buy a house.

<hr />

It's only early October, and it was cool enough to need long pants today for the first time since we arrived in May. At 6,400 feet altitude, the weather is cooler in SMA than I expected, especially compared to Phoenix summers.

I looked at embroidered jackets in the storefront windows as we strolled. A gold one was even in my size, so I'm thinking about it. Not exactly the camel corduroy blazer I had been envisioning for the fall and winter here. My clothes sense is changing; a corduroy blazer would be out of place. I haven't needed any really warm clothes since we left Michigan in 1994.

At first I thought it was terrible for gringos to be wearing clothes inspired by Mexican Indian traditions—cultural appropriation was the label we politically correct activists applied to trends like Afros and dashikis on whites.

Now I'm wondering. We live here, these are the kinds of clothes that are sold in the stores, the money benefits the local economy, and the clothing is more appropriate to the weather here than what we brought from Phoenix. I'm thinking, I'm thinking.

I'm letting my hair grow longer for the first time in 30 years. "Old ladies" here aren't expected to wear modest short dos that "suit" their age. I want some warmth at the back of my neck. In about a year it should look the way I want it to, and until then I'm shaggy. Oh well, this is Mexico. A year will pass whether I get a haircut or not.

We attended a showing of what was simply called "Prisoners' Art" at Belles Artes. We bought an oil painting of white calla lilies (called *alcatraz* in Spanish—I think the prison in San Francisco Bay must have been named for the lilies that were already on the island, and not the reverse).

The lilies are painted sitting in a rust-colored pot on a window-sill against beautiful tiles with a Moorish influence.

The frame of the painting is highly worked tin, and the painting is about 3' x 4'. The entire painting and frame cost $40. The frame alone would have been many hundreds of dollars in the States.

So now we have a focal point for our living room, along with three green paper maché pear slices that range from ten inches to two feet tall ($12), and a big Mexican frog ceramic planter on the entertainment center ($5). A bit kitschy, but we like it. We are starting to make this casa our home.

We took a drive to the town of Celaya, about 25 miles away, in our continuing search for comfortable furniture to be purchased soon, plus my computer monitor had started to do an imitation of a strobe light.

Buying a 17-inch CRT monitor (the fat old style that fits into my desk which has a recessed spot for it) would be easy in the States, probably costing around $60, available at hundreds of places. Ordering online would cost the same, but the duty on any imported electronics is horrendous.

Costco and Office Depot in Querétero had only the new flat-screen monitors that wouldn't fit in my desk, at a cost of around $600-$700. For that price I'd get a new system in the U.S. somehow. The computer stores in town said they couldn't order one.

So Norma got hold of a 1999 yellow pages for this region (phone books are not easy to find) and discovered many computer stores listed for Celaya, a town of around 350,000 (similar size as Mesa, Arizona). But its downtown had a wide, car-jammed main street fed by tiny one-way streets and stores spilling into the streets and people walking everywhere, disregarding traffic, bicycles taking precedence over cars.

We dared the traffic and lousy signage and our lack of language skills, and we found a store that indeed had a 17-inch Viewsonic for $225, though we had to go back the next day to pick it up. After two days fighting the streets we think we now can manage to find almost anything in Celaya.

Celaya has a new Sears. While we were there we checked out the large-size women's clothing department. The clothes seemed dowdy and too expensive for us. Nothing grabbed us in the sofa department, either. La-Z-Boy recliners were $1,200 to $2,000 U.S., which I think is more than they sold for in Phoenix.

We saw a McDonald's, Pizza Hut, and KFC in the same area and decided to splurge on KFC—big mistake. Norma ordered a "Big Crunch" sandwich. The thick chicken breast was bloody red in the center. Visions of amoebas and salmonella danced in our heads.

I faltered in my Spanish with the counter clerk who insisted it was *roja* from *marinara*—red from tomato sauce. Never mind there was no tomato sauce on the sandwich. She gave us a replacement when we insisted, and it was just as red. I shared my thoroughly cooked wings with Norma.

Then we spotted a little gold dog not much bigger than Lacey, with Lacey's same big brown eyes, out on the patio. The dog was so skinny she got in through the bars around the outdoor eating area.

Norma fed her the chicken breast and juice-soaked roll, and the dog was so happy she raced in circles all around in the grass. Her nipples were saggy. It was all we could do to not bring her home. We're still thinking about that dog but Lacey would have had a fit. She's been an only dog for ten years and isn't about to share now.

On the drive into Celaya is a town called Comonfort, the main street lined with cheap ceramics stands. Since then we've gotten a bunch of brightly painted bowls and planters there. Entering into Comonfort is Muelbles Diana, probably the largest furniture store in the region, which will make any kind of furniture you want. (Later we had them make a stand alone kitchen island so that Norma has more working counter space.)

Now for some follow up on stuff I've reported before:

Our current appointed maid apparently got chewed out by the landlord and has been coming five mornings a week again. She even did a flurry of window washing and bathroom wall washing. We gave her a big tip for the month in response. (Well, $15 doesn't seem like a lot to us but it is to her.) She became really nice after that, though the animosity between her and Lacey is still palpable.

But we really could eat off our floors when she's done, and now we expect our floors to be spotless. We wonder what kinds of slobs we were before. We're still doing the dance with the landlady, who is still hinting we should hire the maid with the broken arm when she gets back.

The gardener has been fired. He worked four days instead of three the last week before our neighbors got back, which didn't quite make up for all his absences. And then they found he had been charging the neighbors below them the same full amount for the same work, unbeknownst to either family!

So he is gone, and he could very well sue our neighbors. That would take some nerve since he knows both families could tell the judge they'd been charged for the same work. Now we have a flourishing lawn that needs mowing badly, and flowers running rampant and going to seed. Our neighbor seems to enjoy doing the gardening himself anyway. I don't expect him to hire a replacement.

One day the neighbors came home from a walk and one of the stray cats started bleeding all over their porch to greet them. We loaned them our cat carrier and together we managed to catch the limping animal. Norma drove them to the vet.

Dr. Vasquez was surprised they were paying for treatment for a cat they didn't even own. The cat received injections of antibiotics for the weekend and was neutered in the process. He's home and happy and even lets our neighbors pet him. So I think they own a cat.

He's a gold, fluffy longhaired two-year-old we thought was old, but he was hurting from a badly bitten leg that had gotten infected. They're calling the cat Goldie, fine name for a male. When you name a stray animal, you've already lost the fight.

We're trying not to name any of the others. Umm, except Pinky, a scraggly underfed Siamese mix given that name because he has pink eyes from conjunctivitis. He's next on the list to be sterilized and treated.

Our park model in Arizona is in escrow. It all happened so fast, it's hard to believe. Finally it is starting to sink in: we have chosen to move to Mexico for the rest of our lives. It's been four months, and I feel as if I belong here, I've lived here forever, I'm home.

It is 7 A.M. Sunday, the one day we can sleep in without worrying when the maid will show up, and the fireworks and church bells have started. That would be fine except that I was up until 3 A.M. reading a new book. I'm halfway through the 1,038 pages of *Aztec* by Gary Jennings, which he researched and wrote in San Miguel over a period of 15 years.

I also read a very short but important book for my Warren Hardy Level I Spanish class, called *Mexican Etiquette and Ethics*, by Boye De Mente, who has written a series of books designed primarily to help U.S.-based businesses expand into different countries and cultures. (A more recent book of his is called *There's a Word for It in Mexico*.) He sees Mexican values and customs as very much like those of Asian countries, which are stereotypically called "inscrutable."

Mexico is a land of masks—not just the masks worn for so many ceremonies, in which the men in particular feel free to express with great emotion all the vitality and feelings men are usually uncomfortable displaying.

Mexicans hide their true feelings a lot from foreigners, with good reason. Thousands of years of oppression, first among their own bloodthirsty tribes before the oppression by the Spaniards and the Catholic Church, decimated Mexican tribes and cultures.

Mexicans have learned to be agreeable on the surface, De Mente points out, nodding yes that such and such a vital request will of course be accomplished by such and such a time, and believing in their hearts that of course this will actually happen, while accepting no responsibility for engaging in any conflict or major upheavals which might be required to actually bring this happening about.

It will happen, if God wills it, if only it happens, *ojalá, mañana*, which is not necessarily tomorrow. Even the language has developed to allow individuals to accept no responsibility for things that go wrong, things which could cause them to be killed if they did accept responsibility under the Conquistadors.

Even the words for the weather show this evasiveness. Good weather is caused by God, bad weather happens. The piece fell off the shelf, it happened, nobody knocked it off, certainly not me. I'll be back from vacation and to work on the day I say, though I'll add "*¡ojalá!*" –if only it will be so, God willing. My decision to stay on at a relative's place where family is more important to me than your deadline has nothing to do with your problem.

I'm not sure I understand all the subtleties of this different approach to life; it's important that I realize that the differences are there, and I am not necessarily right when I disagree.

I can see where it can be good to place family and fun ahead of a business deadline, to see that there is some benefit to being easygoing rather than tense. Not that past employers in the States would have understood.

I am coming into conflicts with some aspects of Mexican culture revolving around machismo and class. I still go back and forth in my head on having a maid each morning, appreciating the cleanliness but not liking someone in my house, cleaning up "my" mess. I continue to wear Bermuda shorts when it is hot, though some say we shouldn't.

One woman who has lived in Mexico for many years tells me that gringas should wear what a Mexican woman of similar age and class would wear. On this she and I disagree.

At times in my childhood I was very poor, and a very poor Mexican woman in her '60s would be wearing a *rebozo* covering her hair and shoulders like a Muslim veil, with skirts almost to her ankles. At the same time an upper class Mexican woman would feel free to wear absolutely anything and to shed her bra on a Costa del Sol beach in Spain on vacation.

The elderly women and men sitting on the sidewalks begging would be even more horrified to know all of my lifestyle, not just my wearing shorts. There is no way I could fit into their expectations, and no way that I would want to. But still, I do not want to offend local customs.

A Mexican male online wrote to me to say I should wear whatever I like, that more and more Mexicans are wearing shorts, male and female, young and old. He reassured me that the Mexican spirit is one of freedom and acceptance, and those few older Mexicans who might glare at me, so what. I think I'll listen to him.

There is no way I could ever blend in as a Mexican, and that was not at all in my mind when I moved here. Yet some expats think that should be our goal, that we should be totally unobtrusive.

At the same time I see many Mexican men and children and a few adult women wearing shorts themselves, and I personally think it is a good thing that women should be as free as men to wear shorts and cooler clothes in hot weather, and to express their individuality in their clothes and postures and ways of conducting themselves.

I didn't fight for the freedom of women to wear pantsuits to work in the early '70s to now say we should wear *rebozos* and long skirts here. Am I imposing my U.S. feminist beliefs on Mexico? Maybe my example will allow some Mexican woman to dare to do something her society says she shouldn't—and is that bad?

I doubt I'll ever find a totally comfortable answer to many dilemmas here. Meanwhile, if it's over 80° F, I'll wear shorts.

When Norma and I see a young Mexican woman in a miniskirt narrowly covering her crotch, its "waistline" riding low on her hips, her deep-plunging blouse exposing the rest of her midriff and most of her back, balancing on stilettos, we say to each other, "At least she's not wearing shorts."

I'm in a book club of U.S. women reading Latin American books to help us gain a better understanding of local cultures. An author considered by many to be the foremost Mexican writer of all time is Juan Rulfo, who wrote only two 1950's books in his lifetime, but they were masterpieces to establish his reputation.

We read and discussed both books: the novel, *Pedro Paramo*, and the short stories, *The Burning Plains and Other Stories*. None of us in the book club could say with any certainty we had any idea what either book was about! But they were so beautifully written, so full of wispy dreams and fragmented characters and magical realism, that we all had to admit we loved the books anyway.

Here's what the book flap inside *Pedro Paramo* says: "A masterpiece of the surreal, this stunning novel from Mexico depicts a man's strange quest for his heritage. Beseeched by his dying mother to locate his father, Pedro Paramo, whom they had fled years ago, Juan Preciado sets out for Comala. Comala is a town alive with whispers and shadows—a place seemingly populated only by memory and hallucinations. Built on the tyranny of the Paramo family, its barren and broken-down streets echo the voices of tormented souls sharing the secrets of the past."

This author is my first exposure to "magical realism," where you can never be sure what is real and what is sorcery. I'm looking forward to reading other great Latin American writers known for magical realism, including Carlos Fuentes, Mario Vargas Llosa, and Gabriel Garcia Marquez. To think, I hadn't heard of these names a few months ago.

This week we went to one of the best concerts I have ever attended. Paco Renteria is a classical guitarist who includes an electric violin in his backup band, along with several other guitars, bass, and drums. He and the electric violinist did a sort of "Dueling Banjos" competition that got more and more complex and rapid as they accelerated to an exhausting climax.

Mexican audiences don't seem to give up standing ovations as easily as U.S. audiences, but this crowd was on its feet cheering constantly. Someone told me Renteria has been the opening act for Luciano Pavarotti when he has performed in Mexico. I believe it. We heard he was gong to go on a concert tour in the States soon.

Norma starts a class in batik fabric dying tomorrow, the same hours I am in watercolor class. Because of the lack of suitable quilting fabric here she is going to dye her own.

As usual she has a most ambitious project in mind, a Laurel Birch cat and dog wall hanging design that she bought for a quilt but now she will adapt to batik. She always starts with a highly complex project.

When we both studied stained glass back in Michigan I was doing dozens of small animals of glass and selling them while she struggled with her first project, a 4' span of geese tiptoeing through tulips. We moved away and sold all our supplies before she finished that one. I'm hoping to see the Laurel Birch design on our living room wall someday, however. Norma is going to use bright Mexican colors.

We're both on pins and needles waiting for the house in Arizona to close. So much is going on. While the U.S. celebrates Christopher Columbus Day Oct. 12, here it seems to be a day to celebrate Mexican diversity and the pride of the indigenous people who survived the Conquistadors. Spain makes a big deal out of Christopher Columbus, too—naturally.

In much of Latin America there are protests on Oct. 12 against colonization. All I could find on the internet about U.S. protests this year was a controversy about whether *The Sopranos* cast should be allowed to march with Italian-Americans.

Our friend Tom invited us to his house for dinner, along with another gay man. His house is fabulous—you walk through the door and up a stairwell painted like a floral jungle. Predominant color of the house is deep rose, and he has patio views overlooking the city. His Jacuzzi is on a glassed-in porch so that he can luxuriate in bubbles while enjoying sunsets, sipping Margaritas.

We got to see three more scrumptious houses when Nancy treated us for a present to the weekly House and Gardens Tour sponsored by the Biblioteca. Profits from the $15 fees fund the scholarship program. Each Sunday the tour visits three different houses by bus.

We hadn't wanted to go because it is such a tourist thing to do, but we're glad we did. What different homes lurk behind innocuous plain doors.

Speaking of doors, be sure to read Robert de Gast's book, *The Doors of San Miguel,* full of wonderful photographs of the fancy carved wood doors here. I keep taking photos of doors myself, I can't help it, same as I've taken probably a hundred different shots of the Parroquia alone, standing right there next to the latest tour bus load of amateur photographers. This town is so photogenic.

The first home we visited belonged to a teacher at a private school in the U.S. who hosts students for extra credit projects in his seven-bedroom mansion outside SMA. The pool comes right into the master bedroom suite, and the engraved wood dining table seats 24.

The second house was on what was called "the smallest lot in SMA," 40' on each side. It was a three-story classical Italian masterpiece, with framed photos of the owner's little white French poodle in every room.

Unbeknownst to him, the poodle had defecated on newspapers in his laundry room during the tour, and we all giggled at this sight that would have horrified him.

The third house was wrapped onto a formerly abandoned, long, narrow lot that took months to clean out the rubble before construction could begin. It, too, was a dream house, with a restaurant-sized and equipped kitchen. Oh well, we love our inexpensive rented beauty.

Tom gave us vague directions to the Querétaro Liverpool, a big department store chain that is a cross between Dillard's and Neiman Marcus. We never could find it driving, so we parked in the Costco lot and took a taxi there our first visit. Now Norma could get there blindfolded, we enjoy the store so much.

We found a yellow-gold goose down-filled sofa and two big overstuffed chairs for $1,600 that we visit almost weekly, waiting for escrow to close on our Arizona house.

Norma comes downstairs each day from her batik work with arms and clothes spotted in jewel tones. The bees love it when she uses the beeswax between each session of dyeing. She's been stung several times already.

She keeps learning new ways to bleach and wax patterns into the strong cottons she uses. Norma's precise mathematical and account-ing accuracy comes into play as she plans which layer of color to dye next so that all kinds of shades come out of the three primaries.

After each color is dyed, Norma applies melted beeswax to the areas she wants to stay that color, and then dyes the material the next color. Whatever she wants to remain that color, she coats with beeswax, and so on. At the end, she'll have all the wax dry cleaned out of it and see what she's got.

※

We got word tonight that our Arizona park model fell out of escrow days before closing. We're heartsick. Another buyer will ap-pear, we know.

The whole issue of gringos and Mexican culture keeps com-ing up. At the last book club meeting one woman wanted to dis-cuss U.S. vigilantes on the Arizona border who are trying to do the work of the border guards. Stories about border vigilantes are in the Mexican papers daily, and the book club members think that the image of all of us from the U.S. is being damaged by these vigi-lantes. One woman said that to make up for the abuses by others, we should step off the narrow sidewalks to let Mexicans pass eas-ily, to show our respect.

Norma said, look at that suggestion in the reverse: would any-one say Mexican visitors and undocumented workers in the U.S.

should step off the sidewalks to let U.S. citizens pass to show proper deference? Shades of the South when blacks could not look whites in the eye and had to shuffle on past, looking down, letting whites have the sidewalks. Shades of the way women were taught not to look men in the eye and to "guard our eyes," as the nuns taught me, looking down demurely so as not to appear wanton.

Teenagers and groups of excited friends of any culture often block sidewalks and require everyone else to step down and give them room. I try to do some selective stepping off the sidewalks myself, always letting a disabled person or someone very elderly or someone with toddlers or packages or rambunctious dogs on leashes have the space.

I kind of expect a young man, either Mexican or foreign, to step off a narrow sidewalk for me—but then I was raised that any young person should give up his or her seat on a bus to a pregnant woman or an elderly or disabled person. That really dates me.

This whole amorphous issue of taking up space is important, I think. I go back to my anti-racism workshops and to my feminist consciousness-raising talks. A single black man looms much larger than another white person in an otherwise all-white group, and vice versa. A single man in a room of women changes the dynamics of that room, and vice versa.

Because there is such a range of color and class within Mexico, a single gringo may or may not stand out in any particular setting, but a light-skinned, taller, heavier gringo would certainly change the dynamics in a roomful of shorter, darker-skinned Indians. It would be very hard for the lone "different" person to feel accepted and to actually be fully integrated--not that it doesn't or can't happen. I keep thinking of the shot of Bill Murray in the elevator in *Lost in Translation*, towering over the Japanese people around him.

So these are all issues I think about living in Mexico. We more or less concluded in the book club that all any of us can do is the best we can, to be aware of how we come across, to do our best to learn Spanish and Mexican customs—and to continue concentrating on Latin American books.

The club discussed again whether we should stick with Latin American writers. Some wanted to change to U.S. best sellers. We voted to stick with Latin American books only, with Gabriel Marquez and Sandra Cisneros as our next authors to read. I think some members will drop out. Group dynamics can be complex whatever side of the border. (Later—I've been in three different SMA book clubs now, all with their own style and customs.)

So far I can think of only three unpleasant incidents we've had involving Mexicans. The first was the drunken guy who jumped on the back of our car after the Running of the Bulls. The second was a guy in a gourmet cheese shop who was insulting to us because we lived here and still didn't speak fluent Spanish.

The third was a guy who made some comment we didn't understand when we were walking on a narrow sidewalk. We apparently took up too much room and he wanted us to step down into the street instead of him.

That actually did happen—the issue is not purely theoretical. We didn't know exactly what he was saying, but that was the gist of it, we're pretty sure. We think he was drunk as well.

So three incidents in five months when we've had thousands of passing encounters with Mexicans who were polite, usually friendly, is no big deal. We probably would have had far more than three incidents of unpleasantness back in the States from teenagers, drunks, or anyone else who'd had a bad day, in the same five months. I've heard three nasty comments in five minutes in one block back in the States.

The Texas woman we'd met at the real estate session finally arrived in town with her furniture. She had the border crossing from hell. She spent four days living at the Nuevo Laredo border crossing. A two-day trip took a week, and her few pieces of furniture at one point had to be put onto an 18-wheeler, which in no way could make it into San Miguel's narrow streets.

All her furniture ended up in a warehouse outside of town for another two days. Her poor 14-year-old cat didn't eat or urinate in four days. (He's fine now.)

She slept in the cab of the truck while the driver slept in her bed in the back of the truck and offered to share it with her or to trade. She didn't feel comfortable sleeping in her bed and so she let him sleep in it, but then resented sleeping upright in the truck while he enjoyed her comfy bed, even if it was in the back of a moving van.

Seems everybody has a border crossing from hell story, whichever direction you're heading. We've been lucky.

7

November

The town was quiet approaching the celebration of Day of the Dead. This is the time everyone visits the cemeteries and has picnic lunches at the headstones of deceased relatives, who are still considered integral members of the family. People bring favorite clothes and foods of the deceased and decorate the graves with fresh flowers.

Death and life are one continuum in Mexico, which makes many in the U.S. uncomfortable. We want our dead to stay dead, to not be able to slip back into this world at the time of year when the boundaries between living and dead are the thinnest.

This is the same time of the year as Halloween, a pagan feast which the Catholic Church tried to overpower with All Saints Day on November 1.

The first day of mourning is for babies and young children who have died, who are believed to have gone straight to heaven. Nothing like the "limbo" I was taught about from the Baltimore Catechism in the '50s, where unbaptized souls who have not committed a serious sin are kept from seeing God forever though not punished by eternal flames. I wonder if this is official Catholic teaching now, or another local adaptation that the official Church ignores, or what? I'm still guessing.

Friends who live in areas with kids say they've been inundated for a week by trick-or-treaters, who don't seem to know exactly when or what Halloween is, only that they can get *dulces* from gringos. They're stocked up for Friday night to Tuesday night. Kids don't find their way into our courtyard but we usually have wrapped peppermints on hand anyway, so we'll carry them with us next Halloween season.

Day of the Dead week in San Miguel seems to be filled with altars, altars, altars—lectures on their meaning and making, workshops on how to do it, tours, films. I have never felt comfortable going into a graveyard to witness others in what seems to me to be a private party with their loved ones, so we're not taking part in any of those events.

We do tour the altars in the stores and restaurants, though. I was knocked over by the big display of altars in the Jardín in front of the Parroquia. Three streets are blockaded so that families can put up their own altars recognizing deceased relatives—I don't know how families are chosen for this honor.

In front of each altar the ground is covered with orange marigold petals, or chamomile or wheat, or sometimes with boughs of red gladiolas. Sometimes a sand painting is done on the ground and protected from anyone stepping on it or from blowing gusts. Large photographs of the deceased person are on display on the altar, and beyond that, almost anything goes: favorite foods, drinks, flowers, clothing.

The mementos chosen for the altar are obviously very personal ones, the meanings not always immediately clear. But what is clear is that the altars are deeply meaningful to the families. Since in Mexico burial is to be completed within 24 hours after death, the first Day of the Dead after someone dies is especially important to help survivors mourn more completely.

The crowds wanting to see these altars by the Parroquia were so large that they had to be funneled into lines, so many allowed to enter the streets every few minutes. Brightly colored plastic or paper flags the size of place mats, cut into intricate designs for each holiday, are flown on ropes across the streets for many events, and many of the flags for this holiday feature cut out skulls.

I'm used to seeing these strings of bright flags announcing a gas station opening or real estate open house in the States. Here they seem somewhat comforting, familiar, now that I'm used to them. Neighborhoods that are having a party will fly the banners across their streets from rooftop to rooftop.

Churches often fly purple and white flags across their courtyards for some religious significance. A woman in our courtyard purchased three strings of Independence Day flags in red, white, and green for a party she hosted outside.

This weekend there's a big dog show going on so we'll wander over there, too. And that's how we're celebrating Day (Week) of the Dead.

The dog show turned out to be as organized as most we've gone to in the States. We hadn't seen very many purebred dogs in SMA but there they were, probably 100 different breeds represented and competing in three rings.

Mostly we see two kinds of dogs on the streets in San Miguel: small white long-haired mongrels that look like a poodle mix, happy, happy, happy dogs that we call the San Miguel Special; and then the classic medium-sized short-haired dog, kind of like a brown, black and white Labrador retriever mix. But here were Papillons, Irish retrievers, dachshunds, Afghans, basset hounds, standard poodles, great Danes…all coiffed for the show ring.

A woman who is known for having a hundred matching outfits for herself and her Chihuahua dressed up with the dog in bright red, the dog also wearing a tiny red sombrero. They were probably the most photographed sight at the dog show. Policemen put their German Shepherds through their paces in an obedience segment.

The next weekend we took a bus to Oaxaca for four days. If we had seen Oaxaca first, we would have been tempted to choose that city for our retirement, its downtown is so beautiful.

But overall, we still prefer San Miguel. SMA has 80,000 residents in the city limits compared to a quarter million or more in Oaxaca, a mite too big for us. Its Centro is just as art-oriented. There are somewhere around 12,000 fulltime gringo residents of SMA at any one time, and you can get by with almost no Spanish, though it's much better to learn, whereas there are only 500-1,000 gringos living in Oaxaca and Spanish is an absolute necessity.

The drivers in SMA are much more polite and stop for pedestrians, whereas Oaxacans drive like maniacs. You can't even cross a street because they're busy racing around the corners without stopping to let pedestrians cross first, even when the pedestrians have the green light.

Oaxaca has stoplights at almost every intersection, though they're much smaller and only on two corners, and a pedestrian can see them only with difficulty, whereas SMA is a national monument and no traffic lights are allowed in the city limits. Those are the surface differences.

The more I learn, I find that the area outside of the Oaxacan *zócalo,* the historic central part of the city, has far more problems, far more poverty. Some 15 different tribes live in the area, with some 200 different tribal costumes. Many Indians don't speak any Spanish or English at all, only their tribal language.

The question arises again of how much integration should occur for economic advancement, even if that means extinction of these tribes, versus how much should each tribe's language and culture be protected. From the looks of the graffiti on the main streets outside the tourist areas, the city did not have a good feel to it. We love the *zócalo,* though—another area where you might be tempted to call it a Disneyland.

To get to Oaxaca, we took an ETN luxury bus to Mexico City, a four-hour drive, and received a ham sandwich, can of pop and bottled water when we got on. The ETNs have only three seats across, one on the left of the aisle, two on the right, and there's a snack stand with hot coffee in the rear.

We saw two movies in English with Spanish subtitles, headsets at each seat for good volume control, or you could listen to a variety of music like on a plane.

One of the movies was made-for-TV on the '70s, a group of friends at Kent State and how the day of the killings by the National Guard changed their lives. Pretty sappy and superficial. In case we missed it, it played again on our way back.

The bus took us the 160 miles in four hours to the North bus station in Mexico City, which is so big it has three or four terminals. I was pleasantly surprised by the Mexico City bus terminals, which are clean, immense, very much like a U.S. air terminal minus the security hassles. The terminal had lots of restaurants and shops, places to check packages, carousel rides for kids, probably 50 different bus companies represented in neat lines like the car rental stalls in U.S. airports.

The bus into Oaxaca, which is some 360 miles south of Mexico City, took seven hours. It was an ordinary first class bus—four seats across, no sack lunch, but still very clean and comfortable. Toilets were on all the buses, of course, very much like U.S. airplane toilets. Total cost for both of us, round trip, was about $200 U.S.

Gas at Mexican prices (around $2.30 a gallon while U.S. prices soar) and the tolls would have been that much, not to mention the wear and tear of the drive through torturous mountains much of the way, and the hour and a half through congested Mexico City to get to the south side before heading down. Mexican buses are great!

Oaxaca is one of the more remote big cities of Mexico, tucked between mountain chains, and only recently has an ultra-modern highway been built for easy access, which led to a population explosion.

The city of Oaxaca is another colonial historical monument city, with a tradition of exceptional arts and crafts. It is very cosmopolitan in its center, just like San Miguel. The museums have done a good job of capturing Oaxaca state's diversity and history, which goes back hundreds of years B.C. In fact the first writing done in the northern hemisphere was in Oaxaca at around 500 B.C.

One of the most famous pyramids and tombs of Mexico is outside Oaxaca, at Monte Alban. We walked a half mile to the hotel which was supposed to have bus rides to the tombs but spotted the city's Central Market, which is absolutely gigantic. We thought we kept good directions when we ventured inside for a minute, but soon were lost. We came out on an entirely different street than we thought, and so we hailed a cab to Monte Alban. It was $4 going, $8 coming back to the hotel, since there were no transportation alternatives out at the tombs.

The pre-colonization history of Mexico is incredible. Monte Alban was a flourishing city off and on for a thousand years before the Spanish arrived.

Tomb Seven at Monte Alban is where a lot of gold pieces were found. The originals (copies are sold at many fine jewelry stores around town) are on display at the museum adjoining Santo Domingo Church, which is itself almost totally covered with gold gilt inside. It is an amazing church, made to astound anyone who ventures inside.

After the 1910 revolution succeeded in redistributing wealth from the few rich *hacienda* owners and the church itself, the crackdown on Catholicism meant all the churches were seized. Santo Domingo church was used as military stables for many years. I hope the horses enjoyed the view of all that gold.

Our neighbors had recommended we stay at Las Golondrinas, the swallows. It was $46 U.S. a night for a double, easy walking distance to the *zócalo*. The hotel has 18 rooms around three courtyards and fountains. We kept thinking it was raining until we figured out there was a hidden fountain in the courtyard below our room.

The hotel has a breakfast nook, a dozen outdoor tables under a canopy of fruit trees and flowering vines. We started each day with meals like plate-sized tamales steamed in banana leaves with a dark chocolate mole sauce that Oaxaca is famous for, a fresh fruit plate heaped as big as a cantaloupe, a sundae dish full of yogurt, granola and fruit, Mexican eggs scrambled with salsa with a side of *frijoles* and cheese, big bread baskets of homemade rolls, three huge pancakes with granola and bananas, and more. Most of the breakfasts were about $3 U.S. We talked to the other guests, most of whom were a group of friends from San Francisco, over breakfast.

The *zócalo* was filled with vendors, most notably balloon sellers whose offerings overflowed onto the sidewalks. A popular balloon was a knockoff of Nemo, the orange clown loach cartoon movie star. Copyrights don't mean much in the rest of the world—Disney, Snoopy and Spiderman characters routinely adorn toys for sale.

When we had our ceramics store in Michigan, many storeowners would make knockoffs of Disney and Snoopy molds (which is easy to do, you make a mold from a piece that you buy legitimately), and every so often we would hear of a storeowner who got busted.

You wouldn't think that the Charles Schultz estate had interest in checking every little ceramics store in the country, but they do send out representatives to track down their faked competition. But it seems no use when it comes to other countries knocking off U.S. copyrighted items.

One section of the *zócalo* was devoted to a memorial to Indians who had given their lives to the drive for freedom and government recognition. A casket of one hero was on display, surrounded by plaques with the names of others, and vivid billboards and posters explained their cause.

People sang songs of liberty, some of which I recognized from when I was in the LA Women's Community Chorus and we did a concert of Latin American protest songs: "*Hasta La Victoria Siempre*" (Until Victory Forever), "*Hay Una Mujer*" (There Is a Woman, Who Has Disappeared) and others.

More recently the *zócalo* has been the site of demonstrations protesting the possibility of a McDonald's going up in Centro (protestors won that one) and the felling of historic trees for remodeling (protestors lost that one).

※

One night we were walking the downtown streets to some event or another and came across a little Indian girl of maybe five, sitting on the sidewalk all alone, not a soul within a block, playing a nice accordion fairly well. We threw 10 pesos, about a dollar, into her accordion case, and the next night we gave her 50 pesos. She was so thrilled.

I asked her if I could take a photo of her, which she was glad to approve—maybe she thought we'd take back the $5. We worried that she was all alone on that street. I would have liked to kidnap her myself.

I wasn't so lucky at getting photographs of the famous vendors of fried grasshoppers, or *chapulinas*, which many women had on sale in big platters in the various markets. To a one, they shook their fingers side to side, "No!" when I asked permission. I almost broke down and bought a bag of the insects to photograph them alone, but I couldn't bring myself to do it. They're greasy and salty, my two favorite food groups—I'd have eaten them and hated myself later.

Besides their famous Central Market, there are two big markets with hundreds of stalls each under a roof near the *zócalo*. I think the two markets took up two complete city blocks. One section would feature dozens of bread vendors, another would offer fresh fish being cleaned as you watched, another had plucked chickens hanging by their feet.

I bought something like $20 worth of postcards of the people in various regional costumes, since people were less open to having their photos taken than I had hoped.

Oaxaca is also known for its *alebrijas*, colorful wooden statues of fanciful animals that were originally made by fathers for their children. We fell in love with a life-sized peacock in realistic colors, until we noticed it was $1,200 U.S. We bought a brightly painted wooden grasshopper about ten inches long and four inches high for around $12. The animals are made so that the delicate legs, tails and wings can come apart for shipping.

One of the other markets consisted of 300 women artisans who have formed a collective. I bought a floor-length dark green embroidered cotton dress for $12, and a few other souvenirs. Even more than in San Miguel, Oaxacan artists love to do skeletons and other symbols used in Day of the Dead celebrations. We've grown to appreciate them, though all those skeletons grinning at us were disconcerting when we first got to Mexico. But later I bought Norma a 30" tall ceramic skeleton *katrina*, her bony decolatage showing above her fancy gown decorated with *alcatraz* blooms, that also adorn her wide-brimmed hat. We named her Miss Kitty, after the *Gunsmoke* character that wore floppy hats.

Oaxaca is famous for its dark, rich chocolate, and we went through a pound of that in one night. (Not to worry, I'll cut back when we get home.) We found the best pizza we've had out in Mexico, though we weren't so lucky at finding good Chinese—the restaurants ran to chop suey and chow mein, not the Szechuan spicy dishes we favor.

On the streets we couldn't refuse women selling pecan praline candies by the piece—after all, it was one piece, at a time. We ate some of the noted local dishes like a Mexican pizza made on a big fried tortilla at outdoor restaurants bordering the *zócalo*.

At each meal we had to refuse the street vendors a dozen times before they would go away. Musicians played for us while a partner circulated with a cup.

The city has a literary magazine published half in English, and also one of the largest bookstores with predominantly English books in Mexico.

The art in Oaxaca is more varied and the galleries look more professional than in San Miguel. Not so much kitsch on display. Cleaner looking, art displayed so each piece was at its best and not crowded.

Every gallery owner must face the same decision, even in the States: hang a few pieces to classy perfection, or put in as much art as you can cram in so it can all be seen for sale, even if some good pieces are overpowered. The Oaxacan galleries overall also displayed a lot more sculpture than San Miguel galleries.

A place called La Brew owned by an American woman sells varied bagels and U.S. style sandwiches, plus the best coffees I've had in a long time. It's in a courtyard with great tourist art. Oaxacan coffee is considered excellent and it is for sale many places in town. I loved it.

The *tortas* were very good at several places, particularly a Cuban sandwich at one of the outdoor restaurants on the *zócalo*. I had a local style thin steak that was good, too, and inexpensive compared to SMA. I could write a book on Oaxaca and almost have. But it was good to get back to San Miguel.

A burro stopped in front of me the other day, its back draped in bundles of, I think, garden dirt for sale. The kid leading it around made more money from the tourists willing to pay to take a picture of it than he did from any sales. A short distance outside town a hundred burros could be photographed for free standing out in the fields or tethered near the highway where the grass is greenest.

Many local Mexican residents do not want their photos taken, and at first I thought it was because of the old Indian belief that a photo steals your spirit. But I've learned it is more because they know that many gringo artists will take a photo, turn it into a painting, and get hundreds or thousands of dollars for that painting, without having to pay model fees.

A woman selling flowers in front of our mailing service was crying one day because she'd spotted a postcard of herself for sale in the Jardín, and she hadn't given permission for the photo and didn't like her image being for sale as if she were an alien being or something. That's what a friend could translate from what the vendor was saying between tears.

Indians may see themselves in the paintings hanging in the local galleries with $20,000 peso price tags ($2,000 U.S.) and resent it. Sometimes they seem to think every photo being taken of them will lead to a $2,000 sale, not be put into a scrapbook (or DVD) of tourists' mementoes.

And I'm not thrilled myself when I'm walking along, minding my own business, and some tourist snaps my picture without asking because I'm colorful or quaint or something. (I've been told I look happy, which must be a rarity.) I can understand others' reluctance. So I like to ask if people mind if I take their picture and I respect their "No." I have no qualms snapping away at people who have put themselves into the public eye such as parade dancers, though.

It's similar to journalism privacy laws—if people have done something deliberately that puts them into the public eye, they have chosen to give up their privacy. They can be photographed no matter what they do, and that photograph can be printed or run on TV. Private citizens living their lives have a right to expect privacy.

I'm horrified when I see gringos going right up to Mexicans on the street and expecting them to like to be photographed, ignoring their "No." This is an ongoing argument among tourists and photographers everywhere, however. With telephoto lenses, who can tell if your photo is being taken anyway?

I've even seen lenses for sale that make it look as if you are aiming in one direction while with mirrors you're really taking a photo in another direction.

The kids in the Jardín entertain themselves with so little, a balloon, a tiny rubber ball, the pigeons, the street dogs, a Popsicle. They seem so much more self-sufficient than U.S. kids who seem to need to have a lot of toys and attention to be entertained.

They are held more, especially by their fathers, partly because there are fewer strollers to keep kids at a distance from their parents, and partly because it seems Mexican families spend more time with their kids and enjoy holding them.

We found out about it too late but some of our friends got in to see the filming of the baptism scene in the Hotel Sautto courtyard for the Antonio Banderas movie, *And Starring Pancho Villa as Himself*. The hotel and surrounding streets were in pandemonium, I hear.

Most of the filming has been in rural haciendas and the countryside where Villa actually lived most of his life. We've been trying to avoid all the filming in town, my desire to not be crowded and jostled and shuffled on detours overpowering my desire to see movie stars.

I wrote earlier that the movie is based on the real life happening that Villa sold D. W. Griffith the rights to his life story in return for money for the revolution of 1910. Also in real life, a whole bunch of out-of-place Hollywood types arrived in Mexico for that filming, and it was an instant comedy of errors and clash of philosophies.

Compared to the bad feeling left in the town's citizenry from the filming of *Once Upon a Time in Mexico*, this time the film people are trying to do things right. Many of the local schools are being allowed to take classrooms of students to visit the filming sites, to show the kids what is going on and to expand their horizons, as well as to improve community good will.

I know some people who have been hired as extras. The costume department folks apparently dragged a bunch of costumes through the dirt behind horses for a few days to get an authentic look. I heard that some costumes had been used earlier in *Titanic*, the two films from the same era. Local expats got to be the out-of-place Hollywood types, local natives got to play the Mexicans of that time.

In some history books, Pancho Villa is seen as a mere bandit. But he was important to the 1910 revolution because he understood the peasants of the northern parts of Mexico. He was assassinated by a Mexican in 1923 after he had left the battlefield.

The 1910-24 revolution(s) involved uprisings against the church and the wealthy landowners who had turned the goals of the original 1810 revolution backwards. The church had become the largest lenders, and they took in money from tithes, interest, and other payments and used the money to lend to the poor. They became huge landowners and bankers, and many felt the church owned people's lives as well as their souls.

One of the demands of the 1910 revolution was that the state take over all of those loans and the church property, making all the loans now payable to the government. By 1924 it was the law that no priests or nuns could appear outside the churches in their habits, under penalty of death, and many died fighting that rule. Church property was seized along with that of the wealthy.

Many Catholics fought back on behalf of their church during the Cristeros Wars. The Mexican church still celebrates their martyrs from that period.

Graham Greene's *The Power and the Glory* is a beautifully written story of one of the last priests in Mexico around the time of the Cristeros wars, who is trying to get to Chiapas, one of the states where Catholic priests would not be killed. He considers himself a terrible man for being an alcoholic and the father of a child.

But whenever someone needs a priest for a baptism or wedding or for confession and the mass, he travels to provide these church rites, even when his life is thus endangered.

The reader comes to view the priest as truly a saint, doing what a religious man should do, even though the priest himself and those around him consider him a sinner and a failure.

The book is a rich unfolding of both Mexican history and culture of that time and of Greene's own philosophy on what is a good person. But Graham Greene actually hated Mexico while he was visiting. I recommend the book to anyone who wants to understand that time in Mexican history anyway.

We've had power outages around 8 P.M. each night. Apparently some of the renters in this complex are now using electric heaters for this cold snap, and the antiquated power lines will not take it. We're thinking about getting a propane gas heater installed in our casa, which means not only the cost of the heater but of installation and running another gas line into the house, and greater propane costs.

Norma thinks our propane bill will rise to about $100 a month for the November-February period, and less than $50 a month the rest of the year for hot water and cooking. After seven years in Phoenix, this winter seems really cold. It's supposed to get as low as freezing here a few nights a winter.

How quickly we forgot about our $450 a month propane heating bills for our uninsulated country church we were remodeling back in Michigan. Right now we're bundled in the new sweatpants and sweatshirts we had friends bring down.

We've gotten some experience ordering on the internet for delivery here. Norma put in a big order to Dharma Fabrics and Dyes. I had to replenish some of my art supplies from Dick Blick and Cheap Joe's online. Though there are two art supply stores in San

Miguel and several other shops sell a few items, there's no place to buy specialty items like sumi ink sticks, Robert Wood watercolor palettes, Prismacolor sets of 108 colored pencils, Japanese masa rice paper, and Holbein watercolors.

Everything we ordered came through our mailing service intact, with higher duties than we expected, but cheaper than a trip to the States.

We keep thinking about selling our car, which is depreciating day by day as we use it to go about 100 miles a month. The first class buses are much more logical, and we can take the city bus to Gigante and Tuesday Market and ride a taxi home once a week. We're trying to talk ourselves into the sale. Norma would do it immediately. Somehow I still think I would feel trapped without a car—just in case.

If we do decide to sell it, the transfer of papers has to be done back in the U.S. because we "imported" the car here on our FM3. It can stay here legally even without renewal of our license plates as long as we maintain our FM3s, and we can use Mexican car insurance for local travel and buy temporary policies when in the U.S. Of course to drive it in the U.S. we have to have up-to-date license plate tags.

We hear you can get low-cost license plates online from South Dakota whether you live there or not. Owning a car is a whole lot of hassle. Norma is gradually convincing me. Still, I worry about whatever that "what if" situation could be when we need the car.

(Later, we had to do without the car for a month for repairs and Norma decided we'd miss it too much. We're keeping it, even though its resale value keeps dwindling.)

All the ordinary green trees around our courtyard are suddenly blazing poinsettia trees, announcing the holidays. One throws a red screen in front of our second story window. Poinsettias got their name from yet another rip off of Mexico by the United States. *Flor de buenes noches* are native to the Morelia area, but in 1828 the first U.S. Ambassador to Mexico, a man named Poinsett, took out a patent on the red flowers for the United States, so that all future Mexicans would have to buy their seedlings for their own native plants from the United States. (Not that any small Mexican plant growers actually buy their seedlings from the U.S. It's the principle.)

To this day horticulturists in the Morelia area are trying to develop a similar plant that is different enough that they can get a patent on their own national treasure again.

The pomegranates are ripening overhead in our walkway, and a tiny new tiger kitten is bounding in glee on our porch, thrilled to find the kitty soup kitchen is open. Our own cats are in the process of rediscovering the warmth of sleeping in our bed—they've been strangers all summer. We huddled and shivered under the comforter last night while purring and licking was going on up and down the bed and under the covers while they made friends with us again. It was a busy night.

***

Our Arizona house is back in escrow! May this trip go all the way to the end.

Tuesday we went to a *charreada*—sort of a rodeo—but we left halfway through when it became apparent that the small bulls weren't exactly having any fun. One had a bloody spot on his shoulder. Supposedly every gringo should go to at least one *charreada* to appreciate Mexican fine horsemanship. So that we did, but we found it boring. For $3 admission, we can't exactly complain.

Again, we didn't come to Mexico to change it, and we couldn't if we tried, but at least once a week we face a Mexican not treating an animal well. In the States, the number is probably about the same but we didn't see it, passing by in our cars so that we couldn't see much of any human interactions from a distance even if we'd been looking. And we see a hundred Mexicans loving their dogs, walking their own pampered poodles proudly down the sidewalks, in the same period.

I loved rodeos as a horse-crazed kid but don't like them today in either the U.S. or Mexico. And as long as I eat meat from slaughterhouses and devour chickens raised in overcrowded pens where they can't even walk, I can't complain about horsemen roping and riding bulls and horses.

A "ladies drill team" was supposed to take part but only one woman showed, wearing a long full denim skirt and ruffled white blouse. She emerged for the opening procession and was never seen again. This is what *Atención* had said about the "ladies drill team" that had us eager to see them: "The *señoritas* come to the *charreada* in full Mexican ranch dress, riding sidesaddle, to show their ability in reining and riding, which adds a ballet-like beauty to contrast the rough-riding *charros*." I should have rented *Annie Oakley*.

Two boys about six were among the *charros*, on full-sized horses, though they didn't compete. Some of the competition involved riding bulls bareback (though these bulls were even smaller than the ones at the Running of the Bulls), grabbing a running bull by the tail while on horseback and stopping the bull in its tracks within 50 meters (that usually meant throwing the bull over), and roping a running horse by one rear foot and stopping it (no throwing involved in this one).

It didn't help that one of the first events involved each of the dozen or so contestants on horseback repeating the exact same rush at full gallop toward the judges and stopping as smoothly as possible. A dozen times.

A mariachi band stood in the back row and accompanied the events, the cymbalist making sure no one missed anything important. A tiny baby slept only 3' from the cymbals and never budged. There was a raffle for one of the largest bottles of some kind of whiskey I ever saw, and the Texan who won it seemed intent on finishing it right then and there.

The one act I did want to see was at the end, and we'd already left. A *charro* riding bareback on a tame horse transfers while galloping onto an untamed horse and hangs on for as long as possible.

It's called "the pass of death." Probably just as well we missed it.

As *Atención* describes the meaning of these rodeos, "The *charreada* is one of the most genuine Mexican traditions, because of its originality, boldness, elegance, festivity and color. Actually it is an artistic performance, and a festivity that represents Mexican heritage. The *charreada* is also part of Mexican national culture, which emphasizes the *charro*, the horse and the attire, all of which are essential to this tradition."

Okay. I don't have to love everything about Mexico.

The cold spell hitting much of the U.S. is still also hitting here. We had three sunny days worthy of shorts but it is supposed to go down to around 35°F tonight. The landlord "solved" the problem of our electrical heaters blowing the fuses for the complex by installing bigger fuses, so now I can worry about fire. We're going to get the propane heater installed December 3, and then I can worry about asphyxiation. Someone suggested getting a canary.

There was a citywide protest against high electricity costs Friday night. We were all supposed to turn off our lights between 7 P.M. and 7:20. I couldn't see where turning off household lights would register at all on the electrical company's meters. Commercial use continued, and nobody suggested unplugging refrigerators, heaters, computers, TVs and all the other stuff that gobbles electricity.

I looked outside at 7 P.M. and couldn't see that the protest had any impact at all— as many houses were lit as usual.

The Mexican economy, and all of Latin America, as with much of the rest of the world, is in a period of transference to privatization, and the government here used to subsidize many basic needs. Electricity actually cost less under PRI, the political party that ruled Mexico for some 70 years, and so Fox and his party PAN are being blamed for not solving every problem quickly, including those situations which have gotten worse under his administration. But the problems are far beyond one man's control.

I read of a major survey of 14 Latin American countries, which found that 61% of the people, particularly from the middle class, feel that they are worse off today financially than their parents were, and almost as many fear that their children will be worse off than they themselves are.

This fear is not unique to Latin America—I've seen similar statistics from polls in the U.S. While Mexicans working in the U.S. send some $20 billion a year back home, the payments called remittances, it is still the Mexican economy which is most hurt by the exodus of workers to the States. Not only unskilled laborers but the brightest and most ambitious leave home, taking with them talents and energies that could benefit Mexico. Unemployment is higher among the most educated. First there have to be jobs.

The electricity problem is compounded by possible corruption and certainly inefficiency here. Sometimes meters don't get read for months, and suddenly the homeowner gets a huge bill when it is time for catch-up—this happened to Norma in the U.S. as well. Sometimes people link into another's electrical lines, and so one person is paying for two or more households while another gets a free ride.

We hear jokes about "UEL," the Universal Electrical Line that anyone can hook into, even the street vendors who may send up a wire to draw current from somebody's line down into their cart for the night.

Sometimes there seems to be some kind of mistake: One woman reported on an SMA e-mail list that her maid burns only three light bulbs in her whole house, nothing else electric, and she makes around $400 a month. Her electrical bill this month was $250.

Mexican people for generations and centuries have learned to be passive, to not speak up, or you will be blamed and punished. And you definitely do not accuse anyone of malfeasance or in any way cause a "loss of face." You do not accept responsibilty for anything because who knows what the consequences will be? And many people have a very limited education and are unaware of how the system works.

So we have a situation of people who are generally afraid to speak up and fight back unless really strapped, such as in the various revolutions (and there have been many). I'm surprised anyone even came up with the idea of a protest to shut off the lights for 20 minutes.

Many Mexicans cite the success of the recent protests against the Mexico City airport expansion, where they took hostages, and the city backed down. But they also remember the 1968 student uprisings in Mexico City in which supposedly "only" 300 were shot down but it could be thousands. Some progress has been made recently in trying to finally actually assign some blame for that massacre, 34 years later.

The idea of former New York City Mayor Rudy Guiliani coming down to Mexico City to try to solve the crime and corruption problem with U.S. methods is generally laughed at by those we know. And Mariposa County (Phoenix) Sheriff Joe Arpaio, notorious abuser of human rights, has volunteered his services to help solve Mexico City crime. I can see him enforcing pink underwear on Mexican men in prison.

Nancy was burglarized when she was unloading stuff from her last visit to Cincinnati recently—she left a big box that said "Dell Computer" visible in the back of the pickup camper shell, and apparently didn't lock the shell back gate (no evidence of jimmying).

The empty box was stolen, along with some Christmas wrapping paper she hadn't gotten around to unloading yet. She doesn't have an alarm system on the truck, and she was supposed to park it in a guarded hotel parking lot that is locked at 10 P.M. each night, but she left it in front of her apartment on the street and never heard a thing.

Not much taken, actually. She was lucky. She'd put the empty computer box back into the truck because she hadn't figured out where to store it, to keep it on hand in case she ever had to ship the computer back to Dell. The company recommends you keep the original packaging around for that reason.

A few months ago someone else who was unloading at her apartment, the same complex where we used to live, had her car and suitcases stolen. She'd left the car keys on top of the car while she took one suitcase inside the courtyard. She got everything back a few hours later because a neighbor saw everything and reported it to the police.

I have read that there are a couple of instances of violent robberies a year, far less than back in our Phoenix neighborhood. Rumors spread throughout the foreign community after each incident. Soon, who knows what actually happened? We heard later that another friend had her purse stolen out of her apartment, probably by a bunch of U.S. teenagers staying in a nearby unit. Her credit cards were used at an SMA boutique before she could report them missing. We read in *Atención* that one U.S. family was beaten up and $100,000 cash stolen out of their SMA house. (And why would anyone have $100,000 cash in the house?) So there is crime here.

Lacey started sticking out her tongue and licking her nose and lips in a constant, frantic pattern two mornings ago.We rushed her to our vet, who said she had an inflamed throat gland and probably a sore throat causing the licking. He gave her an antibiotics shot, and another one 24 hours later, which solved the problem completely. Cost: $20 first day, $5 next.

Lacey felt good enough the second day to walk all the way to the vet. She sure had a great time sniffing and peeing the whole 2/3 mile each way. We don't usually walk her on the streets because of loose dogs and people walking big dogs on the narrow sidewalks, but we had no trouble either way. She would like more frequent outings.

Not that she doesn't have enough to do keeping the stray cats under control in our courtyard (which is ever more aflame with poinsettias now). A tabby baby who showed up has two sisters and/or brothers who are still on our roof, afraid to come down, and mama is still visiting them and feeding them, though her milk seems to be drying up. So Norma is bringing them bowls of milk mixed with dry cat food upstairs.

One is another tabby, the other looks like a baby Siamese, white with the distinctive dark ears. One nasty old male Siamese makes many contributions to the gene pool around here. We haven't been able to catch him yet.

The word is out: don't go into that box with the food in it because the door snaps down on you and you get a trip to the vet for something unthinkable. I was eyeing a pool cleaning net the other day at Home Depot, wondering if that would work as a cat catcher.

We caught Pinky easily, and his pink eye has cleared up with antibiotics, but we're still calling him Pinky. We tried to bring him inside but he leapt onto the screen and hung there like those toy Garfield cats on suction cups attached inside car windows, howling as if he were being tortured, until we let him back out. He had his chance to become an indoor kitty. (He's gotten so fat in four years that we now call him Pork Chop. He still won't come in the house.)

We and the neighbors have been able to sterilize quite a few of the cats. Otherwise, our generosity in feeding them could get well out of hand.

I joined another Scrabble group, which meets Wednesdays at one of the luxury hotels a half mile away after my painting class. This group is less intense—I actually won! I got the first seven-letter word of my career, "squires," using the Q in the process on a double-word space. And the next turn I was able to add the "e" for "esquires." Since this group is not as threatening in its concentration and abilities, Norma may come along next week. She likes the game but my other group consisted of killers. I learned to be a good loser. Now I must win graciously.

We finally went to the general public movie complex by Gigante and were surprised at what good condition the theater is in: wide upholstered seats with no lumps, lots of leg room, good popcorn, toilet seats and toilet paper in the bathrooms, good screen and audio. It only costs $2.20 U.S. each all day Tuesdays and Wednesdays and the first shows on Sundays, $3.50 the rest of the time. Popcorn costs from $1.90 up to $3 for the jumbo refillable tub. Nothing at the art film venues has intrigued us lately.

It was a clear, sunny, crisp day yesterday and so we decided to drive to a little town called Pozos, once a flourishing silver mine about 50 miles from here. We should have taken a bus tour—we couldn't find a thing in the town when we accidentally stumbled into it after a couple hours being lost. No signs, nothing to call attention to the tourist sites, only cobblestone roads and ruins.

It was once a beautiful town, though, and supposedly there are tours down into the mines and to the tourist area. A tour guide will have to show us around next time.

I understand that two women in Pozos have formed a collective that is worth supporting, and occasionally the town sponsors Pozos Walks, with shuttles out to the town from SMA to tour the art galleries. People who have bought property there are proclaiming it "the next San Miguel."

Personally, I don't think there's a critical mass of population, culture, and activities to make it attractive to most foreigners. And I've read that mining techniques used before anyone knew the word "ecology" have left heavy pollution behind. But I've never guessed right on real estate in my life. Buy high, sell low, that's my motto.

We've been asked to be ushers for the International Jazz Festival here Thanksgiving weekend, which means we get about $120 worth of free concert admissions for six hours standing around handing out programs and telling people where the bathrooms are. Plenty of expat-oriented restaurants are having Turkey Day. Fresh and frozen turkeys are available at several markets for those doing their own. Life is good.

Thanksgiving Day between concerts we're squeezing in dinner at Harry's: fried turkey with oyster dressing and tasso gravy (seasoned with Cajun sausage) plus spicy lobster bisque, sweet potato pie and the usual sides. Only complaint is no leftovers (but also no dishes, shopping and work).

El Buen Café had an all-you-can buffet of all the traditional U.S. Thanksgiving dishes and a dozen desserts for $17.50 each. We'll try them for Christmas.

※

The biggest surprise for me this week was stumbling upon an International PEN Conference for Latin American writers happening in the auditorium right next door to my watercolor class at Belles Artes. The main speaker was being translated into English via earphones, provided through a grant.

Of course I skipped class to hear Brigadier General Jose Francisco Gallardo Rodriguez, who became an international cause for PEN, Amnesty International and hundreds of humanitarian organizations when he was imprisoned for nine years. He was arrested after writing a university master's thesis calling for reforms in military justice and for the institution of an ombudsman, for those who feel they have not gotten justice in the military system.

A journalist obtained a copy of his thesis and wrote an article about his ideas. He called the journalist to thank him for doing the article and the reporter said, "You may not want to thank me when you hear that we are both going to jail."

He and his family fought hard against the various charges brought against him, and during his imprisonment he received 35,000 letters of support. Many were from school children around the world—he is truly an international celebrity.

One of the charges was that he had mistreated soldiers serving under him, and his family did the research to prove that none of those complaining soldiers had actually ever served under him. It was not until President Fox was elected that Gallardo Rodriguez was actually freed. The military insisted on calling him "Mister" instead of "General" in the release ceremonies. A reporter asked him if he felt badly he was being called only "Mister." He replied that it was a step up from "traitor."

He has spoken of his experiences at Harvard, Yale, and many other major institutions in the U.S. and throughout the world, and has had his story told in many publications during his struggle. He is continuing to fight for these reforms in Mexican military justice. He said there are at least 500 political prisoners in Mexican jails at this moment.

Some 200 writers were at the conference, most of them Latin American men, many from a Cuban chapter of PEN for political prisoners. The local members I talked to said that the San Miguel chapter consists mainly of expats, and it was nice to see a truly international and diverse conference.

I may have to get active in this group, no matter what my intentions are about not getting involved in anything public here in Mexico. It's a large enough group that I can remain low-key.

We went to a party at a friend's house who was into networking, with everyone else there trying to make a name for themselves. At one point we were supposed to go around the room and introduce ourselves and tell all the good things we were involved with. Writers, artists, therapists, realtors, all sorts of professionals told of their accomplishments.

Norma and I were getting more and more uncomfortable as our turn approached. When it was my time I said simply, "We're Carol and Norma, and we're nobodies."

Dead silence. "What do you mean?" someone finally asked.

I had the sudden idea to quote Emily Dickinson's poem, "I'm nobody, who are you? Are you nobody, too?…"

More silence. Oh, oh, in trying to be inconspicuous we now stuck out. Someone else at the party who knew us had to quickly intercede for us and recite our accomplishments as she knew them. The party was satisfied and moved on. Some party attendees were very friendly to us after that, others haven't spoken to us. I guess we violated our goal of staying nobodies with at least one group.

And because I have gotten involved in a couple of SMA e-mail lists and started arguing online about U.S. politics, some people do know me now. (I even attracted a cyberstalker and had to quit one list. Not everyone in Mexico is wonderful.)

I'm thinking of going further and turning all my letters into a website and book. (And when we did, we definitely no longer were nobodies. Oh well.)

We weren't going to join any groups either, and now I'm in PEN, the American Legion Women's Auxiliary and a book club. So much for moving here to make complete changes in our personalities.

We were a bit unrealistic, so pained by our experiences back in the States that we thought we had to hide underground to avoid further hurt. Stick your head up, you get shot down.

That happens here, too—it seems to be human nature. But somehow I am feeling freer to be myself, which is not a mole living underground.

At least we are keeping up on our goal of maintaining our weight loss and losing a bit more. That was our most important resolution. We go up and down, we never can seem to achieve stability at our lowest weights, but we're still both down a net 140+ pounds each.

Friday night we went to a small concert called "Something from the Girls," which was basically a lounge act brought to the stage. The leader of an oldies trio did some research on the lack of public knowledge of how many female songwriters there have been. Her act was maybe 20 songs few people realize were written by women.

The act was Feminism Lite 101. She really didn't go into any depth or analysis of how this happened, as I would have liked. She sang some songs and asked, "Isn't a pity nobody realizes how many beautiful songs have been written by women?"

She did do a tamed-down version of Helen Reddy's "I Am Woman" and a woe-is-me comic version of "Nine to Five," which I believe is more of a fighting activist's anthem, not a pity-pot story. Still, it was a nice evening.

A much more satisfying concert was opening night of the ninth San Miguel International Jazz Festival. Brenda Boykin is a fantastic, strong, big black woman with a voice like Sarah Vaughn. My favorite song was "Big Fine Woman" in which she sang out her affirmation of her size, and included an imaginary conversation with a man who was telling her to lose weight. She sang, "I can lose 200 pounds easy by getting rid of you."

She even did some gay and lesbian references. One song, "Have a conversation with your man," was dedicated (and I loosely para-phrase) to all you women out there, whether you're in a relationship where you need to have a conversation with a man or with some-body else, and whether you're actually a woman or not—whoever is the yin to the yang in your relationship, whatever its composi-tion. Lots of audience applause to that one!

The song, a jazz/blues classic, tells some woman listening to shape up, your bird dog is sniffing up my tree, and the fault isn't totally mine. Every time I shake my big fine self some skinny wom-an loses her man. I'm not quoting exactly but that was the gist. We even bought her double CD.

The next two nights also start out with male musicians and end with a black woman vocalist as the closing act. "Mem'fis Mama" sings tomorrow night. Brenda Boykin is bilingual though most of her songs were done in English. The programs and introductions were all bilingual, which I appreciated. I saw more African-Amer-icans in the audience tonight than I think I've seen since the last Phoenix Mercury game I attended. I was amazed at the local jazz talent as well. We didn't even go to the International Chamber Mu-sic Festival and the Guitar Festival that were here earlier in the year. San Miguel draws artists in every medium.

Little things keep happening that make me love Mexico more and more. Tonight at 9, I was in the kitchen putting together cereal and milk when I heard loud music. I thought it was commercials on TV, which are always louder than the regular programs, but then the *Law and Order* voice intro came on and the music continued, even louder.

I grabbed my keys and we went out on our balcony porch to discover nine mariachi musicians down below in the courtyard, serenading the couple downstairs. All the other residents of the eight casas came out to listen in on the serenade, which lasted half an hour.

Four violins, two trumpets, and three guitars of various sizes (the largest may have been a portable bass) entertained the neighborhood with wonderful Mexican love songs, though they ended with an obviously less rehearsed "I Left My Heart in San Francisco." One neighbor asked the guy how much it had cost, and he said "Expensive."

More than $50 US? "Much more." So we decided we didn't have to tip them ourselves, too. What a wonderful interruption of our TV watching. Now back to see *Law and Order* on the VCR.

Other week's highlights: walking two miles steeply downhill home from Gigante on the outskirts of town, to see if we could do it, and playing canasta at Tom's, though his electricity had been out going on three days and he'd had to cook up a beef stew with the 12 steaks defrosting in his freezer. Delicious—ever have beef stew made from filet mignon? He definitely is not living on Social Security and still says it's not possible, even though we're obviously doing it.

I could write a Thanksgiving essay about everything I love about San Miguel, but I think I'm already doing that.

8

December

After our joking about the empty computer box being stolen out of the back of Nancy's Ford Ranger blue pickup, the truck was stolen from right in front of her apartment near the Instituto at 4 in the afternoon. She didn't have an alarm system, and she hadn't put it in the secure parking lot she pays for. The insurance rep came promptly the next day but she hasn't seen a check yet. (It ended up taking six months.)

She got to experience firsthand the three kinds of San Miguel police, starting with the preventive police, including many women, who are walking the streets, preventing crime, and who are the ones who first responded to her emergency call. She'd already run into the Transito police who had taken off her license plate for a parking violation, which had required her to go to the police station to pay a fine and reclaim her license plate.

And now she had to go to the investigative police, the District Attorney's office. She said it was a horrible experience, she felt as if she were being called the criminal.

She was asked if she had driven around town looking for her car. "In what?," she replied.

But a Mexican friend who does drive her some places, and who had driven her around on errands afterward, went down to the office to verify that she had indeed gone looking for her car. The paperwork was issued that she could use for the insurance claim.

She really misses her pickup—it was a 1998 that she called "Blue Bell," and it had only 20,000 miles on it! It might have been chopped up for parts, or it might have been driven to another state. We worried for a bit about ours—quite an unnerving experience—but we have an unusual model, so it wouldn't be useful in a chop shop. It could be painted and driven to another state, of course. We have a good alarm system, though thieves can get around those, and we always park it in a secure lot space.

Nancy bought a new Ford Fiesta, also dark blue, stripped, for only $8,500 U.S. She did get an alarm system put in ASAP and is careful to put it into the secure lot space she rents.

I fell again. Each time I've only suffered bruises and scratches, but too many people here break hips, knees, and jaws when they fall. I'm typing mostly with my right hand as my left protected my face when I hit the cobblestones.

I've been a lifelong foot shuffler, and that won't do. Norma is now being drill sergeant with me, ordering, "Heel first, pick up your feet." Unlearning a lifetime of sloppy walking is not easy.

We've been watching Mexicans walk, and they all seem to do "heel first" really well, and they pick up their feet so high you can see underneath them as they walk. To see under my feet as I walk you'd have to be an ant.

I fell only once in the States as an adult that I remember, and that was in front of a copy shop in Detroit, tripping on a broken sidewalk raised up an inch. Their insurance company paid me $1,500 not to sue, plus they paid for my new glasses and my broken nose.

We used the $1,500 as down payment for our Phoenix RV lot in 1995, taking the check's arrival on the same day and in the same amount as what we needed for a down payment as some sort of sign. Nobody to sue in Mexico, and so nobody sues.

We had another magical night on the Feast of the Virgin of Guadalupe. We'd been to an art film at the Villa Jacaranda and were walking home around 10 P.M., fireworks in full glory overhead, when we heard a rock band playing on the plaza of the Parroquia. What a way to celebrate the Feast of the Virgin, with a Mexican rock band in front of the church.

Lots of folks were dancing, including a gringa about 60 who

was luring anyone she could find onto the floor—men, women, young, old, Mexicans and foreigners. A half-dozen hippies in their early 20s were dancing, too, not too clear who was with whom, doing that kind of loose, kicky, twirly dancing that marks those who learned to dance after disco.

So we got on the floor and did that kind of floppy, hip-swinging, shimmying dancing that marks those who learned first on the jitterbug and then the twist.

We looked up at the fireworks cascading down upon us, and at the diverse crowd dancing all sorts of ways, and the twinkling white lights in the trees, and the Mexican rock band playing U.S. oldies, and we knew once more we were in paradise. Would the Virgin have approved?

By tradition you are not supposed to loan anybody anything December 28, Mexican April Fool's Day, because you have thereby given it away. I did manage to fall for a joke story published in Atención reporting that the facade of the Parroquia, the beautiful signature church in San Miguel, had been sold to a Chicago fast-food mogul to be transported piece by piece to Chicago for the "Mall of Mexico," the largest mall in the world, with our Parroquia as its focal point. None of the above is true, but the story had me running for a bit.

We're having a lovely holiday. Since our escrow finally closed on our Arizona park model, we were able to buy all the big purchases we'd been waiting for: new fridge, microwave, washer, 29" TV, DVD player, made-to-fit-the-space entertainment center, colorful Mexican woven rug, and our lovely gold goose-feather-filled sofa and two big chairs. We have planters filled with assorted indoor trees in every corner and on the porch and roof patio. The place looks fantastic!

Norma is not quite 65 yet, but when she does hit that birthday, we lose a chunk of income and each of us will be only on Social Security. We've been planning for that date for years, figuring out what we would have to have by then so that we wouldn't feel deprived or poor. That's one of our tactics for surviving our remaining years, however many they may be.

We decided not to spend the thousand dollars to paint the interior of our rental. The yellow and blue looks great with all the new furniture and accessories. Picture one heartbroken housepainter, who has been visiting us every week waiting for our escrow to close, and then we changed our mind. We recommended him to someone else, though, so I hope he'll be okay. He wanted the job so desperately.

Our 6' houseplant in the living room is our Christmas tree this year, loaded with lightweight, very inexpensive, paper decorations and garlands. An aisle of booths in San Juan Dios Market sells artificial or real Christmas trees with all the trimmings. Maybe next year.

The rest of the money is in savings for whatever medical emergencies may come up. The co-pays for our Arizona HMO were much higher than the total costs of prescriptions and doctor visits and hospital stays here. We think we'll be okay, pinching pesos instead of pennies.

Every night in Mexico from December 16-23 there is a *posada* someplace in town. *Posadas* are a Mexican tradition reenacting the Bible story of Mary and Joseph's search for an inn and their rejections. Young children play all the roles and memorize the traditional songs and dialogue. Mary usually rides in on a burro.

She and Joseph go from door to door until the final home which is the scene of that night's party. Then, carols are sung, the kids get to beat up a *piñata* or two, mariachis and other entertainers perform, and everyone waves lighted candles and sparklers. Sometimes the whole ceremony is on December 16, sometimes the visits to the various "inns" occur one a night from December 16 until December 23.

Refreshments typically are tamales, fried cinnamon and sugar coated tortillas, a mulled *ponche* (punch, spiked or not), and various forms of *atole*—dark hot chocolate, white hot chocolate, and *atole negro*, a punch that I think tastes like it is made of charred corn husks.

First we went to a *posada* at a school for developmentally disabled children on Refugio in the morning. The kids were a delight. They'd cut out felt hats and scarves of red and green, and they sang the Christmas carols quite well. Each classroom was an "inn," and the small parade went door to door, singing the traditional responses for a *posada*, assisted by a very strong-voiced teacher. The final manger scene was on a small stage.

Mary and Joseph kept grinning like mad throughout the little play, waving at their families from the stage. A toddler boy played an angel, complete with wings, but he wouldn't leave his mother so she was on stage with him, trying to look inconspicuous behind the manger, attempting to blend in with the "sheep." One older boy could speak perfect unaccented English, apparently self-taught.

The American Legion Women's Auxiliary has picked up this school as one of five we now help to support. Each school gives us a "wish list," along with their necessities. We give each school all the notebooks, crayons, pencils and construction paper they need each semester, and so far the other four schools have all received a computer, computer desk, educational software, and a TV and VCR to play the tapes available from the school district.

This school is going to need mats for the floor where the children now do their physical therapy exercises on the cold concrete, We'll bring big exercise balls and other helps, too.

The school itself is in pretty good shape, though it was built originally on a landfill and the sidewalks are cracking. The basketball court is unusable because the net stands look as if they will topple at the touch of a tossed ball. Anyone want to stage a benefit for its repair?

That evening the Hotel Sautto hosted a *posada* benefit for Alma, a home for the aged here. A white burro was stationed in the hotel garden for many hours, chomping on flower plants, awaiting the arrival of Mary who was late. She was a beautiful blonde Mexican girl of about seven.

When she arrived and was placed on the burro, it promptly tossed the screaming Mary and was banished back to the garden. Mary and Joseph made the procession on foot. A well-trained choir sang the songs along with the kids at this *posada*.

Alma was founded by a woman named Margaret Galloway, and it now has 34 residents, with 30 more on the waiting list. Three gringos live there as well as Mexicans, their Social Security checks sufficient to pay for their own care and to subsidize some of the other residents as well.

Alma has an excellent reputation. I'd consider living there myself if I were alone and frail. It always needs money and donations, though, and has a garage sale just about every Saturday. We've become accustomed to a cheap shampoo we can get here and are thinking about donating the dozen bottles of U.S. specialty shampoo we brought with us to them for their sales.

And at the Jardin there is an ongoing *posada* from December 16-23, the kids processional approaching one "inn" each night, singing the traditional appeal for shelter and being refused, until the final night when one innkeeper finally finds room for Mary and Joseph in the stable.

When we got there one night the procession was ending and a classical music concert was going on at the stage. Fireworks erupted overhead every so often. As we strolled the people from many *posadas* were still walking around, women carrying big pots of *ponche* and tamales to their homes, kids rushing around excitedly in their costumes of Mary and Joseph, angels, wise men, sheep, camels, or cows.

We went on a Lions Club three-day tour to Guadalajara earlier this month—one of the most disorganized events we've ever attended but still fun. The luxury bus trip there was fine and the Hotel De Mendoza located right downtown was excellent.

No one had called the Ken Edwards ceramic factory that was to be a highlight of the trip for us, and they closed early at 1:30 P.M. for a fiesta. The tour group got there at 1:35. But that was okay, we'd go first thing in the morning and rearrange our Friday schedule.

We've heard since that the factory has moved, but it was in the art town of Tonalá, actually now a suburb of Guadalajara as that city has grown to 1.6 million, 4 million for the metro area. Tonalá has an outdoor market that must run a mile or more along the main street each Thursday, but the bus couldn't let us out anywhere close.

We had to walk around six blocks, and the bus driver got a ticket anyway for holding up traffic while we all maneuvered and argued about where to be let off and to meet again. We chipped in $1 each to pay his $35 fine. (Cost of the entire weekend with two nights in a 4-star hotel and breakfasts was $155 each, which included a donation to the Lions Club programs for children's health care.)

We got in to the hotel Thursday around 5 P.M. and the Lions Club organizer made sure that the cocktail party at 6:30 for our group went off well.

That night was a Folklorico Ballet at the historic Degollado Theatre across the street from the hotel, and the PR director of the hotel got us all tickets. Beautiful dancing, whirling twirling costumes and whimsy—they even did a Mexican Hat Dance unlike any we'd ever imagined, far better than the one we'd seen in SMA for Brotherhood Week months before. The men in unison beat their sombreros on the floor in a rhythmic pattern as the women swirled their sombreros in visual patterns, the entire stage a fiesta.

In the dance in which the women balance trays carrying bottles of expensive tequila or beer on their heads, I couldn't believe how much dancing they could do and not spill a drop. So far, so good.

The next night was to be *The Nutcracker* ballet and the Guadalajara Philharmonic Orchestra at the same theatre. The Degollado is like a classic European opera hall with five tiers of balconies and embellished boxes, red velvet drapes, red walls, a panoramic ceiling dome painted with reenactments of Greek mythology, and a crystal chandelier the size of a living room. It's probably five times the size of San Miguel's Teatro Angela Peralta.

We were told that *The Nutcracker* would be free if you brought a toy valued at $5-10, so we were all to be on the look-out for toys during the next day's shopping trips.

Tour participants had Friday morning open. We found the Mercado Liberdad, which I had visited in 1970 when it was a sprawling open-air marketplace of hundreds of stalls. Now it must contain a thousand stalls, three stories under a modern roof, and you can buy anything from a cooked goat's head with limes stuck in the eyeball sockets to fine jewelry and excellent leather goods made in the region. We bought most of our Christmas presents for this year from there. (Nobody got a goat's head from us.)

The bus was to leave from the hotel at 1 P.M. to return to Ken Edwards, then travel to Tlaquepaque, a major arts center for Mexico. (There's a very nice arts market in Sedona named after it, though it's on a much smaller scale.) But a construction crew had arrived and closed off the street ahead of the bus. No exit that way.

The only way out of this narrow one-way street was to back around a tight corner onto another narrow heavily trafficked one-way street lined with concrete barriers. The bus driver tried for almost an hour before giving up, irking most of the cars in Guadalajara during that time. We were on our own to get to the factory or to go directly to Tlaquepaque.

We were the only ones who opted to take a cab to Ken Edwards. We had been planning to buy our dinnerware set for six there for months. After the confusion of the day before when they'd closed early, this morning the factory was expecting a busload of customers. Only Norma and I showed up.

Online, Ken Edwards dinner plates alone sell for $67 each plus shipping and handling. A setting for six with all the serving pieces would have been more than $1,000 if bought online. A place setting includes a 10" dinner plate, 8" salad plate, 6" dessert plate, small bowl, large bowl, cup and saucer. We got our set for $400, delivered to our door a few days later. We were able to find some pieces that were seconds to make our cost a little cheaper. It's a blue-and-white intricate pattern they call Vanilla Butterfly.

Still so far so good. I'd managed to strike up a conversation with the cab driver on the way to the factory, and I proceeded to do the same with the cab driver we hailed to take us to Tlaquepaque.

With the earlier guy, we'd talked about it being Friday the 13th, and I'd said it was the day of witches, and he'd agreed. I'd talked about it being a gray day, and he'd agreed. I'd said I loved San Miguel, and he agreed.

With the new guy, I thought I said the same thing, but looking back, I may have told him I was a witch. The Spanish word for gray being *gris*, I may have told him he had a greasy windshield. I may have told him I loved him, not San Miguel.

I saw a drunken guy and said he'd obviously had too much tequila. Or maybe I told the cab driver I wanted lots of tequila. I saw two lovers kissing madly on the sidewalk and said something about hot young love. Or maybe I told him again I loved him.

His arm kept brushing against my breast—at first I thought it was accidental, but then I saw what was happening, and I was edging closer and closer to the passenger door, almost falling out. Norma was in the back seat, not sure what was happening but she didn't like it. She was about to shout at him to stop the car, but we were on a freeway. I didn't let him have it for the same reason.

I knew to use the formal *"usted"* for "you" when talking to him, not the familiar *"tu"* which might indicate I was being forward, but he'd jumped right ahead to believing I was making a pass at him. I think. I'm still guessing.

As soon as we could safely stop we insisted that he do so. He did, only a few blocks from where we were to meet the rest of the tour, at The Restaurant With No Name. That's its name. He seemed so disappointed.

For a few moments I'd had visions of being one of the kidnapped ones, but there was only one of him and we could have taken him, assuming he had no weapons. Of course it didn't help that recently I had finished reading *News of a Kidnapping* by Gabriel Marquez, for our book club, about drug lords kidnapping ten famous people in Colombia in 1991.

I wasn't really worried but annoyed. One of the problems of losing weight: dealing with mashers again, even in my sixties, especially when I'm not sure what I'm saying.

Anyway, we went into The Restaurant With No Name and found red bantam roosters and three blue peacocks strutting their stuff in the courtyard, begging for food from our table. I fed them crackers and tortillas and they were delighted, almost jumping into our laps. Never did I dream I'd be nose to beak with a peacock eyeing my shrimp.

Norma ordered a tequila flambé shrimp dish cooked at the table, and that was quite a show. I was strangely silent with the cab driver who took us back to downtown Guadelajara.

Our tour bus was nowhere to be seen. We were supposed to leave for the famous Guadalajara Zoo at 9 A.M Saturday and then head home. I looked up in the directories where the bus depot was and we counted pesos, in case we had to get home on our own. That night's cocktail party went off well.

We'd found two toy cars in the $5-10 range for the Nutcracker admission that night. But when we got there, those free tickets were all gone, and we were supposed to have turned in the toys to one of the welfare offices to get our free tickets a few days before anyway. So now the score for the hotel's PR director was 1-1.

We gave the toys to a woman and her two sons who were selling gum to those in line, and then roamed the streets on our own for the night. The next morning the bus was in place and the construction barriers were down. Off to the zoo.

Maybe it was that zoo alone, or maybe it is typical of zoos in some other countries, but we could get much closer to some of the animals than we expected. The polar bear was behind a glass wall in its swimming pool, and it came right up to the wall so again I was nose to nose, with a bear this time. Very nice zoo.

We made it back to the hotel to pick up the others and headed home via two other popular expat retirement communities, Lake Chapala and an adjoining town called Ajijíc. Lake Chapala is the largest lake in Mexico. It went down to half its size in recent years, and the lakefront property in both towns was half a mile inland, but I hear the water is rising again since our visit. Lake Chapala's boardwalk was not lakefront when we were there but a pleasant walk alongside a meadow filled with people riding horses.

We snatched up two paper maché dolls of old women, nicely crafted by hand, for $1 each, from sidewalk vendors. The same statues are $12 in some other stores we've seen since.

Lunch was at the Nuevo *Posada* in Ajijíc, a wonderful hotel and restaurant on spacious flower-laden gardens guarded by two scarlet macaws. The hotel had outstanding Christmas displays, including one Christmas tree decorated with dried fruit like pineapple rings and pears. It's simply a beautiful place. Perfectly baked stuffed trout was the day's menu specialty.

We made it to San Miguel around 10:30 P.M. and the tour organizer had 11 cabs waiting to take us back to our homes. It's been a fantastic month. Yes, skeptics, we still love it here!

At Tuesday Market this week, the clothing stalls were full of bright red or gold women's underwear. It is a tradition for women to wear red underwear New Year's Eve for luck in love the coming year, while gold underwear means you'll have financial success.

On New Year's Eve Harry's had a big bash. Men received a white shiny top hat while women were given a rabbit fur tiara. Norma insisted on the top hat. The waiter shrugged and gave her one.

We also were handed a plastic baggie of a dozen Thompson seedless grapes, to be eaten one per chime at the stroke of midnight for luck. Some places hand out the golf ball sized seeded grapes—you'd choke trying to swallow 12 of them in 12 chimes.

The music in the Jardin kept building. and we decided to head for the square before midnight to see what would happen there. We were pretty sure everyone in Harry's would get up and kiss and hug each other and toast endlessly, and we've done that so many New Year's Eves.

In front of the Parroquia conga lines were dancing every which way and two Mexicans motioned we should join their line in front of them. We were thrilled.

When the Parroquia bells rang the first of the 12 chimes we kissed—everyone else was kissing—and hugged a bunch of strangers and kept on dancing.

As we left, a beggar with children got a shiny top hat, a rabbit fur tiara, and two baggies of grapes, along with a ten-peso coin. What a wonderful way to welcome the New Year in our new adopted home.

9

January

We took part in the American Legion Women's Auxiliary Three Kings Day visit to two of the poor rural schools we sponsor, to deliver gifts, candy, and school supplies for the new semester. The two schools are El Tigre, out in the countryside, which has about 35 students in two classrooms, and Doña Juana, in a small village, which has about 75 students.

The Auxiliary for the past six years has given presents to the rural schools as well as class supplies and cleaning materials each semester. Mexican children traditionally receive their Christmas presents January 6, the same day the three wise men brought gold, frankincense, and myrrh to the baby Jesus, according to the Bible. The day before, a dozen of us assembled quart-sized plastic bags of candy—chocolate bars, lollipops, gummy bears, marshmallows, small bags of fried pork rinds and crunchy stuff like Fritos, and many kinds of candy I'd never seen before.

I was really tempted to snatch one of the little cups of something that looked like caramel sugar to see how it tasted. Like I need it.

One of the Mexican women who went along said that she would prefer we not give out candy. Dental decay is a real problem in rural schools, which don't all get visits from the service organizations that try to reach the outlying schools with health care.

But we did bring toothbrushes and tooth paste, too, along with the notebooks, pencils and crayons for the next semester and cleaning supplies for the school.

For some of the kids, this would be their only Christmas. Do we deprive kids of the candy they've come to expect from us for the holiday? Is the real problem the amount of junk food Mexican kids

213

are starting to eat every day, not only on holidays? Weight Watchers lecturers used to tell us that if you only overate on Thanksgiving and Christmas Days, you might only gain one pound in the holiday season. It's eating everything in sight for two months straight that piles on the pounds, to be faced January 2, if ever.

Local newspapers warn that obesity is becoming a serious problem here, though nowhere near the extent it is in the U.S. It's clear that the little stores along the streets in San Miguel have an abundance of bags of chips and candy that kids buy after school, whereas old-timers here say the stores used to have fruit.

Major corporate food manufacturers are part of the problem here as in the US: there's a higher profit markup on a candy bar than on an orange. These outlying schools we visited don't have a junk food shop on every corner, either. We decided to keep the tradition of bringing candy along with presents each January 6. But maybe we'll make smaller bags.

The mothers at the first school presented the Auxiliary officers with a bouquet of alcatraz flowers and a big squash, probably enough food for a poor family for a week. The mothers at the second school made us blue corn tortillas, rice, refried beans, and salsa—delicious. It was an emotionally rewarding experience. Other members were in charge of visiting the other schools we sponsor.

It was fun to hear burros braying outside the schools and to watch shepherds march herds of sheep, goats, horses, cows and burros past the schoolyards as we gave out the presents.

I attended a one-room country schoolhouse in Michigan in the '40s and this trip brought back memories. No burros, sheep or goats around that Michigan schoolhouse, however, just Holsteins, Palominos, and Percherons.

Littlest kids got stuffed animals, the next range of kids were given dolls and toy trucks, slightly older kids received knock-off Barbie-like dolls and soccer balls, and the oldest kids chose among radios, talking clocks, toy jewelry and small games.

The kids at both schools lined up for the toy distribution—so orderly, so polite. Much of Mexico reminds me of the '50s in the U.S. We used to line up, too, to go from class to class. Today in many U.S. schools there's chaos and horseplay and loud talking if you can keep a line together at all. Friends I graduated with who went into teaching complain that city schools are far, far less disciplined than when they started teaching. Here, the kids behaved perfectly for their visitors bearing candy and gifts.

One of the schools recently added 20 more students when a very small school nearby was closed, so a second classroom was added. Unfortunately, the link between the two classrooms was not well constructed. The cracks leaked and let in cold wind. We're going to buy electric heaters for the classrooms now that we see the need, once we check on the availability and cost of electricity for each school. (We found out later the government pays for the schools' electricity.)

The school system gave the teachers materials to repair the roof but none of the adult men in the village were around. They'd all left for the U.S., which is common in many Mexican villages. The teachers had no one to do the work. So the Auxiliary was looking around for a truck and workers to go to the village. Finally, men from another village nearby pitched in and did the repairs. This is how things get done in Mexico. You look and look to find a way to do something that should have been easy to accomplish—with money.

A couple of local musicians are bringing Maria Muldaur ("Midnight at the Oasis," "I'm a Woman") to San Miguel for a concert this month that will benefit Casita Linda, a program that builds very low-cost homes for very poor Mexicans.

We're talking about people living in shacks and ruins, who will now get to live in a small but safe and warm concrete home with a painted cement floor and a roof that has a built in system to gather rain water for a shower and sink. There will be a communal bathroom for every eight houses or so.

Each house costs only $1,100 U.S. to build, and they given free to those selected by the community. The houses are only about 12' by 20', but that is a good size for a typical Mexican house for poor people who are lucky enough to have a house. The organizers expect to be able to build eight or ten more houses from proceeds of the benefit. I can't believe the number of charities in San Miguel doing such a range of activities for the poor.

Friends called in panic when they heard on the news that there was a big earthquake in Mexico. The epicenter was 200 miles to our west, though it was felt heavily in Mexico City 160 miles to our southeast. Right in the middle, we didn't feel it at all. Supposedly San Miguel is not in an earthquake area, though we are at 6,400 feet. We're on solid rock or something. Some buildings here have been standing since the 1700s, without suffering any earthquake damage.

Speaking of high altitudes, Norma has been practicing baking with adjustments for the altitude. The books and online sites say cooked-through deep dish pizza is possible, even here. Norma tried one recipe using mashed potatoes in the dough like foccacio for texture, plus she used less yeast and flour, less rising time, lower temperature, and longer cooking time. She also precooked the crust for 15 minutes before adding toppings. It didn't help. The crust tasted like the dried mashed potatoes left in the pan.

Water boils at around 199°F here, so all cooking is affected. Cooking a pot of beans can take forever. The higher altitude also means less pressure pushing down on rising dough, so usual recipes rise much too fast and often overflow the pan.

The basic secret Norma has found to high-altitude baking: raise the oven temp an additional 25°. She has started to branch out into more cooking now, using a dozen gourmet cookbooks we brought with us.

She is much better at weighing ingredients and counting calories than I am. Whatever special foods we crave and can't find here, she now is learning to cook. She is especially good at Thai and Szechuan dishes. Our new friends keep inviting themselves over for dinner.

But I have to confess, while Norma was perfecting her pizza dough, we had five nights of pretty miserable pizza. I was dreading each new attempt until one night, there it was, the best pizza I've ever had, from a recipe in the California Pizza Kitchen cookbook.

She topped it with Thai barbeque chicken, bean sprouts, onions and peanut sauce. She makes a good Greek one, too, and grinds her own sausages now so that we can have excellent traditional Italian pizza. Hot Italian sausage as we know it does not exist in Mexican stores. Pepperoni is available in small packages at Gigante, though, and in bags weighing several pounds at Costco.

We finished the 24 hours class time for Warren Hardy's Level 1 Intensive Spanish and start the next level next month. We now know our 100 common verbs and 6 power verbs (I need, want, like, have to, am going to, and can) inside and out for present tense, plus about 300 more vocabulary words and word placement in sentences. Next comes past tense. Help, I'm trapped in the present, nothing in the past or future can happen because I don't understand it and can't speak it. Soon.

I felt confident going into Banamex yesterday to start a new checking account, primed with all the words I would need in Spanish, and the manager spoke English, drat. "*Necesito practicar mi Español, por favor.*" But he wanted to practice his English. The peso has gone from 9.1 to the U.S. dollar last May to 10.6 this month, but Norma is keeping on top of solutions for all possibilities.

We still couldn't get a Mexican bank account. Our landlord keeps all utilities in his name, and we were told we had to be able to show a utility bill in our name. Maybe that will change eventually, or some future bank manager will interpret the directions differently.

One of the nice parts of the class was learning the importance of social protocol, making sure to say "*Buenos Dias*" or the appropriate greeting to everyone you make eye contact with, even in passing on the sidewalk. "*Buenos Dias*" is for mornings, and exactly at noon Mexicans switch to "*Buenas Tardes.*" (Any supposed Mexican confusion over time does not apply to this precise moment of transition.)

After dark you use "*Buenas Noches.*" If you're lazy or sloppy you say simply, "*Buenas.*" Mexicans think most gringos are cold and impolite because we don't say the social niceties to strangers;

we avoid eye contact. Of course if you make contact with a stranger in a big U.S. city you may get robbed or assaulted; you've indicated you're fair game.

It is so nice to talk to strangers, to make that effort to recognize each other, to acknowledge each other's value and importance and graciousness. If you don't ask someone's health or say "*perdon*" if you step on their toes, or ask "*con permiso*" for permission before moving in front of them, you're considered ill-raised—and of course it's your mother's fault for not teaching you.

The teacher had a party at his ranch home for all students, and we were talking to a Michigander who was complaining about burro poop outside her rental here.

"But with burro poop you get burros!" I said.

"They could at least put diapers on the burros," she said.

I was pretty upset at dog poop on the sidewalks when I first got here, too. After all, I'd come from an RV park where it was a mortal sin to leave dog poop. But it's no big deal now.

Homeowners and storeowners here can get a ticket for any kind of litter on the sidewalk or street in front of their property, and both are mopped every morning, but it can be a busy day before the next morning's washing. I don't even notice it most of the time. That's one example of the loosening up I can sense in myself. Mexico is working on me.

January 17 was the annual Blessing of the Animals at one of the churches, and somehow I expected to see more farm animals. The 60 or so blessed pets were mostly dogs, plus a few caged cats and birds, a gorgeous falcon that never left its owner's leather-clad arm, and a tarantula in the hand of a teenager. The goat or sheep we'd heard baa'ing that morning was somewhere in town for something else, probably lunch.

Another milestone was reached this week: we went to our first Mexican doctor. Dr. Salvador Quiroz, an internist specializing in kidney disease, did some training in the U.S., and is affiliated with

Mayo Clinic in some way or another. He came highly recommended, and he wrote a column in the local paper about internal medicine in which he seemed to understand the complexities of interlocking diseases. Neither of us have simple medical histories.

We drove up to his office to make an appointment and he took me in right away and spent more than an hour with me. Only $40, with no charge for the upcoming follow-up visit. Last time I saw a specialist in Phoenix it was something like $150 for 20 minutes and it took a month to get an appointment. I wanted to see if I had picked up amoebas. I had.

He and another doctor had run a research study here to see if the presence of harmful amoebas was over-diagnosed, and the results confirmed their suspicion. Overuse of antibiotics is even more of a problem for many in Mexico because you don't need a prescription for them as you do in the States.

But when the $10 lab test here showed I had bugs he sent me to Querétaro for a more sensitive amoeba test to confirm it, instead of automatically handing me a prescription for antibiotics as so many doctors do. The $215, fifteen-day test showed I was one who really did have them, the worst kind (apparently not all amoebas are created equal).

At that price, I can see why many Mexicans simply pick up a box of Cipro or Flagyl when they get diarrhea that Imodium can't cure. And that's what I eventually ended up taking. No more amoebas. I have a feeling in the future we'll be part of the problem instead of the solution ourselves and just buy the antibiotics and skip the $265 and two-week delay.

In Mexico you find your own medical laboratory, take in the order and do whatever is needed for the tests, and then pick up the results at the clinic when they're processed. You bring the results to the doctor, then you drop by in a few days, no appointment needed, to get the interpretation of the results and any new prescriptions or changes in your care.

In some ways that is more reassuring. Since you're responsible for your own records, you've got your papers right with you so you can change doctors easily. You can check with a friend who's a nurse to see if the doctor is doing right by you. For those of us on the internet, it's easier to research every procedure and drug.

I think I prefer this system, though I'm not sure. At the doctor's clinic I attended in Mesa, my file was a foot thick. No one ever read it all for problems like drug interactions, I'm positive. But if a doctor did need my intensive history, it was available at the clinic, not stashed somewhere in one of my own files.

We saw a fantastic play, *The Proof*, a Pulitzer Prize and Tony award-winner from 2001, here in SMA, and it was well acted. The story line is similar to *A Beautiful Mind*, involving a mentally ill mathematical genius.

But the lead character in *The Proof* is his daughter, who has been trying to take care of him, not able to go to college in the process, educating herself to a level that surpasses his genius. Nobody believes she did the math when she presents her work; they think it must have been stolen from her father.

We also were able to see *Frida* here. Loved *Frida*—so did the Mexican crowd, a packed theater on a Tuesday night. We know enough Spanish to actually understand some of the subtitles now.

Mexican critics have complained that it was not shot in Spanish, it was not political enough, and it did not show quite enough how much pain Frida endured and overcame in her life, so that she became an inspirational folk hero for the entire country. I of course was glad for the English, and there was quite enough pain shown for me. The trolley accident that impaled her was done artistically and graphically. The image of the symbolic caged blue bird that flew away in that crash still lingers with me.

I read a review in some U.S. lefty online site that also complained that the movie did not make clear how powerful and important the split was between Lenin and Trotsky. And it didn't. To make understandable all the political conflicts and infighting of those days would have been another movie altogether, of interest only to political junkies.

Geoffrey Rush was excellent as Trotsky. I knew some of what was only being hinted at in the history, but not all. Frida's affairs with both women and men were clearly shown, though not from our sensitivity, of course. Great movie.

Frida's face is on all sorts of souvenirs for sale here, including a sequined portrait sewn onto plastic bolsas (shopping bags). You can only be sure it is Frida because of her one eyebrow.

We saw a terrible concert one night, supposedly the string section of the Guanajuato Symphony, but the director and accordionist (yes, I said accordionist) was the same guy we'd been stuck seeing a few months ago. Back then he was supposed to do piano jazz but instead played his accordion. We walked out at intermission this time, too.

Norma kept whispering during the songs, "That was awfully flat, wasn't it? And wasn't there something wrong with the timing?" Somehow I doubt Beethoven envisioned an accordion in the string section.

January 21 is Allende's birthday, and the celebration was a sight to behold. Real flowers in abundance adorned the statue of Allende at the corner of the Jardin. Soldiers with guns marched in formation, brass bands blared, kids saluted and marched, pretty girls in high heels lined up, the Mayor shook hands all around—a full-fledged patriotic display.

At one point one of the bands really hit a foul, screeching note. My hands involuntarily leapt upward, but luckily stopped before my fingers inserted themselves into my ears. A Mexican man walking next to me beamed and said, "¡*Muy bonita!*" (very pretty). I smiled back.

10

February

The Sunday before Lent starts is one of my favorites in the San Miguel calendar. The Jardín is full of stands selling eggs that have been emptied and refilled with confetti and resealed with brightly colored tissue paper and glue. Kids buy a bag full and run up and down the Jardín bopping everyone and anyone with the eggs, leaving confetti and eggshells streaming down their victims' faces and backs, and then racing away from retaliation.

I was going to buy a bag of eggs myself to use as protection but a Mexican warned me that if I was holding an egg I was fair game. The egg-armed kids far outnumbered me.

The older kids mostly had spray cans of foam, and the cutest girls seemed to get covered in foam the fastest. Along with eggs, stands ringing the Jardín sold artificial flowers of every bright color and crepe paper clown dolls dancing from sticks.

We refurbished our tired artificial flower centerpiece in our dining room with a bouquet of the colorful clowns and lollipop-style chenille flowers. One tourist asked if we were buying them for our grandkids. We said no, they were for our own dining room table.

She looked startled, as if she were thinking, who would use clowns for a bouquet? Lots of us, I think, from the way people were snapping up the clowns.

Hundreds of cameras were aimed every which way at the kids, Mexicans and foreigners alike delighted with the play being staged before us. I decided that anyone who was taking part in the festivities had to know that it was a public event, they were as likely to have their photo taken as to get an egg on their scalp, and so I joined in the picture taking.

There was one private moment I snapped, and I held up my digital camera quizzically and the mother nodded yes before I took the photo. A Mexican father with a very short buzz cut was teaching his toddler how to break an egg against Daddy's head. The little boy was being so tentative, afraid to actually hit Daddy.

Finally he did land a solid blow, the egg broke, and confetti spewed everywhere. Everyone laughed out loud. When I showed the little boy the close up he said, "*Papá.*" Apparently he doesn't yet recognize his own photograph, but he knew Daddy. I wish I'd had a printer with me to give the family a copy of the shot.

On Ash Wednesday one priest made his mark on foreheads with such a heavy hand he looked as if he had left swastikas on his parishioners. I was shocked and puzzled at the first one I saw before I figured it out. Or maybe that priest was going back millenniums to when swastikas have had many different, non-political meanings. I'm still guessing.

Another priest put the ashes on the top of people's head—only those with snow white hair and bald men who nodded their heads revealed the mark.

卍

As in Michigan, the first day of planting season means chaos at all the nurseries. That day happens the first weekend in February here, not Memorial Day as in Michigan, They call February 2 Candelaria Day here (seeds are blessed at the churches). The entire Parque Juárez turns into a gigantic nursery. Aisle after aisle of giant blooming tulips, orchids, and plants I've never seen before formed a maze in which I could have gladly gotten lost.

Boys with wheelbarrows followed us around, waiting for us to make a purchase so they could carry our plants around for us as we finished shopping, and then to a taxi, for a buck tip.

Stands sold fertilizers and potting soil and all sizes of planters. One booth had information on the healthful uses of various herbs, which they would sell to you according to your diagnosis, Food carts sold refreshments so you wouldn't have to leave the park all day long. Several charities had booths. Tourists were enthralled at the sights, camera flashes going off constantly.

We bought dozens of flowering shrubs and herbs and small trees for the front porch and the roof, which now looks like a true blooming garden with bougainvillea, hibiscus, geraniums, petunias, pansies, and daisies. We can pick all the basil, thyme, rosemary, fennel, oregano, and chives we want from the pots on our front porch railing.

Norma used her Spanish to order what she thought was eight bags of potting soil delivered to our roof. She got through—eight bags were carried upstairs—but it was compost and dirt, and not in the right proportions. We've got four bags of rich compost left over, awaiting more dirt to mix it with. Our neighbor has offered to take it to enrich the lawn in our little courtyard.

It is a losing battle with the wild cats digging up whatever lawn manages to emerge, All the trees and shrubs flourish, but the lawn is also shaded, which doesn't help the grass. Plenty of nurseries are scattered around the outskirts of the city, so we can replace any plants that don't make it.

Belles Artes sponsored a week of puppet shows and classes, mostly for children, but one Saturday night the show was Faust, for grownups and teens. What a high quality performance, though we could understand only a few words of the Spanish. The puppeteer came out in royal velvet costume, alternating from being a very scary Satan to an ordinary guy who kept saying, "Don't be afraid."

He recruited a young man from the audience to replace the old puppet of Faust early in the performance. Of course the guy was really an actor who got into the wooing of the beautiful blonde maiden whom he won, in return for bargaining away his soul. Terribly tragic ending when he lost all. We really got caught up in feeling for this young man in love with what was a rag body wearing a blonde wig.

I'm still not sure whether the story of Faust came through in all its philosophical depths, where Faust is faced with a choice that embodies his very essence, the life choice of what it means to be a human being with free will, or whether it was a soap opera, a tele-novela. But we all got emotionally involved, even those of us who had no idea what was being said.

Norma and I were delighted to be invited by a Mexican neighbor to a baby shower for a Mexican woman whom we had seen around, the cousin of our landlord. All the women in our court-yard were invited—I'm not sure the idea of co-ed baby showers has even caught on much in the U.S.—so there were five retired expats. Also invited were two U.S. college students, doing a two-months compressed Spanish language stint at Academia to earn 15 college credits. They were living with a relative of the mother-to-be.

I guesstimate 50 Mexican women were there, teens to 90 years, plus a dozen kids who mostly played outside. Showers are pretty boring but we weren't about to pass up the opportunity to take part in a Mexican family festivity.

We had the usual games of trying to figure out what various baby-related items were by squeezing the packages. In this case it was more interesting because of the many English and Spanish words that could be used for the same item, the English words also including Canadian and British variations. The judges kept marking "nappy" wrong for "diaper" until we protested on behalf of the Brit.

The most fun was a game where everyone got to roll three dice; if you got a pair you could pick one of five prizes, and then you sat up front in the row of prize-holders. The next person after the original five winners who threw a pair could then pick any prize and oust that prize-holder from her seat.

We had ten minutes of frantic prize-switching until the last five people sitting up front with prizes in hand got to keep theirs. I had a set of six multi-colored gel pens in hand four separate times in ten minutes before I actually got to keep them.

We played that game several times, until about everyone won a prize. Norma scored a hand-held folding fan for her purse, suitable for these May days when it hits 90°.

Many of the Mexican women spoke English well, and all of the gringas spoke at least some Spanish, so we communicated. One game involved figuring out the convoluted relationships on a list, in Spanish, though English answers were accepted. The cousin of my uncle's grandmother is *my* sort of thing.

Shockingly, Norma and I both got them all right, but so did so many contestants that we let the prizes go to the youngest women.

Green chile *empanadas* from San Sebastian bakery on Aurora were the main course, accompanied by plenty of salads and snacks. The raw veggies for dipping had been marinated in my favorite chile-*limon* seasoning (*limon* means lime; lemons are harder to find here), so I had a hard time staying away from those. We had tiny storks pinned on our collars as we arrived.

The surprise to me was that the Mexican women clapped loudly and cheered the presents as they were opened, instead of the polite "ooohs and ahhs" at the U.S. showers I've attended. The enthusiastic applause made that part of the shower far more fun. The toddlers got to deliver the presents to the expectant mom on the sofa, which also was a delight to watch. Of course the littlest kids had more fun playing with the ribbons and boxes.

Most people gave cute little outfits—love to shop for baby clothes even though I don't particularly like babies. Some were more practical and gave boxes of diapers.

The shower was supposed to start at 4:30. At 4:15 all the gringas were in our parking lot waiting to be picked up. The cars arrived for us at 4:45, and people straggled in to the party as late as 7 P.M. Several Mexican women said to us, "It's always the gringos who arrive on time."

We left around 8 P.M. and the shower was still going strong, the kids invited back inside for food cleanup in particular. Not as in dish washing, as in gobbling the leftovers.

We were also happy we could communicate as much as we did in Spanish, though admittedly the Mexican women who knew

English saved our necks. Norma and I looked at each other as we left and said simultaneously, "That was the best shower I've ever attended!"

I opened all the windows in the house because it reached 89° today and heard unexpected bird songs; I hadn't even realized I had missed the bird songs all winter with closed windows and doors. Or are these particular arias from birds migrating through, as massive Vs crisscross the skies and we lose our winter visitors who are flying back to those in the north?

A cute little red-and black bird similar to the scarlet tanager that has about disappeared from the Michigan area keeps showing up in our pomegranate tree. I was watching a red and black butterfly of a kind I'd never seen flit from geranium to moss rose in our courtyard when, zap, Pinky ran out from hiding and ate it. I hope that wasn't the last one on earth.

I've never seen so many multi-colored butterflies mating all over the gardens, flopping onto the pathways in abandon. The monarchs have gone back up north in the millions. We didn't get down to Michoacan to see them this winter in their resting grounds, which we've been warned are up some 650 steps into the jungle off a road that's some 10,000 feet altitude. Next year.

You never know what will happen in Mexico. We were driving to Querétaro and looked out the car window and about twenty big fat pigs were wading in the lake. Nobody was around we could see, how did they get loose, wasn't anybody going to get them out of the lake? (The lake is polluted but I've seen a few kids swimming in it anyway, and we know not to buy any local fish. It's a beautiful lake, especially at sunset, since SMA is in the mountains and the panoramas are spectacular.)

I'll turn a corner and have to scurry around three burros on the sidewalk carrying firewood or bagged garden soil for sale, or I'll hear the whistle of the knife sharpener who must be making the rounds that day—each vendor's whistle is distinctive.

I got back to my watercolor class when the two Spanish classes ended and have finished a cute painting of a frog and a lily pad both reflected in their pond, and another of a dragonfly on a tiger lily. Non-challenging, traditional, but I felt the need to start with some small subjects. Some day I am going to tackle painting the Jardín filled with Conchero dancers, but not yet.

Winter visitors have flooded all the art classes in town for January-March. There were 16 on the waiting list for Helen Coffey's class that she bypassed to work me back in. It is so easy to spot the tourists, who are scrutinizing their maps, not watching where they are walking, tripping over each other on the narrow sidewalks.

We hosted the Book Club at our place last week, our first presentation of our house since it was completed, showing off all our new furniture bought since our Arizona park model sold. We discussed the Harriet Doerr books of short stories about her life in Mexico (she started writing at age 73, which is encouraging to many of us). Charming little books, including *Stones for Ibarra*, echo the minimalist setting-rich books of Mexican classic writers like Juan Rulfo, but with nowhere near the centuries-deep levels of meaning.

Upcoming books to be discussed are Sandra Cisneros's *Caramello*, Mario Vargas Llosa's *Story Teller*, Katherine Blair's *In the Shadow of the Angels*, and the classic *100 Years of Solitude* by Gabriel Marquez, all with Latin American themes. *The Story Teller* is symbolic of what is going on in every place that is being gentrified—old housing in desirable areas being bought up by wealthier people who replace the poorer original inhabitants, who now cannot afford to live in their old neighborhoods.

What is the very presence of wealthier foreigners of different cultural perspectives doing to the old ways in Mexico and throughout the world, or, in the case of this novel, the Amazon rain forests? Does even just studying the small tribes there change them by their being studied?

It's like the Hawthorne effect we learned about in college. If people know they are in a research study they will change their behavior toward what the observers want, even unknowingly.

Llosa explores the question of whether a tiny Amazon River society where handicapped people and unproductive old people are killed, children are married off, and women are beaten should be protected and allowed to continue unchanged. Should a few hundred tribe members be maintained at any price, even though hundreds of thousands might benefit from development of the Amazon riverbanks? Who decides what is "better"?

The book even affects my thinking on gringos wearing shorts here. It's like the classic science fiction story where people are able to travel back in time, warned not to even step off the marked paths so as not to distort anything in history, since one tiny ripple set in motion can have huge effects over centuries.

Is the presence of foreigners in and of itself changing Mexico, in bad ways or in good, and who assigns the values?

Would Mexico be changing as rapidly due to the mass media and cultural and economic exchanges, even if not a one of us ever came to San Miguel? Does the good we do in such programs as scholarships and health care outweigh whatever negative effects we may be having on Mexico?

Already hundreds of remote tribal languages are being lost throughout Mexican Indian communities, as in the rest of the world, and the beautiful native dress for many regions is being replaced by jeans and T-shirts for daily wear. Can change be stopped, and should it? Mexican literature presents these issues more clearly than a classroom.

But we're still wearing shorts.

ABC news reporter Sam Quinones' book, *True Tales of Another Mexico*, is another work that is furthering my education. He wrote it in 1999, before Fox's election and the end of the monopoly of the PRI party, though he has an afterword with his optimistic thoughts about what he thinks Fox will accomplish.

In his six-years-only term of office, there was no way Fox could accomplish everything everybody wanted, but this book revels in the joy of the anticipated improvements while it reveals some of the more sordid aspects of Mexican culture.

The tale that shocked me the most was about lynchings that still occur in the dark corners of Mexico, where people have no hope and are ripe to scapegoat anyone for all their frustrations and fears. Quinones says he has a folder three inches high of lynching cases from the period of his research, 1994-1999.

He describes one case in which two poor itinerant salesmen, hawking trading cards that can be turned in for toys when enough are accumulated, made a stupid comment to a young girl in one village about wanting to take her home with them.

By the time the rumors and exaggerations about that comment made the rounds, the salesmen were labeled child molesters and/or they were stealing kids for their livers, One person claimed to have seen the back seat of their car full of tiny livers!

Within hours, despite speeches by the mayor on the truth, a mob formed and broke into the jail to drag out the two men and to lynch them. I have been in conscience-less mob scenes, I can believe it.

Another tale is of the murders of at least 300 young women who worked in the factories in Juárez. Quinones decided from his research that there was no one serial killer, there were many, apparently men who are enraged by the freedom these young women factory workers enjoy, breaking away from all of their traditions.

The women are independent, they make enough money (in comparison to the men in Juárez) to support themselves. Many go to bars alone, where they can even watch male strippers.

The number of murders alone would not be surprising, since Juárez usually has 250 murders a year, mostly related to drugs and alcohol, But these are murders of young women whose only "crime" is breaking away from women's roles.

The book *Caramelo* is simply delightful. Cisneros paints lovely pictures contrasting the old country around the time of the disastrous 1910 revolution that devastated the Mexican civilian population, with the new life for those millions who escaped to the U.S. Fascinating footnotes describe the incursions into the U.S. by Pancho Villa and the retaliatory raid ordered by Woodrow Wilson.

I learned more of the history behind the movie filmed here, *And Starring Pancho Villa as Himself*, along with a greater understanding of what drove the major immigration of Mexicans into the U.S. at that period. Another book club selection that helped me understand this era was *Rain of Gold* by Victor Villaseñor.

The International PEN writers seminar series continued with Beverly Donofrio, who wrote *Riding in Cars with Boys*, talking about how Hollywood films a novel. W.D. Snodgrass, a Pulitzer Prize-winning poet, read a 24-page short story/memoir he wrote about his early life and the death of his sister, and then he read a 12-line poem that covered the same material even more powerfully, and he discussed the differences between poetry and prose. The audience received a semester's worth of literature instruction in one hour.

PEN is such a great group. I tried to get in when I lived in LA and I was rejected for not having written enough books yet, so it feels good to qualify now. I'm getting so busy that I'm going to pass on joining, though. There are so many worthy charities and intriguing classes to choose from.

Norma bought a software program that allows her to design and print out patterns for every kind of clothing for both of us, no matter what our sizes as they go down. She now has it down pat so she can whip out a new pair of slacks or shorts for me in 20 minutes. She hasn't got her own pattern perfected yet—we wear the same size but have totally different shapes.

We also discovered Girasol, a store here in town with designs from a woman in Guadalajara that truly are one size fits all, including us. So we have new wardrobes in bright cotton gauzes and muslins. It feels good to have a decent wardrobe again that didn't come from Lane Bryant.

After eight months without a haircut, trying to achieve the long gloriously waving hair I remembered from my youth, I gave up. I'm too old, my hair is too old, my neck is too old and flabby, and long hair doesn't work any more. So I am back to my usual haircut.

Somehow major weight loss raised some unrealistic expectations in me. I thought losing the weight would bring me back to looking like 21 again, just because I now weigh about what I did at 21. No such luck.

We discovered a British woman (she used to cut Margaret Thatcher's hair) who had a salon in Mexico City for 20 years and now is in SMA, and she did a great job on both of us. So another problem is solved: we have a good hair stylist.

We took another Instituto Allende tour, this one to Mexico City, over the weekend.

This time the bus trip took only three hours to cover 160 miles. The tour organizer had to check that it wasn't a smog alert day, and that it wasn't a day in which the bus's license plate would not be allowed inside the city. (Only certain license plate numbers are allowed in each day, to cut back on smog and traffic in Mexico City. Richer people have gotten around that problem by buying more cars with assorted license plate numbers.) Traffic was jammed downtown because of an anti-war protest of about 50,000.

First stop was Belles Artes, a palace housing dozens of huge murals by Diego Rivera and others. (Many cities in Mexico have their own Belles Artes, as does San Miguel—that's the art center where I take my watercolor classes.)

A common theme of Mexican murals is the rape of the indigenous people by the Conquistadors—wide-scale rape, since no women accompanied Cortez and the early conquerors. The Mexican population is now about 90% mixed heritage. A few purebred

Spanish descendants remain, and many Indians, including one of our tour guides, are proud of their undiluted heritage.

Like in the U.S., there is discussion over what terms to use, indigenous, native, Indian. César was our leader again. He said that the tour guide who is pure Indian jokes he was glad Columbus didn't think he had discovered Turkey instead of India.

We saw the giant yellow metal abstract horse head statue, El Caballito monument, on the way to the *zócalo*, the huge main square of the city. What a sight—I haven't been to Tiennemen Square but I bet it feels like that. I restrained myself from buying anything from the pushy vendors, though a straw hat seemed like a good idea for the sun. Because of the anti-war protest we had to walk what the tour guide said was an extra three blocks, but it felt like a mile through the crowds. César waved a red flag so we could keep track. He joked that maybe a red flag was not such a good idea in the middle of a demonstration.

The heart of the city was built over an Aztec city and pyramid that only recently is revealing its riches, whatever is left that the Conquistadors didn't deliberately destroy. A hundred years ago the city built new sewer lines and ran them right through the pyramid area, not even noticing then that national archaeological treasures were being destroyed. Now they are a matter of pride.

Also in the *zócalo* area are the National Palace, still used for the most formal of government events, and the balcony where the President addresses the population for major speeches. Inside the Palace are the most important of all of Diego Rivera's murals, depicting the entire history of Mexico from earliest days. One focal point is a Spanish Conquistador raping an Indian woman—symbolic of the rape of the entire country.

Diego had the nerve to put both Frida and her sister in his mural, both reading to Mexican children, the future generation. One of the major heartbreaks of Frida's life was Diego's affair with her sister.

One of the most impressive museums I have ever seen is the National Museum of Anthropology and Archaeology. It was too big to see it all, so we concentrated on the age of the Teotihuacan culture, from several hundred years before Christ to a thousand years after, since we would be seeing those pyramids the next day. Have to admit, I had no idea of the richness of the early Mexican cultures. The museum includes the 20-ton round stone of the Aztec Calendar, their original books with highly evolved picture writing, segments of the original temple carvings, and recreations of many of the pyramids and their surrounding civilizations and cities.

One area was for touching, for the sight-impaired, to give them some sense of the sculptures and carvings. Mexico is far behind the States in handicap accessibility overall, but they're catching up in some areas. My favorite statue was in that part of the museum, a ferocious stylized jaguar. Then I realized the hollow in its back meant it was one of the receptacles for the beating hearts ripped out of the still-alive sacrificial victims.

That night those tour participants who weren't totally exhausted got back on the bus for a night drive through the downtown, where the anti-war demonstration was still going at 11 P.M. We stopped at a local favorite "taco stand," actually quite a nice restaurant, with probably the best *carnitas* and *carbón* tacos I have ever had. (We passed on one kind made of fried pork rinds softened with some kind of sauce.) The tacos were served family style on platters, and our group devoured dozens and dozens. (The tour guides got to eat all the pork rind ones.)

While most of the group swigged Victoria beer, available only in Mexico and one of the most smuggled items taken back to the States, Norma and I enjoyed piña colada juices squeezed on site. Wonderful meal.

Our hotel was in the Zona Rosa, the pink zone, where the best restaurants, nightclubs, and hotels are located. The area was swinging on a Saturday night, One park several blocks long is where the mariachi bands hang out, hundreds of musicians looking for customers to hire them for parties and such. I couldn't help thinking it, they looked like the male prostitutes along Santa Monica Blvd. in LA, watching passing cars with eager eyes, dressed in flamboyant outfits. (Sunset Blvd. was where the female prostitutes in LA mainly worked.)

The next morning we headed for Teotihuacan, once a thriving city of 200,000. Yes, the pyramids were where the human sacrifices were made each morning, most of the cultures believing firmly that only the sacrifice of a still-beating human heart yanked out of the chest would appease the sun god and assure that the sun would come up that day.

Parts of the pyramids were painted red so they gleamed totally red and glistening during sacrifices, emphasizing the color of the flowing blood that ran down the sides of the step-pyramids.

Cannibalism was an important part of Aztec culture, while at the same time the civilizations were highly developed in other areas—the same way that this age is still filled with wars and violence while supposedly so highly developed.

First to build the pyramids at Teotihuacan was a civilization that lasted from 100 BCE to 750 AD. One theory why the city died is that it got too big to be supported with corn grown on the overworked region, and so the people moved on. The pyramids were reused by the Toltecs centuries later, then by the Aztecs. And then the ruins were abandoned again and were pretty much buried and lost.

The Conquistadors did their best to obliterate all signs of previous civilizations throughout the New World. Only recently have these pyramids been restored and reclaimed,

The Pyramid of the Sun is the third largest pyramid in the world, though it depends on how scientists measure the pyramids, by the size of their base, height, or mass. Cheops in Egypt, Cholula in Mexico and the Great White Pyramid of Tibet fight for the rankings.

Besides the Pyramids of the Sun and the Moon at Teotihuacan, some 600 smaller pyramids dot the park. I've always been fascinated by the mathematics and the similar designs used by pyramid builders throughout the world. UFO believers have many theories about that.

The bus discharged us at one of the five entrances. The guides said they would pick us up three hours later at the entrance on the other end, which looked as if it were at least two miles away. It was so hot. I bought the first hat I could find, a gaudy monstrosity when I examined it in the reality of San Miguel the next day, but it served its purpose. I only got a little sunburned.

All around us the younger tourists were scrambling to the top of the Pyramid of the Moon and then the Pyramid of the Sun. We just looked. Norma says to tell people that she ran to the top but my camera batteries ran out before I could document her ascent. Being in the middle of that park, I could almost feel the presence of the ghosts of the bustling city of 600 AD.

Overall, Mexico City was beyond comprehension, one of the largest cities in the world. (Some say it is the largest, if you could count all of the people crammed into the outskirts.) I was impressed by the thousands of new apartments—miles of identical rows of bright pink and white row houses—that had been built on the outskirts to try to contain the millions of homeless who keep flooding to Mexico City from all of Latin America looking for jobs.

Our guide explained, "Mexicans will sell anything. Whenever the government tries to sweep away the street vendors, they say, give us jobs and we'll gladly stop selling in the streets. Until then, we're not going to starve, we're going to sell anything we can get our hands on."

Throughout our walk across the Teotihuacan plain, men kept approaching selling small black cat statues made of obsidian (yes, I bought one for $20), pendants of the Aztec calendar stone (yes, I bought one for $5 that turned my sweater black where it rubbed), and gorgeous turquoise and black ceramic ceremonial masks (my spending money was gone by then).

That's it on Mexico City—I could go on for hours. I don't think I'll ever return except on a tour, though—too many tales of crime, and the city overwhelms me. One scheme that seems to happen a lot on Mexican city streets: somebody squirts you with mustard or salsa without your noticing it. Someone else comes up and says you've been dumped on by a bird, and let me help you clean it up. While you're being dabbed and scrubbed with a paper towel someone else grabs your wallet.

Many in the U.S. think all of Mexico is crime-ridden but high-crime areas (primarily Mexico City and border cities) can be mostly identified and avoided. So much is drug-related, and U.S. drug users are as much to blame as Mexican drug suppliers.

I think I am finally getting used to daily life in San Miguel. I heard drums and saw dancers on the way to the Jardín yesterday and didn't even bother to go check it out.

I found out later it was the Celebration of the Lord of the Conquistadors, and there is one statue in the corner of the Parroquia that is devoted to this particular aspect of Christ. Why would Mexicans celebrate being conquered and their own religion destroyed? I can't believe that Mexico finds so many holidays to celebrate.

11

March

We have no more maid, and it's the dog's fault. We never knew when (or if) the maid would come between 9 A.M. and 4 P.M. on a particular day, and she was terrified of our dog, who reciprocated by nipping at her ankles and yapping viciously. So we either spent the whole day waiting for the maid to arrive and finish up, keeping the dog on our laps when the maid was actually here working, or we put the dog in the quilt room when we go out. Since the maid is not always careful about keeping the outside door closed while she works, we put the cats in the quilt room, too.

And our downstairs neighbor complained about us today that our dog's yapping and banging on the door and scratching to get out and hurling herself in a generalized frenzy disturbs him. Don't know why. We didn't know Lacey kept it up even after we left. No wonder she's frothing at the mouth when we get back and let her out. The quilt room is 12' x 12', so we never dreamed she would feel so caged.

So our choice was either to spend every single day waiting for the maid and holding Lacey on a lap while she cleaned, or get rid of Lacey, or fire the maid. She's history. We will have to do our own sweeping and mopping and trash removal and toilet scrubbing, unless we find someone who will come at a specific hour we can count on so we can plan our day without having to throw Lacey in the quilt room all day long.

We were not thrilled with the maid lately anyway, because we paid her in advance to do some extra work while we were in out of town, and she never showed.

Since the maid technically is employed by our landlord, we don't have to worry about the stringent labor laws that would have required us to give several months' severance pay even if we had grounds for firing. Discharged employees in Mexico almost always sue and win.

One Saturday night we decided to walk down to the Jardín to see what was going on. We took off with no purses and no money except for two pesos Norma found tucked in her slacks pocket. She gave them to the first old Indian woman beggar we saw so we'd be free.

Along the way we ambled into an art opening, enjoying pepperoni and cheese on crackers as we tried to figure out the abstract paintings that didn't grab either of us. We did try to appreciate the paintings, in exchange for the appetizers. SMA is famous for its freeloading attendees of art gallery openings who go only for the wine and cheese.

The adjoining jewelry store had finally changed its annoying window display—beheaded Barbie dolls with flashy rings on their necks, the longhaired heads hanging from a dried branch in the same window. The Barbie ring holders were now in a back shelf and gorgeous custom silver work now shone out into the night from the new window display. More future Christmas and birthday present choices were duly noted for each of us.

We passed Harry's restaurant, which has now opened a larger restaurant in Centro Querétaro—hard to go by the SMA place without turning in for fried oysters and jambalaya. New women's dressy jackets made of woven ribbons drew our eyes to another window as we neared the Jardín.

Banners in front of the Parroquia celebrated the last of the Celtic Festival, a week-long commemoration of the Irish immigrants (many promised U.S. citizenship if they joined the U.S. Army) who fought alongside Mexican soldiers during the Mexican-American War of 1846-48. They abandoned Gen. Zachary Taylor when they saw they were fighting a devout Catholic country, plus they were mistreated by the U.S. officers who looked down upon the Irish.

The San Patricios Batallion was defeated in the Battle of Churubusco in 1847, a Waterloo for Mexico in that war, but Mexican President Antonio Lopez de Santa Anna said that if he'd had a few hundred more soldiers like the San Patricios he would have won the battle and the war. Most of the survivors were court-martialed for desertion and executed. They are heroes to the present day in Mexico. Villa Jacaranda Hotel usually runs a half-dozen Irish films during St. Pat's week, in commemoration of these Irish soldiers (and some Scots and Germans) who deserted the U.S. and fought on the Mexican side.

Fire dancers performed in front of the Parroquia, an inviting rhythm maintained by four drummers, all in face paint. A pixie-haired Mexican woman, her face painted mime white with a black line down the center, showed the men how it was done, swinging her fire-tipped batons like samba partners.

Someone yelled in English, "I have a camera," and expected the crowds would part for her so she could get a close-up, but nobody moved.

Already the vendors who weave palm fronds into fantastic religious images and flowers were at work, selling the completed palms for blessing at Palm Sunday masses. A Cuban exhibit alongside the Jardín in a long tent sold books, Che Guevara T-shirts, and handmade wood and leather drums ranging from 50 to 500 pesos ($5 to $50 US).

Fireworks overhead and loud music channeled down the narrow San Miguel streets in our direction told us there was something going on at Civica Plaza two blocks away. We had to check it out. Almost no foreigners there—what a difference two blocks can make.

We got close in to the masked and costumed dancers who were going round the plaza as if it were the Day of the Locos parade. Well-amplified salsa and rock music was just below the decibel level that would have had my fingers plugging my ears. A smirky Bush-masked guy kept shrugging his shoulders as if he knew nothing as he danced. He kissed a gorilla and chased a large Indian-costumed woman and tried to look up her skirts. She danced with him and swung him into a deep backward dip. Then she held her nose as if Bush had let off gas.

A Vicente Fox was there, flirting with all the women. A Satan scared a small boy who ran away from the circle, his parents chasing him to comfort him. Little kids in costume made the circuit as well, dancing right along with the adults. Who could tell who was male or female, young or old, neighbor or stranger? That was the point.

A white-masked guy in cream velvet pants and jacket over a white T-shirt spotted Norma and swept her onto the floor and made a full circle, escorting her under a bridge of people's upheld arms and adding her to a conga line. Fox came over and shimmied at me so I shimmied back but waved bye-bye to him, not ready to follow Norma's dance circuit. I was tired watching the costumed dancers salsa on, dance after dance after dance. Once in a while a rock song I recognized came out of the amplifiers. Mostly it was purely Mexican high energy music, great fun. We kept dancing in place as we watched.

Fireworks kept exploding overhead. They were being set off a few feet away from people around the bigger-than-life statue of Allende on horseback that is the centerpiece of the park. Safety regulations? Who needs safety regulations?

Another books exhibit, mainly of children's materials, under a long tent ran parallel to the dance circuit. It could be that proportionately more people actually read books in Mexico than in the States these days, where computers have taken over. At least I see far more books for sale on the streets. (Oh, never mind, I forgot the U.S. grocery store and drug store mass market paperbacks, where most of the books in the U.S. are actually sold.)

A live band performed on the steps at the other end of the Civica Plaza. Clowns tried to sell us highly intricate balloon creatures. Old men offered roasted sunflower seeds. Indian women scraped the thorns off of nopales cactus pods and bagged them for sale.

We walked around a bit more and spotted two Flexi shoe stores that we'd been told carried sandals. We're ready to drive to Leon, a leather center of the world, to find shoes that fit, rather than go back to the States or order over the internet, since we both have big feet compared to Mexican women. But no, the largest size in women's sandals at both shops was a Mexican 28, and Norma wears a 29, I wear 30. Off to the shoe stores in Leon soon.

We're finding lots of ways we save money now—bulk cereal at Bonanza for $1.40 for the same amount that is in our former $4 a box name brands, for example. Norma dared to go to the woman who cuts hair in the unisex barber shop near our home, 60 pesos for a cut and blow-dry styling, $6 compared to the $20 we were paying to our hair stylist who caters to gringas.

More palm frond weavers worked in front of other churches we passed, snacking on tacos from street stands that smelled heavenly, as they wove crucifixes and flowers from the palms. More stands sold those delicious-looking but oh so tough gigantic ears of white corn, grilled over charcoal or steamed, then brushed with mayonnaise, grated white cheese, lime juice, and chili powder or hot sauce.

We haven't been able to find the tender small yellow ears of corn that spoiled expats back home, though some friends have found them from farmers selling off of trucks in the early morning. I buy frozen ears at Costco for my corn-on-the-cob fix.

Kids of five or six pushed baby carriages containing their younger siblings as their parents worked.

We passed Petit Four bakery and chocolateria, workers beating dough late into the night for Palm Sunday purchases, and next door a live jazz band was warming up at Tio Lucas steak house. Teatro Angela Peralta has new lighting for its entire three stories, the historic opera house finally revealing its architectural intricacies.

A glossy black and orange banty rooster moved into our courtyard, followed by a speckled gray female banty who also arrived out of nowhere. They had nine baby chicks, tiny as they could be, scratching in the dirt and scurrying for cover under Mama whenever a cat appeared. Then the chicks became teenagers, their yellow downy coats replaced by scraggly pinfeathers.

One day there were nine chicks and two adults, then there were no chicks, and now Mama is huddled in a way that looks as if she has about 20 legs under her—more babies.

I've heard that guys who work for our landlord got permission to take the chicks. I have to remember that chickens are a cash crop, not pets for me to enjoy while not having to take care of them.

In our courtyard, we dodged walking under the rooster perched up in a tree and patted the outdoor cats we have tamed slightly as they learn to trust their reliable feeders. We could still see fireworks overhead, another magical evening in San Miguel.

⊠⊡⊠⊡⊠⊡⊠

Meanwhile, many gringos in town are on fire over the introduction of a Dunkin' Donuts sales display cabinet on the back wall of Dolphy's ice cream parlor on the Jardín. There is no sign, it isn't visible from the street, and only the most discreet historical-appearing signs are allowed in the historic district anyway. The city recently ordered all neon signs banished.

But many who are frightened of any U.S. corporate invasion into "their" town are upset. The camel's nose is under the tent, next will be a McDonald's, they say at the slightest opportunity. (Over the next two years, the Dunkin' Donuts signs got bigger but they're still only inside Dolphy's.)

Others are saying, hey, it's a Mexican-owned business trying to serve a need, even if that need is feeding grease to gringos anxious for any sign of the familiar. Lots of Mexican bakeries sell donuts already. Dunkin' Donuts is affiliated with Baskin Robbins and Togo sandwich shops. Many franchises include two of the stores in one outlet, since ice cream shops and doughnut shops in particular supplement each other and draw in all-day traffic to keep the number of customers constant.

Everywhere in the world, popular tourist attraction cities worry about the effects tourism and development will have on their towns. I read that Venice, Italy, gets 14 MILLION visitors a year, for a population of 65,000, slightly smaller than San Miguel, and they fear Venice is being "adored to death."

Santa Fe, Sedona, San Francisco, Los Angeles, Austin, Asheville, lots of areas face exactly the same fears of the effects of their popularity as San Miguel faces, and many of them are also in areas where water availability might not keep up with the exploding populations. That to me is the most serious concern. Maybe we'll finally come up with desalinization programs like Israel's.

The town is full of *Semana Santa* (Holy Week) spirit, with many employees and students having three full weeks off for Easter. Tourists are everywhere. I cringe hearing them saying some of the things I said, too, my first days here. Semanta Santa is celebrated in full pageantry in San Miguel, and the nicest part of it all to me is that the people do it for themselves, they couldn't care less whether there are tourists to watch or not. They were doing it long before the hordes arrived.

Friday night before Palm Sunday is a display of shrines around town for Our Lady of Sorrows. Even street fountains are cleaned and decorated beautifully, using flowers of white, purple and orange, the colors of mourning; bitter oranges, which represent the tears of the Virgin; and wheat, for resurrection and renewal of life.

We ran into one display on the corner that shocked us—a young girl was playing the Virgin Mary in a silent unmoving tableau that had us convinced she was a statue, until she blinked. We always fell for the immobile street artists in Ghiradelli Square and other tourist attractions as well. This one was not collecting money, "merely" demonstrating her reverence.

On Palm Sunday vendors in the Jardín sell intricately woven palm fronds, which are blessed at masses. At 1 A.M. is the procession from El Calvario chapel down toward the Jardín, with participants representing the 12 disciples and various New Testament characters.

At 11 A.M. a figure of Christ on a donkey comes out of the church next to the Parroquia. This particular Christ statue was made in the 18th century and so it is in a scarlet coat, knee breeches, hose and buckle shoes popular at that time.

Tuesday is the Apprehension of Christ, with mass at the Oratorio near Plaza Civica. Christ is behind bars.

Wednesday is a procession carrying a bier of *Nuestro Senor del Golpe*, Christ carrying the cross, which goes on until dark when candles and lanterns appear, to light paraders' way.

Holy Thursday, which is the day traditionally celebrated as the first Lord's Supper with the consecration of the bread and wine, is the day all practicing Catholics in San Miguel are supposed to visit at least seven different decorated altars throughout the city. Each church also has a commemoration of the washing of the feet of the 12 disciples.

The entire city is on foot, walking from church to church. Women hand out crusts of bread to be eaten in front of the altars, and sheaves of wheat, also embodying the bread and a symbol of new life. (Pigeons were happy.) Vendors on the sidewalks sell all kinds of pastries and tacos and drinks to the throngs. If you visit at least seven different altars that night, your sins are supposed to be totally forgiven. We stopped at six just in case.

Even though it was a solemn evening, a *Las Tunas* group of musicians gathered in front of the Parroquia and sang for all the tourists in town for *Semana Santa*.

Good Friday has spectacular processions starting mid morning from San Juan de Dios church, following a small statue of St. Roque, who is traditionally shown with an ulcerated leg, accompanied by his dog with a Mexican bread roll called a *bolillo* in its mouth, to feed its master. Atotonilco villagers proceed the five or so miles to SMA's Parroquia with a large wooden cross originally carried each year by Padre Alfaro, the priest who insisted that the Atotonilco church be built.

Around noon believers reenact the trial with Pontius Pilate condemning Jesus, and the crowd chooses Barrabas to be freed rather than Jesus. This is a highly emotional, intense procession and re-enactment. I wouldn't miss it.

I could not imagine that one small town could turn out so many people for the Good Friday processions. Hundreds of Mexican men in tunics wearing real crowns of thorns carry wood crosses and are "whipped" by tall men we think are gringos in Roman soldier attire.

Young girls in their First Communion white dresses or their *Quincieñera* (Sweet Fifteen party) gowns lead the floats, strewing flower petals, chamomile, and stalks of new wheat, a symbol of rebirth. St. Peter, who according to the Bible denied Christ three times during the hours leading to the Crucifixion, is a stop on the parade route.

A bit of shocking theatrics takes place during this procession. At the end of the march, the Christ statue comes face to face with his mother. A mechanism is operated so that the Christ statue raises its head to look directly at Mary. Those who don't know the moment of drama is going to happen are startled into silence.

After the time Christ dies on the Cross, at around 5 P.M. another procession leaves the Oratorio with the Christ statue in a gold and glass coffin on a velvet float. Tall men, I think mostly gringos, in Roman soldier costumes lead the solemn procession, marching in cadence.

Mourners dressed in black, accompanied by sorrowful orchestras and drum beats, carry floats reenacting many scenes, such as St. Veronica with the cloth she used to wipe Christ's face and which retained his image. There are men's and boy's choirs and full orchestras. The procession lasts until dark, returning by candlelight to the Oratorio.

Every male who knows how to play an instrument is in the bands interspersed among the floats, some groups wearing their best mariachi band uniforms, muting their horns in deathly cadences. It reminds me of a U.S. presidential death tribute. High stepping horses could be from the JFK funeral procession in 1963.

We sat ourselves on folding stools on Mesones for this parade and I took a hundred more photographs. At one point a boys' choir was stopped in front of us and one cute boy right in front of me kept wanting to see my photos as I checked them in the back of my camera.

He mugged and begged to have his photo taken, so I did, even though he was supposed to stay in solemn character in his altar boy clothes. He was so thrilled! He sang even more loudly after that.

The choir director kept motioning to the kids to bring it down, softer, but they were bellowing their little hearts out. The boy's friends then wanted to see the shot and have their photos taken, too. The choir director glared at me, and I blamed him for my stopping as I told the kids, "*No mas.*" I bowed my head as if I were praying to return the boys to their mood.

Two twin girls about 1-1/2, in yellow pinafores, made the long waits before and during the procession quite enjoyable, playing with anything in sight, chasing each other, lifting their dresses to irritate their parents, making friends with everyone who passed by, dancing in the street.

The little girl next to me had a sword fight with me using our sticks left over from our cotton candy buys. Hadn't had cotton candy in some 55 years—there's a reason, I forgot how little flavor it has. But the melting sensation on my tongue somehow added to the magic.

I asked permission to take her photo before we disbanded, too, and her father was so proud. In English he told her to say cheese. She looked at him like, what the heck are you talking about, but she smiled broadly anyway, a femme fatale in the making. I'd practiced my Spanish on her mother, she'd practiced her English on me.

After the last float and band, we greeted new friends we'd made as we walked home in the perfect weather. The evening couldn't have happened anyplace else I've lived.

On Saturday is another procession from the Oratorio at dark, in which women in black, wearing white gloves and black lace mantillas on their heads, carry floats such as the Virgin of Dolores, who has a very long black velvet and silver train. They stop every half a block to rest, ladders appearing from discreet hiding places to hold up the heavy floats for a few minutes. I can't help checking out the shoes worn by the women carrying their heavy burdens for several miles. Some of the younger ones do the entire route in stilettos. At 10 P.M. at the Oratorio and Parroquia are solemn ceremonies welcoming the Risen Christ as the Light of the World.

On Easter Sunday are early masses, low key compared to U.S. churches, no show of fine new Easter bonnets here. Around 11 A.M. is the explosion of the Judases. About 30 life-sized paper maché effigies are strung in front of the Police Station at the Jardín as if from high clotheslines.

Each one has a wick that is set afire, one at a time. Each paper maché statue then revolves to a loud whistling hum, and blows up in a loud gunpowder explosion, sending pieces of paper maché legs, arms and faces throughout the crowd that scrambles for the pieces.

Originally people made the statues to resemble their enemies and political figures. Now it is more of an honor to be chosen, and people pay the cost to have an effigy of themselves hung and exploded. Each effigy has the name of its sponsoring San Miguel business or civic leader written below it.

Every explosion is excruciatingly loud, and the kids riding on their fathers' shoulders scream at the sound and try to bury themselves in their fathers' hair. Dogs wail. It is funny hours later to see a youngster walking down the sidewalk still grasping tight to a paper maché arm he captured that morning.

Great fun. *Semana Santa* is not to be missed in San Miguel. And the whole week was free, except for a few donations thrown into passing church baskets and into a *Las Tunas* tambourine.

Since then the flood of activities has continued, though this is low season. Snowbirds have gone home, while sunbirds escaping Texas heat and those on summer vacations are yet to arrive.

Fireworks were so loud tonight that car alarms were set off throughout the city. We walked down to the square a couple nights ago and a parade broke out, no reason we could tell, only a few young people who dug up their Day of the Locos costumes and decided to let loose. A masked woman in a turban made sure to collect donations from anyone willing to give—which is why I think it was some kids who decided to see if they could make some money from their energy. Or maybe it was a neighborhood trying to collect funds to pay for their colonia's festivities. We're still guessing.

Usually parades are not vehicles for people collecting so blatantly—though the churches and neighborhood groups get donations to pay for them all some way. Of course at most events there are always a few nurses in white taking blood pressures in return for a donation to the local battered women's shelter, which we are happy to support. Never had my blood pressure taken so much in my life outside of hospital stays.

A drug prevention program has a different tactic—their volunteers slap a little smiley face sticker on your shoulder indicating you've donated, so most people then feel required to actually donate. The sticker wards off the other collectors the rest of the day.

The beggars and kids selling Chiclets turn out in high numbers for all big events and on every weekend when the DFers pour into town. (DF is the abbreviation for the Federal District of Mexico City and so tourists from there are called DFers.)

Oh no, the maid showed up at 9 A.M. and did a fantastic job! The hotel owner apparently didn't give her the word. Was it my bad Spanish? Lacey didn't bark, and we felt guilty because the maid outdid herself in cleaning. Maybe she did get the word and decided to ignore it. And we thought this problem was solved. It was as if I'd spit in the wind. She keeps coming.

But now Maria, the maid who worked independently in the afternoons until she broke her arm a few months ago, has reappeared with a doctor's note saying she can return to work. The neighbors next to us snatched her up for 1-4 Tuesdays, Thursdays, and Saturdays, and we hired her for 1-4 Mondays, Wednesdays, and Fridays. The landlord seems pleased and the maid who hated our pets is history. This time apparently she got the memo.

Maria actually moves everything when she cleans. The dust bunnies under the sofa are gone. She snatches glasses out of my hand when I go to put them in the sink and washes them immediately. She dusts, even using a long-handled feather brush to reach high places that have never been dusted before.

She looks for clothes Norma has washed in the washing machine and rushes up on the roof to hang them for us. She shakes them out before hanging so that they don't need ironing. She collects them before she leaves and has them folded neatly and put into the right drawers and shelves.

She's figured out the weird storage arrangements we have for various "stuff" and gets it right almost all the time. She's even unafraid of the vacuum cleaner! Our rug thanks us. She loves our pets, though Lacey still would as soon nip her if she could.

The neighbors have talked to us about the possibility of going in together to buy Maria her first television set ever next Christmas, in addition to her required Christmas bonus. Or maybe she will prefer a stove or refrigerator. One of our more cynical friends here says he wants to hear our next report on her in a month when the honeymoon is over. Honeymoons don't end, do they?

The month of *Semana Santa*, whether it falls in March or April, is as busy as September Indepedencia festivities. But every month has its highlights.

12

April

This month is peaceful after the packed Easter ceremonies. April and May are the hottest months. We're glad we had ceiling fans installed in three rooms of our apartment.

Norma's daughter came to visit for a week, and to ease her insecurities about visiting Mexico after her coworkers kept telling her she would be kidnapped, etc., we drove into Querétaro and then took the bus to Mexico City Airport to meet her, rather than letting her take the shuttle.

We try never to drive at night, but with her in the car with us from Querétaro to San Miguel we had three near catastrophes as dusk encroached.

A big tan cow walked onto the highway and the car ahead of us hit it. The car spun and the cow hit the road and it spun, and we were able to stop in time before hitting either one. The cow got up and ran off the road! The people in the car that hit it were in shock but otherwise seemed to be okay, as were we. Their car wasn't. One was using a cell phone so we knew help would be on the way.

Then a few miles farther we missed being in a collision between a car and a man on a bicycle. The bicycle rider got up and was walking, if shakily, so he seemed to be okay, too.

Right after that we almost hit a big dog running across the road. Once in Michigan we hit and killed a big dog that ran right out in front of us at dusk. The accident caused something like $600 damage to our car, not to mention the horror and guilt we felt. So we know that hitting a dog is not a minor event.

I am still picturing that cow spinning in the road, cars braking and veering all over the place, and then the cow getting up and running off to its herd mates on the side of the road. I doubt I will ever forget that image. Norma's daughter kept saying, "Does that happen all the time here?" Otherwise, she loved SMA and is already thinking about retiring here—in another 25 years.

We love to dance and went to Club 27 for another fantastic evening. What excellent dancers we have in SMA. A half dozen of the older foreign men could have been Arthur Murray instructors. One tall guy with a gray ponytail outshone all his partners and everyone else on the floor. He had the '50s moves down as well as the big band style and more current dance steps, too.

Two preteen girls who obviously had taken dance lessons were a hoot dancing with each other and with various parents and other elders throughout the evening, when they weren't dashing up and down the aisles showing their age. Several couples performed the tango with all the prerequisite ankle twists and dips, very cool.

Music alternated between a half-dozen Latin beat tunes, then rock from the '50s and '60s, followed by Sinatra and big band, more salsa, rock from the '70s and '80s, tango, etc. Something for everyone.

For those who complain about the high costs of drinks in SMA, entry was $5 each, which included two drinks and peanuts as well as the dance floor. It's a fun little club with life-sized photos of John Travolta, Elvis, and Astaire around the walls to inspire your steps. Norma and I thought we were pretty good but we were surrounded by really hot dancers, as entertaining to watch as to dance ourselves.

It's every Thursday night, on Hidalgo between Mesones and Insurgentes, closer to Insurgentes. (The building, also called The Ring, used to host cock fights.)

We happened upon a ceremony in the Jardín and after asking around found that the day is the blessing of the municipal vehicles, including around a dozen brand new shiny white garbage trucks. Also lined up around the Jardín were dump trucks, road graders, police cars and motorcycles. School children in plaid uniforms and sanitation workers in blue jumpsuits stood in attendance as government officials made speeches and the priest swung the holy water, climbing inside every vehicle to bless the interiors as well. Another day is the blessing of the taxis—don't plan on catching a cab that morning.

We went down to the Jardín around 9:30 P.M. and one of the three *Las Tunas* musician troupes was doing a concert on the sidewalk to the left of the Parroquia, a dozen men in medieval costume performing under the arches.

The lead singer tonight had shoulder length blondish red hair, waved and curled to my envy. He pretended to be a woman throughout the performance, cuddling up to the handsome young men in the audience, who were not too horrified. We clapped and sang along, and the audience rocked to the songs. The lead had a great time doing almost a burlesque, at one time pretending to strip, but never turning off anyone that I could see.

The group did polkas, traditional Mexican songs, and a sort of limbo where the leader brought a conga line under a couple's bridged arms, which kept slipping lower with each pass, until most of the audience could no longer go under. The kids smirked when they could still do it easily.

Some group members circulated through the crowd passing out plastic cups of wine, selling CDs, and taking up a collection. Mariachi bands could be heard competing elsewhere in the Jardín. Several clowns blew up and tied balloon animals for kids with a rock music accompaniment.

A group of drummers performed on the right side of the Jardín with a guy twirling the currently popular streamer-ball combination toy that kids have been enjoying all week in the Jardín. He made a real act out of it.

Church chimes rang out like mad at 10:40—was it a call to 11 P.M. Mass? A few fireworks went off someplace out of sight but we could hear their pops and streaming hisses. The tourists in town took more photos of the Parroquia glowing pink in the night, and teenagers flirted with each other and older folks smiled in memory.

Another sight—a Harley-Davidson that must have cost $20,000 or more with all its chrome was parked at one end of the Jardín, accompanied by less glistening cycles. Kids were blowing bubbles shining against the evening sky everywhere we looked. Mama Mia's looked packed with salsa dancers.

Just another perfect evening in San Miguel.

13

May, Coming Around Again

As we approach our fourth year anniversary here, we keep going back to most of the events we have described that make up a year in San Miguel. We're as enthusiastic as in our first year, though some gringos get jaded: "If you've seen one redwood, you've seen them all."

If you've seen one *Semana Santa* weekend, you've seen them all. If you find Midnight masses Christmas Eve inspiring and beautiful, would you never go to more than one in your life? I don't think I will ever stop wanting to take part in the whole town's involvement in these intense religious ceremonies, even if I'm no longer a Catholic. It's part of belonging to San Miguel.

As others told us would happen, we decided that once was quite enough for the Running of the Bulls, and we don't always run outside every time we hear the sounds of drums and bands to see what parade has sprung up someplace.

We don't even hear the fireworks much anymore, but when we do, especially at 6 A.M., we're more likely to curse and throw a pillow over our heads and try to get back to sleep. We don't always stop to think why we should be tolerant of the noise. But then again we don't usually hear them.

The board members of our Arizona RV park's HOA used to say that organizing lesbians was like herding cats, not exactly an original analogy. Today Norma and the neighbors literally are herding cats, trying to keep up with new felines who stray into our courtyard before they have or cause a litter

We're not the only ones doing this. We keep running across many people, expats and Mexicans alike, who feed stray dogs and cats and sometimes manage to get them fixed. My art teacher brings in grain to feed the pigeons on the classroom patio in Belles Artes. And of course there are benefits all the time to support the Society for the Protection of Animals and Amigos de Animales.

Norma catches the cats by putting canned cat food in a dish inside our pet carrier and then placing the carrier so that its half-opened door is against our porch wall. When Norma sees the tip of a tail disappear into the cage, she opens the front door fast. The front door pushes the pet carrier flush against the porch wall and closes the carrier's door, trapping the cat inside.

It takes two of us to keep the container's door shut on the thrashing cat while we fasten the lock. We hear there are some Have a Heart cages in town that we should have tracked down. Sometimes we think our vet charges for the sterilizations based on how wild and mean each cat is.

A vet back in Michigan told us that outdoor cats live an average of three years, indoor-outdoor cats have a life expectancy of about seven years, and a cat kept totally inside will likely live to seventeen. Our two old cats we brought to San Miguel did not quite make it to seventeen.

Maria, our new maid, filled the gap in our lives, though. She brought us a tiny piece of mewling fur that she'd found crushed in a rock pile. Dr. Vasquez saved the drab tabby's life, though he had to amputate her front leg at the shoulder. Bibi hops around the house like a rabbit and is unaware she is disabled, though she'll work that shoulder lump as if it were a complete leg. She'll have to be an indoor cat all her life, unable to survive an encounter with a wild male.

And then Maria found a tiny orange male wailing on a fence post and brought him to us after Calicat died and we needed a kitty fix desperately. We called the baby Ali, short for either Alejandro or Alejandra, since we didn't know yet if the cat was male or female, and also short for Ali Baba, Alley Cat and Alley Oops because of his propensity for breaking expensive ceramics and glassware.

Maria also brought us two nondescript male puppies that she'd found abandoned in the garbage; we brought those to the SPA and have told Maria, *"No mas."* So doing our part in solving Mexico's unwanted pet problem is one aspect of our life here.

Everybody we know is involved in some charity or another. A friend moved here and helped the wonderful maid and cook she discovered start her own business, showing one Mexican woman the way to more income—but now she has to find another maid.

This same friend learned almost accidentally of the three orphanages in San Miguel, the one that is farthest away from Centro has the most severe financial problems. The young orphan girls are sent out to beg on the streets when their home's money runs out. Our friend has now joined a group of women on a crusade to help this orphanage, and to help the girls learn other ways to raise money besides begging.

This is how newcomers to San Miguel get involved: they find out about a need that hits their interests and talents right, and they dive in. There's no way anyone with a good heart can be bored in San Miguel. The needs are too great. And there are dozens of excellent charities helping to meet the needs. Some cynics say that many expats would rather found a new charity than try to work with an existing one.

A big part of a non-wealthy expat's life in Mexico is worrying about health care, not that we didn't worry about health care back in the States, too. A new 60-bed Class Three hospital is being built outside of town, between the new municipal offices and the jail. It should be able to handle almost every medical problem short of something like a liver transplant.

We have heard from informed sources that it will offer a health insurance plan open to anyone, even with pre-existing conditions. If that insurance plan comes into reality, it will make all of our lives much easier.

Medicare does not cover care for anyone living outside of the U.S. Some private U.S. health insurance plans cover medical emergencies for those on vacation outside of the U.S., though you'll

probably have to pay up front and then submit your bill for reim-
bursement. A few expensive private plans will cover you anywhere.
Anyone considering moving outside of the U.S. should check medical insurance options and existing policies thoroughly.

Since prescription costs, doctor visits, and hospital stays are so
much cheaper in Mexico for exactly the same drugs and services,
expats often find that paying their medical bills out of pocket here
costs less than their co-pays did back in the States. Those with more
money may maintain their U.S. private insurance or find a Mexican insurance plan that will work for them.

Mexico has a low-cost (maybe $300 a year) government-sponsored
health insurance plan, IMSS, but we understand that you cannot get
in with pre-existing conditions, and a thorough medical exam is required. More likely some days in some offices we could get in, other
days not. That's something we have to check into soon. We've heard
some expats rave about their care under the program, while others
have reported bad experiences—the same as with U.S. hospitals.

Some of us hope that we will be able to get to the States to use
our Medicare coverage for a serious condition, and we keep what
we hope will be enough in the bank to pay for emergency care here
until we can be stabilized enough to get to the States. A friend who
had a critical heart attack was revived three times at Hospital de la
Fe. His total hospital bill was about $4,000.

Later he went to Querétaro for an angiogram that involved an
overnight stay, his wife remaining in his room on a sofa bed with
him. Total cost was $3,000 out of pocket. I think that was my co-
pay for my angiogram in Phoenix.

Another friend with melanoma goes back and forth to the States
for her treatment, having MRIs and other expensive medical proce-
dures done in Mexico and bringing the test results with her back to
the States. Another friend had to move back to the States when she
developed a serious heart condition requiring very expensive spe-
cialized care for which she needed to use her Medicare coverage.

We think we're so much healthier here, with all of our walking
and eating better and less stress, that we'll do our best to remain
in San Miguel even if a serious medical problem develops. Angeles

Hospital in Querétaro and hospitals in San Luis Potosi, Guanajuato, and Mexico City are as good as most in the U.S.

Getting good health care is not a given in the U.S., either. Norma has had three close relatives die from hospital misdiagnoses.

I had a very serious medical problem after living 14 months in San Miguel that required that I go back to Phoenix for three months for major surgery. Doctors there said the Mexican doctors had done everything right. The surgeon I'd finally seen here had said I needed immediate surgery or I would die. That was a Wednesday afternoon.

The next morning we were on the road back to Phoenix, where we had a place to stay and were familiar with good doctors. I'd been told by surgeons through the years that the next time I needed major surgery, I probably would not survive. I did not want to have risky surgery in a small hospital with less access to substantial quantities of my blood type and no experience with my unusual problem.

I won't go into all my medical history, just to say that this time the surgeon assured me my entire insides were rebuilt and it's possible I will have no more medical problems, at least not of the same kind I've suffered from for more than 30 years.

Many times Norma has been told I would not make it through a surgery. And yet here I am. Norma thinks it's some gene that goes pop at an appointed time that determines when you die. I've got a multi-million-dollar body, if not a house.

I've been hospitalized twice at Hospital de la Fe, the first time before the Phoenix surgery, for a blockage that the doctors helped unblock by doing exactly what doctors across the U.S. had always done for my numerous blockages: insert a naso-gastric tube and an IV, stop all eating, and require me to walk continually around the hospital corridors while hospitalized until the blockage broke free.

The experience was almost the same as in U.S. small hospitals, except for the use of manual gravity-driven IV drips rather than the expensive computerized electronic IV drip machines I was used to.

The daily rate at de la Fe for a private room was $75 U.S. My total bill for a two-day stay including the ER entry care and doctors was around $270. Immediate cost to a patient in the U.S. who is hospitalized under Medicare is more than $850 before Medicare kicks in.

Mexican hospitals expect patients will have someone accompany them to attend to personal needs, such as fetching pillows and even assisting in feeding, that we in the States expect a nurse's aide to do. There will probably be a cot and meals provided for the guest if needed. Interesting fact: there are no elevators or stairs in the hospital side of de la Fe, only a long ramp between floors so that the male attendants have to push patients on a gurney.

Other things were different—in each room was a stack of thick, plush, fur-like blankets, far warmer than the thin sheets handed out at U.S. hospitals, but I doubt if they were washed between each use.

My IV pole was the plain metal gravity only kind, not the mechanical pump IVs that keep very good record of how much medication is delivered and how fast, and that sound an alarm whenever there is a slowing of flow to the vein. With the manual ones, the first sign of a problem was when my arm started swelling, indicating a blockage or blown vein, very painful. A mechanical pump would have indicated the problem before pain and tissue damage occurred.

And when I had to walk with my rusted old IV pole, the wheels wouldn't turn on the irregular tile floor. I ended up carrying the whole thing around, until I realized that I only needed to carry the IV bag above my head, minus the pole. Duh. I had to use the bedside list of English-Spanish medical phrases a couple of times with the nurses, though the doctors all spoke pretty good English.

These are the kinds of differences to take into consideration when deciding whether a retiree's medical care can be handled in Mexican facilities.

The second time I was hospitalized at de la Fe was for a minor

biopsy and surgical removal of some stitches that were still causing problems two months after I'd returned home from the Phoenix surgery. The surgeon performed the operation in the de la Fe
emergency room, with no assistance.

Once the overhead surgical lamp went out. He called to a nurse
who came and shook the lamp until it went back on. For two hours
in the ER, the surgeon's fees, $150 for the biopsy, and all the sup-
plies, my total bill was about $250 U.S.

After four years in SMA I had a third experience with a San
Miguel hospital, this time the Hospital General, the public facility.
I'd gone to a meeting that day and had five cups of strong coffee,
though I'm supposed to drink only decaf. At 3 A.M. I awoke with
tachycardia, rapid heart beat.

Quickly I read up on it on the internet and decided it wasn't serious, there were many ways to make a heart slow to normal, such
as rubbing your eyes hard and splashing very cold water on your
face. The medical information websites recommended getting an
EKG afterward anyway, just to be sure there wasn't some continuing serious problem. Since it wasn't serious, and we figured an EKG
can be done anyplace, we decided to try Hospital General.

It took only half an hour to be seen (sometimes I've waited 16
hours in a U.S. ER), and the doctors spent a full hour with me and
did the EKG. I'd typed my entire medical history out on two computer pages, though I hadn't had time to have it translated accurately into Spanish. Norma was ready to start calling around to find
a friend fluent in Spanish if I needed it. The doctors were surprised
I had done my own medical history, they didn't know quite what
to make of it, and they took turns trying to read and understand
what I'd written. Most had at least some knowledge of English, and
though I could tell them what I thought I needed, I couldn't understand the nuances of what they were telling me in return.

They were able to find a young English-speaking doctor. The
SMA Hospital General takes part in a Spanish language immersion

program for U.S. doctors who want to learn Spanish in a medical setting so that they can better treat Mexican patients in the States.

The U.S. doctors are mainly there during the day, and it was
too early for one of them to be around, but this young Mexican
doctor was able to explain to me that I was fine, and I should see a
cardiologist to review my meds since my life had changed so much
since I was last reviewed.

He said there was no cardiologist connected with Hospital General yet, but there was an internist that the hospital used, and he
gave me the contact information. He said the internist would be far
less expensive than the cardiologists who treated primarily gringo
patients, and he felt the doctor would be almost as good,

So that's another decision to make: start up with a local cardiologist, or go to this internist who works out of Hospital General. Everything will change when the new 60-bed Hospital General
opens sometime in 2006. We'll see who's on staff then.

The EKG machine wasn't a sleek portable model the size of a
laptop U.S. hospitals use now; it was a bit clunky. A man was being
taught how to use the machine by another man in the process of doing my EKG, so I wondered how thoroughly people were trained.

There were no hospital gowns, not even a skimpy one, and the
drapes didn't reach totally around the ER bed, so people walking
by could look in to see me naked above the waist. But I was given
my EKG printout to take to the next doctor with me, and I was assured the internist had reviewed it and I was fine.

I went out into the waiting room and got Norma, and we headed for the patient accounts window, dreading what we would be
charged. Are you ready? Six dollars! Only 61 pesos, total! I'm optimistic that charges at the new Hospital General will be low, too. I
think $2,000 is the least I've ever gotten charged at a U.S. ER, and
around $900 was the patient's cost before Medicare kicked in.

We are often asked if someone with a disability can live in Mexico.
It depends on the disability and often on the town being considered.

In general, Mexican cities are not adapted to mobility problems.

We see some Mexicans walking on the narrow, irregular sidewalks with metal walkers, and some people in wheelchairs, though their path must be carefully planned to take advantage of driveways instead of curb cuts and to avoid the worst sidewalks.

Several blind beggars make their rounds on the streets with apparent ease, knowing the hazards well. I don't think even the best-trained guide dog could distinguish every single Mexican sidewalk hole and eye-level window box hazard.

The mile-high altitude of cities in the central plateau might be a problem for some people with breathing problems, though most people seem to be able to adjust after a few days. I saw one parking space on Mesones reserved as a handicapped space for a couple of months, but there was no sidewalk cut anywhere nearby to make the space usable, at least not if the disability required a wheelchair.

The Jardín was renovated in 2005 and handicap cuts were included in many places for easier access. New sidewalks and streets generally have curb cuts, but so many of the sidewalks are so tiny and the streets are so narrow and stairs are so prevalent that San Miguel could never be totally handicap accessible.

The big box stores in Querétaro have handicap spaces but usually there is a thick chain or row of grocery carts across the entrance so you have to drive around looking for a parking lot attendant to open access to the space. There is no understanding that some people have "hidden disabilities," like heart or breathing conditions that make it hard for them to walk any distance. If you're not actually in a wheelchair you're not considered handicapped.

SMA is not alone—the other Mexican cities we've visited may have regular smooth cement sidewalks in some places, but you'll still find a utility pole sticking up in the middle of a narrow one so that no wheelchair or walker could possibly use it, and no curb cuts nearby to help. You have to keep looking down to make sure there isn't a hole, marked or not by something like a red-painted brick, or a metal plate for utility access that doesn't fit tightly, leaving a gap to catch a toe or a ridge to trip you.

Especially in hilly areas like in SMA, a store or home may not have access at sidewalk level. Half the narrow sidewalk is taken up by a step or two leading into the store or home, or there is a sunken step leading to that door that an unsuspecting person could fall into. And step heights are never regular.

Even in Mexico City where there are many blocks with "normal" sidewalks, the drivers don't drive carefully enough to allow you to cross the street with confidence if you're not agile. SMA drivers in general seem more polite. The streets are narrower, many are one-way, and they are so crowded that drivers can't get up much speed, so they're more likely to stop and allow you to cross if you need some time. Taxi drivers in particular seem very polite here.

But Oaxaca? I felt in fear of my life every time I had to cross a street. I can't imagine trying to do so in a wheelchair or with a walker.

Another question that the two of us are often asked is about gays and lesbians living in Mexico. This book grew out of my editing of our first three months' letters to friends about our retirement in San Miguel for an internet website on Mexico. The column was from the point of view of two open lesbians falling in love with San Miguel, like so many others fall in love with SMA.

We are not the first to have decided within three days of arriving in SMA that we were going to move here. It is a common story—lots of people fall in love with San Miguel.

Others don't, not wanting any part of Mexican life outside of vacations. Others choose to move to other areas of Mexico or Latin America, cities or remote areas, mountains or beaches, whatever fits their needs and wants. Each person's decision-making process is unique.

We find we are totally accepted here as lesbians. I have not run into a single word of negativity here, less than I experienced in the gay ghettos of Los Angeles.

(Four years later one woman said she didn't consider our 27-year relationship as valid, though. And one guy on an e-mail list insulted my sexuality until I put him on block. That's it in four years. I received worse than that at some family gatherings.)

Plenty of gays and lesbians live here, plus some I think could be considered bisexual and others who might consider themselves transgendered, though none have had any reason to tell me their sexuality.

It isn't like LA where we immediately sought out the gay and lesbian communities and were fairly segregated within them. We fit in well even in groups like the American Legion Women's Auxiliary, which I always pictured in my own bigoted way as full of bigots, but they're wonderful women and totally accepting of us.

The American Legion back in a Michigan town where I lived for seven years was definitely not accepting, as a comparison—my dad was a member and he surely never mentioned me or introduced me to his friends. Gays were extremely closeted there, though we refused to be, and we knew several had had negative experiences and comments. It's been easier here.

❦

There was one gay SMA bar, 100 Angeles, which was only open late Saturday nights, but it closed in 2002. In August, 2005, it was replaced by Proud, a disco bar. Its flyers and ads proclaimed all were welcome, with symbols showing men and men, women and women, and women and men.

We went to opening night. It was supposed to open at 9. When we got there at 10, after seeing *Kinsey* at Villa Jacaranda, only 20 were there, half of us older gringos, no one dancing to the slow music with videos on the screen.

At 10:15 they switched to '70s disco and a light show. Suddenly there were 35 people in the bar, almost every one of them on the dance floor, including us. Lots of gorgeous young Mexicans, women and men, some of the women in stilettos and tight skirts, others in jeans and boots, all dancing together, not at all clear who was with whom and who was gay or straight. Fantastic! Beautiful people, fun to watch, men and women.

By 11 older Mexicans started to come in, including more men, and I counted 75 before I gave up. Some of the younger Mexicans came over to talk to us, thrilled to see us there. At least one of the older gringas was a lesbian who used to live in SMA and now lives someplace cheaper in Mexico, visiting friends in SMA. She was happy to see we have a gay bar again.

We were tuckered by 11:15, having danced our fool tails off, and more people were still streaming in. A gay friend who used to go to 100 Angeles three years ago had said that the older gay men probably wouldn't show up until much later. We couldn't keep up that long to check it out later—still recovering from a flu bug or something. I didn't want to make a splash my first night falling off the elevated dance floor.

One man behind the bar said that he was happy we came and to tell all our friends. A woman at the door who seemed to be the owner said that she was going to place announcements in Atención and that Proud would be open every Friday and Saturday night, available for parties, too. On Wednesday nights she hoped to eventually have live music, perhaps a piano bar.

We'd danced in just that way, everybody together, gay and straight, total acceptance, at Finnegan's restaurant when they had Irish music Friday nights, two owners ago, and at Club 27, which has dancing open to everybody on Thursday nights. This bar felt very appropriate for San Miguel.

I can't imagine any of the younger Latinas at the LA bars coming up to us and saying how glad they were to see us. Older women were ignored, and Latinas and gringas tended to be separate even in the same room. I got the feeling the same was true for older gay men at their bars. Here, the unity of all of us having fun together was really important to me.

Next door at Pancho & Lefty's, same entrance as Petit Four, crowds were in the streets. Mesones near the Teatro Angela Peralta was a very swinging street now. Folks were dining at Nirvana and Tio Lucas, too. The music levels at Proud were about right for us. I think I've heard that the music can get too loud into the morning at Pancho & Lefty's, and I've always felt that the younger crowd there was not at all inviting to us as we passed by. At Proud, everyone was welcome. Another perfect night in San Miguel!

But when a gay friend we'd told about Proud went the following week around 11, there was no one there except him. The only gay bar in San Miguel might not make it this time, either. Last time we walked past the door, there were no more posters up for Proud. I don't know if it will return. (Later there were no signs it had ever existed, and Pancho & Lefty's is gone, too. Months after that, a new sign, Rincon de la Alebrije, went up over the former Proud's wooden door. Rincon means corner or hideaway. Alebrijes are wooden sculptures of whimsical toy animals made near Oaxaca. Sometimes when we're walking home late on weekend nights, the door is open. Is a gay bar there or not? Will one be there the night you want it? We have no idea.) SMA hosted a festival of sexual diversity in July, 2006—plenty of gays here.

<hr />

The whole issue of why people socialize with some people and not with others, especially across racial and cultural and class and international boundaries, is highly complex. You'll get no simple answer from me because I don't see any.

The isolation many single people, gay or straight, feel in a coupled world applies here as well, though I see older single women here having more opportunities to have fun and enjoy activities than in most places in the States.

Single straight gringas outnumber single straight gringos probably four to one, some say six to one. And I know several expats who have found wonderful Mexican spouses or partners. Other cross-cultural couples have not survived the problems.

My lesbianism is a small part of the total of who I am, and I make friends usually on the basis of all that I am. A Mexican lesbian and I who had nothing else in common but our sexuality would have no reason to be friends, even if my Spanish were better.

The straight Mexican man in my art class who is my age, who paints in a similar style, who can give me help when I can't seem to get the perspective right, and I can help him point out where he needs to have more contrast, who enjoys the same music, who laughs at the same things, might turn into a friend even if I'm constantly looking up words on my pocket translator to communicate.

Come on in, the water's fine. (Oh, not the actual water, you still need to drink bottled water.)

People of color have asked whether they will feel comfortable in San Miguel or other parts of Mexico. As I've written earlier, I don't feel as if I know very much about racism any more, now that I see it in a far broader perspective. I can make a wild guess that only a handful of African-Americans live in SMA, though many more visit, often on a regular basis.

From conversations with some of them, they say they do not experience as much discrimination in SMA as they do back in the States—their being from the U.S. or Canada outweighs their being black.

And like being called a *gordo*, a fat person, is not an insult here as it is in the States, many words that would be racial insults in the U.S. are only common nicknames denoting color in Mexico.

Not that Mexico is not color-conscious. Color-consciousness has been a part of Mexico from the days of the Conquistadors when Spaniards born in Spain had much higher status than those of full Spanish descent who were born in the New World, and both were considered much higher in status than anyone of mixed heritage, and all of the above had higher status than Indians.

In the same way, Mexicans of African heritage often are quoted as saying that they are invisible in Mexican history and awareness. At some periods in Mexican history there were more African-Mexicans than Spaniards. Slaves descended from Africa worked the mines as well as Indians.

The controversy in 2005 over official Mexican post office stamps that carried a cartoon character with what would be considered stereotypical African features stirred the issue across national boundaries.

African-Americans were furious that thousands of the official Mexican government stamps were coming into the U.S., while many in Mexico said that the U.S. had no right to criticize Mexico on racial issues, since Mexico had none of the enormous history of legalized segregation that the U.S. did. The fight ran deep.

I cannot give fair balance to the story now, nor to any real understanding of the complexity of race relations in the U.S. or Mexico, or whether any particular person of color will be comfortable living in San Miguel or any other part of Mexico.

My feeling is that there is less prejudice against African Americans and against Asians in Mexico than in the States. Each individual person of color reacts to situations differently and is probably treated differently depending on many issues—skin color, overall likeability and personality, previous experience and attitudes, and individual encounters with racist or welcoming persons in Mexico.

As with any expats, some have wonderful experiences here, while others may have one overwhelmingly negative occurrence that will override all other experiences and send them back to the States.

There is no one answer for whether one particular person of color will like SMA any more than whether one gay or lesbian will like SMA, or a person with a disability will be able to live in any one area of SMA or Mexico, or whether a single woman or man will find happiness here, or whether anyone else will find Mexico is for them.

That isn't a copout answer. Everyone is unique. Our story is ours alone. Remember the five blind men describing the same elephant based on what they touched in front of them.

Another question we are frequently asked is exactly what do things cost in Mexico. We've given the prices we've paid throughout this book. Here are some more examples.

We splurge on Sunday brunch as our main meal of the day maybe once a month. The rest of that day we eat cereal, fruits and veggies. We usually go to Cafe de la Parroquia, and the bill runs

147 pesos for two (about $14.70) for this menu: French toast, migas scrambled eggs (with various things like onions and ham and cheese and tortilla strips and jalapenos stirred into the eggs), *chilaquiles* with chicken, Diet Coke and coffee.

With the meal comes a basket of three baguettes, butter, strawberry marmalade, pancake syrup, four corn tortillas, a wonderful salsa verde with avocado pieces in it, and a small bowl of homemade black beans. The place is usually about half gringo and Mexican, and there's usually a wait of 15-20 minutes. While we wait we take turns going into Tecolote book store in the same courtyard.

The menu has maybe 40 choices, mostly traditional Mexican dishes. Our other favorites there include their side of thick-sliced bacon, tamales either in husks or in casserole baked with cheese and green salsa, meatballs in gravy with rice and beans, or chile rellenos. Our brunch meal has been as low as 110 pesos, $11 U.S.

Today we went to Harry's for Sunday brunch. When we sat down at noon (no waiting, the place is big, with four rooms and the bar) there were four tables of Mexicans and three of gringos. By the time we left three more tables of gringos had been seated. These are of course sloppy guesses—that light-skinned couple in the rear, woman with blonde hair that looked natural, might have been Mexicans of more Spanish descent. I couldn't hear whether they were speaking English or Spanish.

One of the couples I guessed to be Mexican could have been born in the U.S. and speaking primarily English since I only heard a Spanish phrase when I passed by. Obviously I didn't do a scientific survey, but we usually go by surface appearances anyway, such is the pity.

Our bill was 180 pesos, about $18 US. The menu has at least 50 food choices, including Sunday brunch and the day's specials, and there is a full bar, with mimosas the specialty for weekend brunch.

Dishes include Cajun specialties, traditional Mexican dishes and U.S. choices. One of the day's specials was a 21-ounce Angus aged T-bone, $21, plus the usual fresh crawfish and oysters. Other dishes we love for brunch include a U.S.-style huge breakfast burrito, crab cakes with poached eggs, eggs benedict, banana and pecan hotcakes, and seafood crepes. The waiter brought two small free margaritas with the menus.

This time we had a small order of *chilaquiles* with about seven ounces of marinated tender skirt steak, a Monte Cristo sandwich, bread and rolls tray with butter and apricot marmalade, two fruit cups, coffee and a Diet Coke. In the background was live jazz from two local musicians.

The wait staff at both places spoke both English and Spanish, and at both places the service was excellent. The owner of Cafe de la Parroquia is a Venezuelan and French woman who works herself silly all during the rush hours pouring coffee refills and seating newcomers. She's very gracious, greeting everyone, stopping occasionally for a smoke break herself out on the patio.

Many people bring small children to Cafe de la Parroquia; that's rarer at Harry's. I didn't smell any smoke at all this morning at Harry's, and the owner, Bob, worked the tables, making sure everyone was fine, remembering names and favorites.

Both are lovely experiences, and the live jazz, free margaritas and included fruit cups make up for the slightly higher prices at Harry's. Harry's is a half block off the Jardín, Cafe de la Parroquia is a short block and half a long block away from the Jardín. Take your pick, we love them both. We could have just as nice a breakfast at other Mexican-owned restaurants for under $9 for two. Some smaller breakfasts at some Mexican restaurants are around $2.50.

Housing prices are extremely variable, the greatest demand for lower-cost homes. I happened to pick up a recent Real Estate Review, a 52-page giveaway representing 30 real estate agencies. Twelve houses were listed at more than $1 million, 24 homes including condos were listed at under $150,000 (certainly none in Centro), and hundreds more fell in the middle. I'm not counting lots and commercial properties. And the realtors who advertise in the expensive glossy booklets will have the highest priced properties.

I know of three friends who have found houses recently for $80,000 to $125,000, knowing the houses would need at least $25,000 renovation. (Remodeling costs much less in Mexico because of the lower labor expenses.) One of these houses has been completed and could probably sell for a profit of $55,000 in six months. But the owners love it, it's home for the rest of their lives, they hope.

One friend saw a house listed for around $135,000 one day but was told it was sold. A week later the same house was back on the market, no remodeling done, for more than $200,000. That is the kind of turnaround that is being done right now in this housing bubble.

Another friend found a three-level gorgeous house full of architectural details on two lots with two parking spaces for $150,000, a long walk from Centro but on a bus line. He put $20,000 remodeling into it, and he could probably sell it now for $270,000. But he loves it, and it's now perfect for him to spend the rest of his life here.

I know a gringo who paid $160 a month for a studio in a Mexican-owned complex a few blocks from the Instituto, and several who pay $200-450 a month. You have to look a bit to find the bargains, but they're out there. If you're lucky you'll find a decent two-bedroom under $500 near Centro, less the farther away you get from the Jardín.

More likely you'll easily find a spacious nice place for around $600—check always on what utilities are included. Or you can look for a $1,200 a month and up rental and find plenty to choose from. Some go for $5,000 a week! These rentals seem high to some gringos but low to those coming from housing bubble areas.

⬛◥◤◢◣⬛

Those of us who are renters living in less expensive homes have very little contact with those who are buying the million-dollar homes. In the U.S., I didn't know any millionaires personally, I mixed mostly with people in my same economic level, we moved on different planes from the rich. Same here, among Mexicans and foreigners alike. That's the reality of the housing bubble in SMA to-day. We're not all millionaires in SMA, though sometimes people who don't live here get that impression.

But one day I actually looked for clues in the lives of the people I like and sometimes socialize with, and I realized that eleven of my friends are probably millionaires. I could no longer say that millionaires and folks on Social Security never interacted. It's not that hard to become a millionaire these days. A house in a prime location that escalated wildly in value over the years is enough to do it for many people. None of my millionaire friends ever rub their wealth in my face, though. There are plenty of others in town who do flaunt their money. I've heard that some have even been warned by police to be more low-key.

If you need parking you'll pay $35-$60 a month for a secured lot if parking isn't included in your rent. The new El Cardo 700-space underground parking lot near St. Paul's Episcopal Church charges 90 cents an hour and $94.50 a month for covered park-ing, though free shuttle service to the Jardín less than a mile away is promised.

Electricity can range all over the place—you can pay as little as $15 a month if you're lucky, or more likely $40-$50, or you can get a strange deal where many freeloaders are plugged into your line and you can get bills of several hundred dollars. If you want A/C and electric heating and freezers and Jacuzzis, who knows? You'll probably need special electrical lines run to your place for that kind of load anyway. I don't think most Mexican power lines can handle it. Our lights may go out if a neighbor plugs in an elec-tric space heater.

For a propane fireplace-style heater and hot water heater we spend about $100 a month in the winter to fill the tank monthly, and then $100 about every three months in the summer. Gasoline is around $2.30 a gallon if you do all the conversions from liters to gallons and pesos to dollars—cheaper than most places in the U.S.

A taxi is 20 pesos, around $2, in Centro by day—hand the driv-er that amount rather than asking what the fare is. City buses are four pesos, 40 cents. We used to drive at least 40,000 miles a year in

Phoenix, and now drive less than 1,200 miles a year, excluding if we have to drive to the States. Intercity buses are excellent and cheap compared to driving when you consider tolls and gas.

For those interested in food prices, I kept my receipt from one of our occasional runs to Gigante. We'd gone to the Gemelos for a movie and decided we'd stock up on Diet Pepsi in the 1.5 liter bottles, since we'd brought the car. So of course we threw all sorts of odds and ends into the cart, items we usually buy at local shops. How easy it is to slip back to U.S. practices. Here are some of the prices:

Diet Pepsi, $1.20 the big bottle

Giant white onions, 90 cents a kilo (2.2 pounds)

Green bell peppers, $1.39 kg.

Red bell peppers, $4.29 kg.

Big U.S. style tomatoes, $1.39 kg.

Tomatillos, 99 cents kg.

Jicama (kind of like a white radish the size of a cantaloupe), 79 cents kg.

24 replacement 12-hour mosquito killer tablets to go into a plug-in: $2.30

8-ounce low-fat strawberry yogurt drink, 58 cents

Haas avocado, large, 58 cents

Carrots, 69 cents kg.

Large white baking potatoes, $1.69 kg.

50-teabag size box of Lipton's black tea, $3.15

C-Light, like an envelope of diet Kool-Aid, 39 cents.

Jalapenos, 99 cents kg.

Serranos (small green chiles), 99 cents kg.

Big tube (not the giant size) Colgate toothpaste, $1.33

8 Johnsonville brats (surprise—we've never seen them here before, only at Costco) $4.25.

Granny Smith apples $2.60 kg.

Bananas, $1.49 kg.

A giant papaya, nearly 2 pounds, $1.07.

Packet of Pedigree soft dog food for small breeds over 7 years, 65 cents.

Plastic bag of dried hibiscus blossoms to make many gallons of Jamaica tea, $1.55

Twelve extra large brown eggs, $1.05

Small can of sliced pickled jalapenos for nachos, 40 cents

Roll of Ritz crackers, 75 mg, 18 cents

Campbell's can of condensed soup from squash flowers, $1.23

Campbell's can of condensed chicken soup with fine noodles, $1.23

A liter (about a quart) carton of low-fat *crema*, similar to sour cream, $1.20

Tin of Brunswick *picante* sardines, 90 cents.

Pound of unsalted butter, $1.62

Two 40-watt light bulbs, $.43

Liter (about a quart) bottle of green salsa, $1.40

Cantaloupe, $1.09 kg.

Package of dried laurel leaves (bay leaf spice), 89 cents

Fancy whole-grain mustard, small jar, $1.39

Normally the produce would have been a little cheaper at a neighborhood market. SMA does have several gourmet imported food delis where you can spend $200 U.S. for a bag you can carry in one hand. Or, you can shop at Tuesday Market, Ramirez Market, or San Juan de Dios Market for fresh produce and come away with enough to feed you well for a week for $20, if you use beans, corn, rice, and tortillas as your main protein sources. Meat you can get from 50 cents a pound for lesser cuts (even for chicken livers, which are a high-price delicacy in the States), all the way to $25 a pound for imported jumbo shrimp.

Primarily we buy chicken from Bachoco next to Plaza Civica. A kilo of boneless, skinless chicken breasts pounded flat to the size of a plate, an average of seven breasts in a kilo, costs about $4.90.

On restaurant prices, you can get three very tasty small burritos or tacos (six-inch flour or corn tortilla, usually one filling) for $1.05. At one fish taco stand owned by an expat near Espino's a hefty piece of fried fish in a tortilla is $1.50, same for a chili dog. A hamburger runs around $2.25, and a cup of good coleslaw is around 50 cents. Or you can spend $100 each for dinner at higher-end places.

At Sierra Nevada a mixed drink may be $10, compared to $4 or so many other places, and many restaurants have two for one specials. On some nights Mechi Cano's and other places offer free Margaritas to all *senoritas bonitas*—and don't try to tell us over-60 gringas that we're not pretty young women.

At some of the small Mexican lunch stops you can get a huge meal for $2.50—chicken leg and thigh, rice, beans, and salad plus tortillas and salsa. A can of soda pop can be 40 cents or $2 depending on the restaurant, averaging around $1.25. Coffee can be 45 cents a cup with refills at a small Mexican restaurant to maybe $5 at a gourmet gringo favorite—I think it's around $1.50 most places I go. I buy a kilo of deluxe imported decaf, freshly ground, for $15, which lasts me a month, and I do love my coffee.

I find lovely scoop neck T-shirt style blouses for $4-8 a lot of times in the local shops, though blouses at the boutiques can cost $25 and way up. Good sandals are around $25 at Tuesday Market. Knockoff Nikes are around the same. You can buy a knockoff DVD at Tuesday Market for around $2, or spend $20 for it at a legitimate shop. The Gemelos first-run movie prices are $2.20 Tuesdays and Wednesdays, $3.50 the rest of the week. The $7 admission for an artsy movie at Villa Jacaranda includes popcorn and a drink. Classic movies at the Biblioteca are $5.

Most lectures around town are around $5. Topnotch entertainment at Teatro Angela Peralto can be free, or average around $15 for the best seats down to $8 for the third level. Free entertainment happens many nights at the Jardín. People-watching is always free.

A *paleta* (fruit bar) at Dolphy's on the Jardín is a dollar, or only 50 cents a block away, Dolphy's has a one-scoop small sundae for $2. Or, you can buy a two-scoop sundae of deluxe ice cream at Santa Clara for $4, or buy a dish of ice cream for a buck a block away. Domino's has two-for-one Tuesdays, the basic prices similar to the U.S.

You can trade books with your friends, or there are second hand books at Tecolote bookstore, many for very little, or at Buster's Used Books or at garage sales. New books will cost more than in the U.S. to compensate for the shipping. You can order them from Tecolote bookstore and probably pay about what you would online, counting shipping, duty, and mailing service costs.

Cable TV is as low as $25 but we paid around $50 with a selection of English language channels.

Now we're on Satellite DISH TV, and we can't remember what installation and the dish cost, but it was a lot, maybe $400, plus around $50 a month for a hundred channels, plus $150 or so for a year's service contract and the connection to U.S. channels.

High-speed internet through TelMex using Prodigy Infinitum is around $50 a month. We pay $16 a month for Vonage for our long distance phone service for 500 minutes to or from the States. Unlimited calls are a few dollars more. Our basic TelMex bill for local calls is around $18 a month.

A five-gallon bottle of purified water delivered to our doorstep is $2, including tip, and we use two or three a week. You can get a decent haircut from a Mexican haircutter for around $2.50, or you can go to a high-end salon for $40 or more.

The daily English-language newspaper, the Mexican edition of the *Miami Herald*, is 70 cents if you buy from a newsstand or the two stands in the Jardín, or 80 cents if you buy from a guy taking it door to door, restaurant to restaurant. The weekly *Atención* with an excellent calendar is 80 cents. Other publications with calendars are freebies.

To have a pet spayed at the Society for the Protection of Animals is $27, or the top vet in town charges $40-70 depending on sex and age and shots needed. Poor people can get their pets sterilized for free at the occasional spaying weekends by Amigos de Animales.

Teeth cleaning at our dentist is $40, a simple filling is $40. A woman in town advertises she does really deep dental cleaning for $55—people say it hurts, but if you've got gum disease, that's what you need. Some expats drive to Querétaro for a specialist dentist who is higher.

Doctor visits are as low at $20 ($2 if you drop in to some of the pharmacies and need a prescription written on the spot by their staff doctor), to a high of $50 for most specialists, though a cardiologist can charge double that. You get in right away, and they spend lots of time with you. A private room at Hospital de la Fe was $72 a night my last visit, and an ER visit at Hospital General was $6 U.S.

Instead of Lipitor at $80 a month many people take capsules of *nopales* cactus powder for around $5 a month and find it just as effective at lowering cholesterol naturally. I now take the NSAID Indocin, marketed as Malival in Mexico, for $12 a month instead of $70 for Vioxx for arthritis pain.

But a printer cartridge for an HP photo printer is much higher—$35-45 for each of the three cartridges I need. I bought a refilled photo cartridge in town and it only printed out yellow and blue, no red. Electronics seem to be higher overall.

You can get a small TV for $90 that would be $75 in the States, a tiny black and white one for $28, or a huge flat screen monster for $5,000. Computers cost more overall, though you can have a good basic system built for you here for around $600, not including monitor and printer.

A small stove with oven is around $200 in the local appliance stores, and an excellent standard size one is $400-600. We've seen deluxe gourmet stoves for more than $1,000. A small fridge is as low as $250, all the way to $1,500 for a double door one. A custom built-in would be even more.

When you move into an apartment you can expect to have to do lots of repairs and replacements. Tenants usually take things with them like towel bars, because they replaced them themselves when they moved in. You may face hanging bare light bulbs and a charred hot water heater, for example.

A new propane hot water heater installed ran us around $180.

We had it replaced ourselves rather than cause any problems with our landlord, since we've got such a good deal on our rent. Gringo tenants who complain about every small repair often are the ones whose rent is raised.

A friend bought a stripped four-door Ford Fiesta for $8,500 U.S. Tiny cars you see a lot here are even cheaper. But many new cars are more expensive here, and check on what all your payments will be beyond purchase price. Check in particular what your car registration will be the first years for an expensive car. I don't know the prices for a kitchen sink.

People say we are so happy here, and we are. But one thing drives me crazy: the difficulty in learning Spanish for some of us, and the occasional snide remarks putting us down for our lack of ability. Sometimes Mexicans' attitudes depend on whether they lived in the U.S. themselves and encountered nastiness there because they couldn't speak English right away. Fair is fair.

We have now taken two conversational Spanish classes in Phoenix and the first two levels of Spanish at Warren Hardy (total cost of more than $1,000 U.S. for the two of us and, believe me, on a budget, that hurt). We had a tutor for half a year.

We went to the *Destinos* PBS course on learning Spanish at the Biblioteca for the first 14 classes before it was totally over our heads. We have a dozen books and CDs on learning Spanish, and we are still stumbling around like first graders stuck in present tense.

I can get across quite well what I need and want, but I freeze when someone then decides I must speak Spanish well and so they buzz right on past my comprehension at full speed. I ask them to repeat, *mas despacio por favor*, and I still have no idea what they said. I am reduced to sign language. It doesn't help that my aging ears don't even hear English very well any more.

I know it is terrible to be able to express my own needs but then not be able to understand any response. I cringe at my own self: *Necesito esta*, I need this, said while pointing like a

fool. And don't tell me why I can't have it now because I probably won't understand.

I would love to be fluent. Ideally all of us could be. But I have
tried and tried, and I know I will never, ever be fluent in Spanish.
I was lousy learning languages in school, too. My German teacher
in college gave me a B after three semesters though I deserved to
flunk, saying she wouldn't ruin my grade point average too much
if only I would promise never to take another class from her.

I absolutely could not memorize those 12 most common irregular past tense verbs, nor figure out where all those *se los* go (indi-
rect or direct objects, I'm not sure which.). I can understand that
adjectives go after nouns but when does *la* or *lo* or *se* go before or
after a verb, and when should it be added onto the verb, and which
verbs can take a *lo* or *la* or *se* ending and which don't?

I am very bright, and I am even a word person, as a writer, but
I absolutely cannot learn another language.

To which those who are able to learn other languages fairly
easily say, "Try harder." I am trying, I have tried, I will try, I could
have might have possibly will have tried, in whatever tense you can
come up with. But it is not easy for this particular senior to learn
another language.

I can pick out of my limited vocabulary, with the help of a
Franklin pocket translator, whatever I need to say, and I can usually stumble through about every necessary interaction, but not
with any ease or grace.

Recently I told a cashier that *Mi tia es muy viaje*, when I meant
vieja. (My aunt is very travel, not, my aunt is very old.) I couldn't
hear the different pronunciations: vee-ah-hay versus vee-a-ha. Yesterday I was trying to find the specific word for Romaine lettuce,
not lettuce in general. The clerk thought it strange I didn't just use
lechuga for lettuce in general, what in the world was I trying to say?
And then she was very slow and enunciated clearly when she picked
up the next item: *manzana*, assuming I didn't even know the word

for apple if I didn't know the word for lettuce. At those moments I want to die.

And so thanks be for San Miguel where there are enough Mexicans who are tolerant of their economic base, and who have learned enough English that between the two of us, we can stumble through a transaction. An occasional taxi driver on whom I am inflicting my Spanish will actually say I speak Spanish very well, but I'm sure he is going for a tip.

Our housekeeper has learned to work around what she has figured out we do know in Spanish, and so we converse away, she limiting herself to words we know in present tense, and we rushing to the pocket translator when we need to know another word. We talk a lot about the weather, our health, families and pets.

Friends who visit here hear me rattle off some stock phrase and they are totally impressed, they tell friends back in the States that Carol is fluent, but of course they would be impressed by a rapid restaurant order.

I know enough that I appreciate having Spanish subtitles on a movie because, when my poor hearing causes me to lose the phrase in English, I can usually pick up the meaning from the Spanish.

I can read a Spanish newspaper and get the gist of the stories, though I may not be sure whether the event already happened, is definitely going to happen, or is threatening to happen. I am learning more each week. But I know it is not enough.

I advise others that they must learn Spanish. What if they are in a car accident and the family in the car they've hit is surrounding them, accusing them, and the police who arrive don't speak any English? What if they're taken to an ER and no one there speaks sufficient English to get them the right help or medications? What if they think they understand something they're agreeing to but they've misunderstood a crucial legal detail?

I never thought I could totally assimilate into Mexico and become a light-skinned Mexican, and that was never my goal. I was very active in the civil rights movement in the '60s, and even when living with a black man in a black neighborhood, I knew I would always be the outsider.

Norma and I are quite happy to live within our own world; we don't think we're hurting anyone else by our presence. Gringos who have lived here 40 years say that they will never be totally accepted, even if they are fluent. Only if you marry into a Mexican family do you have a genuine chance at assimilation, and even then friends who have done so say they are never truly accepted.

If I can engage in my simplistic Spanish and certainly do not expect a Mexican to know English, though I am so grateful when someone does, and I can love this country and this city and this culture even if I will never be able to totally understand it, I am okay with that. Most Mexicans seem to be able to sense that I do love Mexico, and I am trying to learn Spanish, and I am not faulting them for what is my lack. Not all gringos who have become fluent are as accepting.

I appreciate San Miguel as a place where I can exist. I couldn't live in a town where no English was spoken at all, even when other Latin American cities could be much cheaper. I love San Miguel for what it is, including the number of foreigners, even though many people put San Miguel down for having so many foreigners. We're 15% of the population inside the city limits, and 8% of the population of the greater region called San Miguel. San Miguel is certainly not all English-speaking. An occasional Mexican will reply to a tourist's Spanglish with an English phrase, but that doesn't make that Mexican a fluent English speaker.

English is becoming the number one language in the world, spoken as the second language of the greatest number of people in the world, and it is becoming the language most people in other countries want to learn as their second language. Mexicans should not be faulted if they are also trying to learn English, practicing their fractured Spanglish on us as we practice our fractured Spanglish on them.

I never, ever told a Mexican living in LA or Phoenix that they must know English fluently or else they should go home. It was quite acceptable to me that Mexican-Americans could live their entire lives in parts of LA and Phoenix without ever having to utter a word of English.

Now if they wanted to work with the general public or get ahead in a career, why then they probably should learn the majority language of the country where they lived. But if they were retired old people living in their own community, let them live out their days happy. Their kids would be fluent soon enough.

Not everyone can become fluent in another language. The important thing is to try, and to be gracious and humble when you know you are making a mistake, and not have the attitude that the world should cater to your language and to you.

So that is the end of my rant on learning Spanish. Anyone considering moving to Mexico who does not pick up languages easily needs to hear it.

The remaining big issue many people have about moving to San Miguel is this town's image as too gringo-ized and too expensive. They say we're the subject of far too many articles on how wonderful it is to live in San Miguel, so more and more people keep coming.

Seems to me that a whole lot of the people who are complaining the most about the new interest in SMA are fairly recent arrivals, whose arrival set up the same kinds of complaints in those who had arrived before them.

Those who have been here the longest seem more likely to accept that change is inevitable, and SMA will never remain exactly the same town it was whenever anyone in particular arrived. It is changing every minute, I think mostly for the better.

Frommer's and some of the most "in" guides of trendiness long ago decided SMA was over the hill—in the words of Yogi Berra, "It's so crowded that nobody goes there any more."

It's more of a populist crowd who finally heard about SMA, the news filtering down through many layers of media into more of a mass consciousness, rather than a secret among only the rich elite and artists. (I wonder if the prospective real estate flippers are learning about SMA through some sort of financial advice channel.)

Besides, more and more people in the U.S. dislike elements of U.S. culture so much that they want to escape it, not just for money reasons, same as those of us who live here already may have wanted to escape parts of U.S. culture.

For many of us, Mexico is a positive draw in and of itself, not a place to escape to. Others come just because it is the latest fad. Like lemmings, we will come, to whatever hot spot catches the media's interest, and life will go on, and change will happen, everywhere in the world. Look at the Amazon rain forests.

I was talking about this to a friend who first started visiting SMA 40 years ago, and she remembers that people even then were complaining, "You should have seen SMA in the '50s when it was great."

Every couple of years there's a great cry about all the new gringos who arrive not knowing Spanish or Mexican customs, who are scrambling for cheap houses that they hope will make them a millionaire (as they did previously in LA and other popular destinations), and who want to take advantage of all the English-language entertainment and amenities instead of trying to totally assimilate like a good gringo "should."

A friend who has visited SMA for 40 years and lived here forever, married into the Mexican upper class, which would have been likely to give her access to that assimilation process. She says even she will never, ever be accepted as a genuine Mexican, and why not enjoy all the expat English-language activities SMA has to offer, without guilt?

Those complaining about development say, "Look at Centro, no Mexican could afford to live there any more." I say, look at Centro, it was the Spaniards who got land grants who lived in Centro in those huge haciendas which are now being carved up into hotels and B&Bs.

Poor Mexicans never could afford to live in Centro, and it is like the most popular areas of any city on earth, not only SMA.

Poorer Angelenos got pushed out farther and farther from desirable areas of LA. I have relatives who ended up driving 90 miles each way to work because they wanted to buy an affordable house and ended up in Moreno Valley and farther out. I couldn't afford West LA/Santa Monica almost from the day I arrived there in 1970.

And Silverlake/EchoPark? First it was farmland, then it became the hot new site for summer homes in the hills for the wealthy from downtown L.A., Then it was headquarters for the Max Sennett film studios.

Next it was a nice neighborhood of Mexican-American lower-cost homes, before it became gentrified as gays and lesbians moved in and fixed up the lower-priced homes. All along it was home to a dozen gangs who fought viciously with each other—African-American and Mexican-American gangs uniting sometimes to fight off Samoan-American and Vietnamese-American gangs.

And now the $72,000 home we owned in 1980 today sells for $500,000. Talk to me about change.

We can go way back to the roving migrations of Indian tribes throughout earliest history, cultures supplanted by peace and war and ecological changes and famines and disease. More and more evidence shows that the image of the peaceful Indian tribe wiped out by cruel white people misses the entire picture—very few tribes were that peaceful, and there was plenty of warfare and encroachment on land and changes in land use throughout history. The newest expats who complain that more gringos will destroy SMA lack historical context.

Yes, it would be very good if as much planning as possible is done to try to control the changes and at least channel them into the least harmful paths. Yes, water shortages worldwide are a big part of what needs to be taken into consideration, and probably won't be, same as in Phoenix and much of the U.S. and much of the world.

It's the pattern of history: overpopulation of the most desirable areas, causing those areas to become less desirable, so that those who can most afford it move on to the next "most desirable area" and change that, too. I'm not saying this is good, only that this is fact, not unique to SMA.

Already newly arriving foreigners are looking to the outskirts of SMA and neighboring towns for their affordable housing that they hope will make them rich in a few years. That also happened in LA. It made many of my friends well off, to be able to afford a good retirement on the appreciation in their LA house price, while I never could afford to hang on to a house long enough to develop that kind of nest egg.

In LA, in Phoenix, in thousands of areas current and past, the exact same trends have occurred. You might as well try to stop the wind. Or change human nature.

A new factor in San Miguel's image is crime, particularly a serial rapist who was captured in July, 2006, after raping five foreign women in the nine months starting in October, 2005. He confessed to at least two of the rapes and to various cat burglaries, and his DNA matched that left at the crime scenes. More than 30 suspects' DNA was tested in the nine months.

The man who was arrested was a 58-year-old Mexican from a nearby town who had worked in the U.S. in construction and as a locksmith, and he had served at least five years in a Texas prison for a robbery. He was released from prison in October, 2005. The first rape here was days later.

This sick individual made many people reexamine their views of San Miguel as their own safe little haven. With the addition of so many new wealthy homes, robberies have also risen slightly. San Miguel crime rates are below those of similar-sized tourist towns in the U.S. Many U.S. citizens picture all of Mexico as the border towns of Tijuana, Nuevo Laredo, Cuidad Juárez, and Mexico City. Many serial murderers in the U.S. have gone uncaptured for years, even decades, and sometimes have never been caught, but nine months and five rapes in San Miguel brought strong calls for more police action. Everyone's attitudes changed.

Mexican women's groups are working hard to educate women to report rate and domestic violence, and to insist these crimes are prosecuted and police take the reports seriously. We learned later that Mexican women had also been raped by the serial rapist, but none of them reported it. The experience of the five foreign women standing up and coming out about their experience was new. The demands on the police were also new.

Mexican law is based on Roman law and the Napoleonic Code, under which you are guilty until proven innocent. The police system is divided into the local preventive police who respond to emergencies and work to prevent crimes, and the district attorney's office which investigates and prosecutes only crimes which are reported to them. They are clearly separate, and the division is more distinct than the 30 minutes each allotted to the capture and then the trial of criminals on a typical *Law and Order* episode.

San Miguel and Guanajuato State officials reorganized many programs, shifted personnel, and initiated patrols on every street where a foreign woman lived alone. A team of specially trained state investigators was brought in to lead the case. A bilingual police officer was hired as liaison to the foreign community, on call 24/7 to help crime victims navigate the Mexican legal process. At least 50 undercover officers were brought in to run down tips, including one from a woman whose house was being broken into and she got a clear glimpse of his face. Finally local authorities were able to obtain a mugshot of the suspect from the U.S. F.B.I. from a previous arrest, which led to his capture here. At this writing, he is awaiting his trial before a judge. He could get more than 60 years for his crimes.

News of the serial rapist spread internationally. Women contacted us, afraid to vacation in SMA. Some financial interests worried that SMA's image would suffer and property values would fall. City officials made it clear that women's safety and capturing the rapist outranked concerns about investments.

Norma and I, who had lived in LA during the Hillside Stranglers and the Night Stalker, reexamined our casa and realized the window on our metal roof access door could be used to get into our house. We immediately ordered metal bars for the window. Until they could be installed three days later, we piled baking racks and pot lids on the circular stairway to the roof, and upended chairs so that anyone coming down our stairs would slide off and impale themselves on the chair legs. And the first night one of our cats knocked a lid off the stairs.

The repercussions of this one man's terror continue to ripple. In a few months there may be no lasting effects, beyond a higher safety consciousness, which is always a good thing.

Meanwhile, people are still coming to San Miguel, reassured by the response of the city and state to the crime concerns and realizing that crime happens everywhere. Property values did not fall, there is not a surplus of cheap apartments, inexpensive houses still have to be sought intensively.

Norma and I still walk home from cultural events in Centro at night, enjoying one magical moment after another, grateful every day that we discovered San Miguel and that we have found a place where we can live well on Social Security.

There are still residents who wish that the flood of new residents would stop, especially those who are here just to make money on the real estate boom. I am sure we as the authors of this book will be criticized for alerting even more people that it is still possible to live better in Mexico on Social Security than it is in the States, even in a desirable town like San Miguel.

The people would be coming anyway. San Miguel de Allende continues to rank near the tops of lists of the best places to retire in the world by many respected national publications. Television shows continue to air shots of blissful retired couples strolling past the Parroquia, predicting that the coming baby boomer retirees will be flocking to Mexico and other countries because they can't afford to live in the best parts of the U.S. on Social Security.

And word of mouth is the best publicist. We have former friends in the U.S. contact us constantly asking if life is really as good as we make it sound. We think so. Everyone's experience differs.

Those who say, "I got mine, now shut the doors," would prefer that all the favorable stories about San Miguel instead read something like this:

First, instead of a photo of our beautiful Parroquia to illustrate the San Miguel story, editors should use 1950's file photos of the old cardboard shacks of Tijuana.

Writers should say that if you walk the SMA streets you will be run over by rampaging burros and buses reeking of bleating goats and squawking chickens.

All menu items include tripe, and all prices are in dollars.

If you speak English someone will spit at you.

If you speak Spanish someone will spit at you.

Every day is the running of the bulls, and they don't announce which streets the bulls will be charging down that day.

If you get sick only shamans will be available to heal you with cow dung.

All paintings on sale were bought wholesale from the "Starving Artists" factory, painted in Taiwan by assembly lines of lepers.

Book early and often.

Conclusion

For sure, come for a visit first—you may fall in love with San Miguel in three days or you may leave knowing it is not for you. We do hope you don't fall literally on the cobblestones in the process, as Carol did our first day.

Check out other areas of Mexico with many expats, such as Lake Chapala-Ajijic, or discover a town where no one else speaks English, but you fall in love with it anyway. Don't make any big decisions immediately. Settle in to a place, let it get into your head and heart. If it doesn't, try someplace else. Life's too short to live where you don't love it.

For us, moving to Mexico, and in particular to San Miguel, has been the best decision we ever made. Our hearts sing every day we wake up. I keep taking photos of the Parroquia's rose glow every time I round the corner and there it is, in all its stunning beauty. I smile every time I see a Mexican child call out "*dulce*" at a parade, asking for someone to throw wrapped candy. We have to try every new restaurant that opens, a new experience, even when our old favorites disappear in this changing city.

We still can't believe we can buy armfuls of fruits and vegetables for almost nothing, and the gigantic pineapple for two bucks will actually be ripe and luscious. Norma bought maybe one fresh pineapple in her life before we moved here; now we eat one or two a week.

We walk along a street and rejoice in the riot of colors and the pink, lavender, burgundy, coral, and bronze bougainvilleas hanging down over the garden walls. We come across a plein air painter capturing the exact same view from Aldama as a thousand others have painted, and compliment the artist no matter how the attempt looks, glad to see someone else who feels truly inspired.

We round a corner and come face to face with burros, or men on horseback clip-clopping down the street, or a child selling squash blossoms for stuffing empanadas and quesadillas, or a man selling hand woven reed mats and baskets. We hear drums and if we have time, try to find the source, knowing another parade is starting somewhere. We hope everyone can find a home where they can be as happy. This book is our personal love story to San Miguel de Allende.

ABOUT THE AUTHORS

Former newspaper and magazine writer and editor, Carol Schmidt was public relations director for the medical research programs at Harbor-UCLA Medical Center in LA. She published three mystery novels now out of print: *Silverlake Heat, Sweet Cherry Wine,* and *Cabin Fever.* Her writing is in seven anthologies, including the Library of America's Reporting Civil Rights (*www.reportingcivilrights.com*). Her freelance articles have appeared in hundreds of publications, including the *Los Angeles Times, Long Beach Independent-Press Telegram,* and *National Catholic Reporter.* Born and raised in Detroit, she moved to LA in 1970. She met Norma in 1979 when both were on the state board of directors of California NOW. Carol and Norma RVed full-time for more than three years and then lived in retirement RV parks in Washington and Arizona. Carol also studies watercolor in San Miguel.

Former accountant and tax preparer, Norma Hair was director of accounting for a major mortgage company. Born and raised in Pontiac, Michigan, she reared three children before going to college at 39, and has four grandchildren and three great-grandchildren. As treasurer of Sunset Junction Street Fair, a Silverlake community effort that soon grew to a quarter million attendees in LA each August, Norma also did volunteer accounting and tax work for several community service organizations. She was honored by such LA groups as El Centro del Pueblo, a social services organization that works with local street gangs, for her community contributions. When she and Carol owned a hobby ceramics store in rural Michigan, Norma ran two statewide trade shows of the Michigan Ceramic Dealers Association. She is a batik artist and gourmet cook in San Miguel.

Breinigsville, PA USA
13 September 2009
223994BV00002B/5/A